Using Turbo C®

Using Turbo C®

Herbert Schildt

BORLAND·OSBORNE/McGRAW·HILL
PROGRAMMING SERIES

Osborne **McGraw-Hill**
2600 Tenth Street
Berkeley, California 94710
U.S.A.

For information on translations and book distributors outside of the U.S.A., write to Osborne **McGraw-Hill** at the above address.

A complete list of trademarks appears on page 419.

Using Turbo C®

1234567890 DODO 8987

ISBN 0-07-881279-8

CONTENTS

FOREWORD

It had to happen.

It was inevitable that Borland, which is first and foremost a language company, would create software developer's tools for C, one of the most popular programming languages. It probably is equally inevitable that Herbert Schildt, noted author and veteran C programmer, would write a book that helps serious programmers make the most of this elegant language.

Turbo C follows in the tradition of Turbo Pascal and Turbo Prolog in demonstrating our commitment to bring superior development tools to market for the thousands of C and BASIC programmers in this country and abroad. With this language development environment, serious developers have the tools to build the most portable software applications possible. And because of C's usefulness in multiple CPU environments, programmers will be able to move these applications among many machines.

It has been a pleasure to work with Osborne/McGraw-Hill and Herb to produce the kind of book programmers like best about the language they like most.

Philippe Kahn
President
Borland International, Inc.

PREFACE

I have been programming in C since the mid 1970s and have been writing about the C language for the past several years. Although I am fluent in the most popular computer languages, including FORTRAN, BASIC, Pascal, Ada, Prolog, and assembler, it is C that I choose for my own projects. I like the philosophy behind C: it offers freedom, elegance, and consistency. Just before Borland announced Turbo C, I—like many other C programmers—was fairly sure that C compilers for microcomputers had nearly scaled whatever heights they could reach, and that any improvements would be small and insignificant. Frankly, I think that a large part of the C programming community had become a little complacent. Needless to say, Turbo C certainly changed that!

First and foremost, Turbo C is a "C programmer's compiler": it is fast—really fast—both in compilation and in execution. If you have never used a C compiler before, you might be surprised to learn how slowly some of them compiled code. Second, Turbo C adheres to the proposed ANSI standard. This means that code that you write in Turbo C will be as good ten years from now as it is today. Finally, Turbo C's integrated environment has simplified program development.

Is This Book for You?

This book assumes that you have never programmed in C before. Although programming experience is not technically necessary, it will be helpful if you have programmed (even a little) in some computer language.

Part One begins with a discussion of the C language's history , followed by a look at Turbo C's integrated environment and editor. Part One finishes with some Turbo C essentials. Part Two contains the "meat" of the C language. Part Three finishes the book with coverage of some advanced concepts. By the time you finish Part Three, you will be an accomplished C programmer.

This book will help you learn to program both in Turbo C specifically and in C generally. Because Turbo C is ANSI standard, you can apply many concepts of the Turbo C language to other C compilers in other environments.

There is good news and there is bad news about learning C. First, the bad news: While C, in general, is a sophisticated language that gives virtually unlimited power to the programmer, the price of this power is a greater potential for error. In almost all other computer languages, the compiler is constantly watching over your shoulder, trying to keep you out of trouble. In C, however, you can do just about anything you like without so much as a stifled snicker from the compiler. The good news is that if you know Pascal (including Turbo Pascal), Modula-2, Ada, or any other contemporary structured language, you will find yourself right at home with Turbo C.

This book contains many useful and interesting functions and programs. If you're like me, you probably would like to use them, but hate typing them into the computer. When I key in routines from a book, I always seem to type something wrong and spend hours trying to get the program to work. For this reason, I am offering the source code on diskette for all of the functions and programs in this book for $24.95. Just fill in the order blank on the next page and mail it, along with your payment, to the address shown on the order blank. Or, if you're in a hurry, call (217) 586-4021 and place your order by telephone. (VISA and MasterCard accepted.)

H.S.
Mahomet, Illinois
May 1987

Please send me ___ copies, at $24.95 each, of the programs in *Using Turbo C*. For foreign orders, please add $5.00 shipping and handling.

_____
Name

_____
Address

_____
City   State   ZIP

_____
Telephone

Method of payment: Check ___ VISA ___ MC ___

Credit-card number: _____

Expiration date: _____

Signature: _____

Send to: Herbert Schildt
        R.R. 1, Box 130
        Mahomet, IL 61853
        Or phone: (217) 586-4021

Introduction to Turbo C

PART ONE

▲

Part One of this book lays the groundwork for your study of Turbo C. Chapter 1 offers a history and overview of the C language. Chapter 2 teaches you how to use Turbo C's integrated programming environment, and Chapter 3 examines the editor. Chapter 4 introduces some Turbo C basics.

▼

Turbo C in Perspective

C H A P T E R   1

Before you can begin to explore the exciting world of Turbo C, you should first place it in perspective, in relation both to other programming languages and to other C compilers. The purpose of this chapter is to present a general overview of the C programming language, its origins, uses, and philosophy. If you already know something about C and are a fairly experienced programmer, then you might want to skip to Chapter 2.

This chapter begins with a short history of C and its uses. The chapter also explains the reason that C has become the world's most popular and important computer language. If you are completely new to C or to programming in general, you will find this background information valuable.

The chapter then covers the differences between compilers and interpreters. If Turbo C is the first compiled language that you have worked with, you should read this section carefully. Finally, the chapter ends with information specifically for Turbo Pascal users who are moving up to Turbo C.

The Origins of C

Dennis Ritchie invented and first implemented C on a DEC PDP-11 that used the UNIX operating system. The C language is the result of a development process that started with an older language called BCPL, which is still in use primarily in Europe. BCPL was developed by Martin Richards. BCPL influenced a language called B, which was invented by Ken Thompson and which led to the development of C in the 1970s.

For many years, the de facto standard for C was the version that was supplied with the UNIX version 5 operating system and described in *The C Programming Language* by Brian Kernighan and Dennis Ritchie (Prentice-Hall, 1978). With the growing popularity of microcomputers, many C implementations were created. In what could almost be called a miracle, most of these implementations were highly compatible with each other on the source-code level. However, because no standard existed, there were always some discrepancies. To change this situation, a committee was established in the beginning of the summer of 1983. This committee began to work on the creation of an ANSI standard that would define once and for all the C language. As of this writing, the proposed standard is nearly complete, and its adoption by ANSI is expected in 1987. Because the ANSI C standard is a superset of the UNIX standard, programmers who are migrating from a UNIX-based compiler to an ANSI-standard compiler will find all the features they have come to rely on. In addition, they will find some new features that will make programming easier.

When Borland began its Turbo C project, it defined three goals. The first goal was to implement the complete ANSI standard so that Turbo C users would have the most up-to-date C compiler available. The second goal was to produce the fastest, most efficient compiler possible. Borland knows, as you will understand, that C programmers are an uncompromising bunch when it comes to speed and efficiency in the programs that they write. The final goal was to provide an integrated C programming environment that would streamline the development process. It is a pleasure to report that Borland succeeded in accomplishing all three goals.

Now that you know Turbo C's lineage, let's examine what kind of a programming language it is.

C Is a Middle-level Language

C is often called a *middle-level computer language. Middle-level* does not have a negative meaning. It does not mean that C is less powerful, harder to use, or less developed than a high-level language, such as BASIC or Pascal. It also does not imply that C is similar to assembly language with its associated troubles. C is thought of as a middle-level language because it combines elements of high-level languages with the functionalism of assembler. Figure 1-1 shows the way that C fits into the spectrum of programming languages.

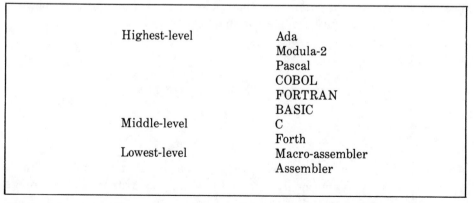

Highest-level	Ada
	Modula-2
	Pascal
	COBOL
	FORTRAN
	BASIC
Middle-level	C
	Forth
Lowest-level	Macro-assembler
	Assembler

Figure 1-1.   C's place in the world of programming languages

C code is very portable. *Portability* means that you can adapt software written for one type of computer to another type. For example, if you can move a program written for an Apple II+ easily to an IBM PC, then that program is portable. Turbo C's support of the ANSI standard assures you of the portability of the code to other environments.

All high-level programming languages support the concept of data types. A *data type* defines a set of values that a variable can store with a set of operations that the computer can perform on that variable. Common data types include integer, character, and real. Although C has five basic built-in data types, it is not a strongly typed language like Pascal or Ada. C will allow almost all type conversions. For example, you may freely mix character and integer types in most expressions. In general, C compilers perform little run-time error checking, such as array-boundary checking or argument-type compatibility checking. The same is true of Turbo C. These checks are the responsibility of the programmer. The reason for this lack of run-time error checking is that run-time error checking slows a program's execution. Therefore, you as the programmer decide whether or not any error checking is necessary.

As a middle-level language, C allows the manipulation of bits, bytes, and addresses—which are the basic elements with which the computer functions. This ability makes C well suited for system-level programming where these operations are common.

Another important aspect of Turbo C is that it has only 38 keywords (32 that are defined by the ANSI standard, and 5 that were added by Borland to allow you to make better use of some special aspects of the PC environment). These keywords are the commands that make up the C language. By comparison the IBM PC BASIC has 159 commands!

C Is a Structured Language

Although the term *block-structured language* does not strictly apply to C in an academic sense, C is commonly referred to simply as a structured language because of its structural similarities to Algol, Pascal, and Modula-2. (*Note:* Technically, a block-structured language allows you to declare subroutines inside other subroutines. However, since C does not allow this, it cannot formally be called block-structured.) The distinguishing feature of a structured language is its *compartmentalization of code and data*, which is the ability of a language to section off and hide from the rest of the program all information and instructions that are necessary to perform a specific task. One way to achieve compartmentalization is by using stand-alone subroutines. (A *stand-alone subroutine* defines its own variable, which may be used only by that subroutine.) The use of stand-alone routines makes it possible to write subroutines in such a way that the events that occur within them will cause no side effects in other parts of the program. By developing compartmentalized subroutines, you only need to know *what* they will do, and not *how* they will do it.

Here are some examples of structured and nonstructured languages:

Nonstructured	Structured
FORTRAN	Pascal
BASIC	Ada
COBOL	C
	Modula-2

Structured languages tend to be more modern, while nonstructured languages are older. In fact, a mark of an old computer language is that it is not structured. Today, it is widely agreed that structured languages not only make programming easier, but also make maintaining a program easier.

A Replacement of Assembly Language

C's inherent efficiency compared with its ability to operate directly on the bits and bytes of the computer's memory allows you to use C in place of assembler in many situations. This cannot be undervalued as a factor that contributes to C's popularity among programmers. Assembly language uses a symbolic representation of the actual binary code that the computer directly executes. Each assembler operation maps into a single task for the computer to perform. Although assembly language gives programmers the potential for accomplishing tasks with maximum flexibility and efficiency, assembly language is notoriously difficult to work with when you develop and debug a program. Furthermore, since assembly language is unstructured by nature, the final program tends to be *spaghetti code:* a tangled mess of jumps, calls, and indexes. This characteristic makes assembly language programs difficult to read, enhance, or maintain. Perhaps more importantly, assembly language routines are not portable between machines that have different CPUs.

As this discussion implies, even with all of the shortcomings of assembly language, it was often used because it offered the only way to produce programs that ran fast enough. However, with the advent of Turbo C, it is difficult to justify the use of assembly language programming in all but the most unusual circumstances.

What Can C Be Used for?

Initially, C was used for systems programming. A *systems program* is part of a large class of programs that form a portion of the operating system of the computer or its support utilities. For example, the following are commonly called systems programs:

- operating systems
- interpreters
- editors
- assemblers
- compilers
- data base managers

As C grew in popularity, many programmers began to use it to program all types of tasks because of its portability and efficiency. Before long, C became the most popular, general-purpose programming language. Now that C has been standardized, there is little doubt that its dominance will last well into the next century.

A Programmer's Language

C is a programmer's language. You might respond to a statement like that with the question, "Aren't all programming languages for programmers?" The answer is an unqualified *NO!*

Consider the classic examples of nonprogrammer's languages: COBOL and BASIC. COBOL was designed not to make the programmer's lot better, not to improve the reliability of the code produced, and not even to improve the speed with which the programmer could write code. Rather, COBOL was designed to enable *nonprogrammers* to read and presumably (however unlikely) understand the program! (*Note:* The reader is cautioned that the merits of COBOL are not under assault here—it does have its uses. The point is that COBOL was not designed to be the ideal language for programmers.) On the other hand, BASIC was created essentially to allow nonprogrammers to program a computer in order to solve relatively simple problems.

Indeed, C stands virtually alone because it was created, influenced, and field-tested by working programmers. Its success was largely due to "grass-roots" support. The result is that C gives a programmer what a programmer wants: few restrictions, few complaints, fast code, and efficiency. It is amazing that, by using Turbo C, a programmer can produce programs that are nearly as efficient as those programs coded in assembly language, while still enjoying the benefits of a high-level language. It is no wonder that C is easily the most popular language among top-flight professional programmers.

Compilers Versus Interpreters

Turbo C is a compiler. By contrast, the standard BASIC that came with your computer is an interpreter. If you have never worked with a compiler before, it will seem different. So, if compilers are new to you, carefully read this section.

The terms *compiler* and *interpreter* refer to the way in which a program is executed. In theory, any programming language can be either compiled or interpreted, but some languages are usually executed one way or the other. For example, BASIC is generally interpreted and C is usually compiled. The way that a program is executed is not defined by the language in which it is written. Interpreters and compilers are simply sophisticated programs that operate on your program source code.

An interpreter reads the source code of your program one line at a time, and performs the specific instructions that are in that line. A compiler reads the entire program and then converts it into object code, which is a translation of the program source code into a form that the compiler can directly execute. Object code is also referred to as *binary* or *machine* code. After you compile the program, a line of source code is no longer meaningful to the execution of your program.

When you use an interpreter, it must be present each time that you run your program. For example, in BASIC, you must first execute the BASIC interpreter, load your program, and then type **RUN** each time that you want to use your program. The BASIC interpreter will execute your program one line at a time. This slow process occurs every time that you run the program. By contrast, a compiler converts your program into object code that your computer can directly execute. Because the compiler translates your program one time, all that you need do is execute your program directly — generally by simply typing its name. Therefore, compilation is a one-time cost. Interpreted code incurs this overhead each time that you run a program.

Not all compilers are created equal. As you probably know, Turbo C is, at the time of this writing, the fastest C compiler available. This situation is not expected to change because Turbo C performs special manipulations called *optimizations* to the code that it generates. Code optimization is still in the realm of magic — not every C compiler developer can do this as well as another. Although there is no way to know how many "spells and incantations" Borland used, it certainly managed to create some clever optimizations.

Two terms that you will see often in this book and in your C compiler manual are *compile-time* and *run-time*. The term *compile-time* refers to the events that occur during the compilation process. The term *run-time* refers to the events that occur while the program is executing. Unfortunately, you will often see these terms used in connection with the word *error*, as in *compile-time error* and *run-time error*. Happily, as you become a better Turbo C programmer, you will see fewer of these messages.

A Word to Turbo Pascal Users

If you are a Turbo Pascal programmer, there is good news and bad news. First, the good news: in terms of basic language elements, Turbo C is similar to Turbo Pascal. For example, although some of the names are different, the loop statements and the conditional statements are virtually the same. Thus, you already know most of the essentials of programming in Turbo C. In fact, among the elements that are similar between Turbo C and Turbo Pascal, those in Turbo C are generally more powerful, more flexible, and more efficient. Because of the way Turbo C treats such basic elements as variables and operators, you will have more direct control over the computer and the way that the computer actually executes your program. To give you an idea of what programming level you are moving up to, Turbo C is roughly twice as powerful as Turbo Pascal—and, as you know, Turbo Pascal is no slouch!

Now for the bad news: there is a price for all of Turbo C's power. Turbo C (and C in general) does not do much to keep you out of trouble. With Turbo C, you no longer have automatic strong type checking, for example. In Turbo C, the rule is "the programmer is king": Turbo C will more or less do whatever you tell it to do, even if what you want cannot conceivably work. For example, in C, you can call a function that should take integer arguments with floating-point arguments. Doing this will cause the function to misbehave, but the Turbo C compiler will not give you any warning messages. As you will see later in this book, there are ways to cause Turbo C to "look over your shoulder" (not as much as Turbo Pascal, however) but you must explicitly request it to activate these ways. In a different vein, you will find that, while Turbo C's I/O capabilities are much more powerful than Turbo Pascal's, they are also more complex, so be patient when you read Chapter 10, which covers this subject.

Start Your Engines

Now that the stage has been set, it's time to start your engines. By the time that you finish this book, you will be able to enjoy true turbo-power programming at its best.

The Turbo C Environment

CHAPTER 2

Turbo C has two separate modes of operation. The first mode, which you will almost certainly want to use as you begin to program, is its integrated development environment. In this environment, you can control editing, compilation, and execution by using single keystrokes and easy-to-use menus. The other mode of operation utilizes the traditional approach, where you first use an editor to create your file, then compile it, link it, and run it manually. This mode is called the command-line approach. The first part of this book will use only the integrated environment because it is easier to work with and because its on-line help will aid you if you need it. Using the compiler from the command line will be covered later.

The purpose of this chapter is to show you the Turbo C integrated environment—in other words, to get you acquainted with Turbo C. Many of the options that you will see may seem cryptic now, but as you progress through this book they will become clear. If you are already familiar with the way that the integrated environment functions, you should skip to Chapter 3 at this time.

The rest of this book assumes that you have properly installed Turbo C according to the instructions given in its manual. If you have not or if you have had trouble with installation, please refer to Appendix A, which describes this process.

Executing Turbo C

To execute the integrated version of Turbo C, simply type **TC** and then press ENTER. When Turbo C begins execution you will see the screen shown in Figure 2-1. This is called the *main menu screen* and consists of four parts, listed here in order from top to bottom:

- The main menu
- The editor-status line and window
- The compiler message window
- The "hot key" quick-reference line

To exit Turbo C, press ALT-X.

The rest of this chapter examines each of these areas.

The Main Menu

You use the main menu either to tell Turbo C to do something, such as execute the editor or compile a program, or to set an environmental option. There are two ways to make a main menu selection, which you should try at this time. First, you can use the arrow keys to move the highlight to the

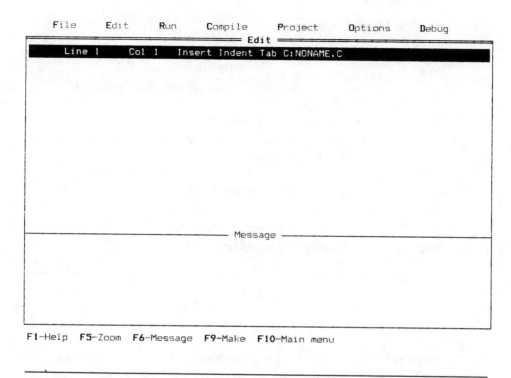

Figure 2-1. The Turbo C main menu screen

option that you want and then press ENTER. Second, you can simply type the first letter of the menu option that you want. For example, to select **Edit**, you would type **E**. You may enter the letter as either uppercase or lowercase. Table 2-1 summarizes what each menu option does. Let's look more closely at each option in turn.

File

Move the highlight to **File** and press ENTER. This process activates the **File** pull-down menu, as shown in Figure 2-2. To make a selection from a pull-down menu you either move the highlight to the option and press ENTER , or you type the first letter of the option. To exit a pull-down menu you simply press ESC.

Table 2-1. The Main Menu Options

Item	Options
File	Loads and saves files, handles directories, invokes DOS, and exits Turbo C.
Edit	Invokes the Turbo C editor.
Run	Compiles, links, and runs the program currently loaded in the environment.
Compile	Compiles the program currently in the environment.
Make	Manages multifile projects.
Options	Sets various compiler and linker options.
Setup	Sets various environmental options.
Debug	Sets various debug options.

The **Load** option prompts you for a filename and then loads that file into the editor. The **Pick** option displays a menu that lists the last eight files that you loaded into the integrated environment. You can select one of these files by using the arrow keys to move the highlight to it and pressing ENTER. Selecting **New** lets you edit a new file. The **Save** option saves the file currently in the editor. The **Write to** option lets you save a file under a different filename than you used previously. **Directory** displays the directory, while **Change dir** changes the default directory to the one that you specify. The **OS shell** option loads the DOS command processor and then lets you execute DOS commands. Under this option, you must type **EXIT** to return to Turbo C. Finally, the **Quit** option quits Turbo C.

At this time, press ESC to return to the main menu.

Run and Compile

The **Run** option of the main menu attempts to compile, link, and execute the program that is currently in the editor. There is no menu associated with **Run**.

Move the highlight to the **Compile** option and press ENTER. There are

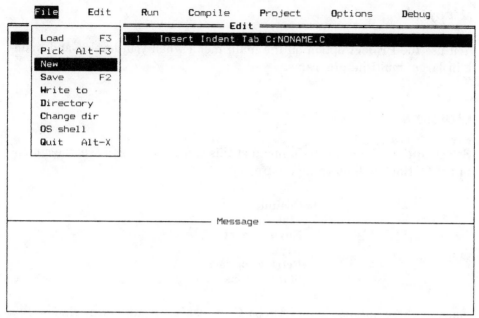

Figure 2-2. The **File** pull-down menu

five options on the **Compile** menu. The first option allows you to compile a C source file to an *.OBJ file*. An .OBJ file is a relocatable object file that is ready to be linked into an .EXE file that Turbo C can execute. You will learn more about the .OBJ files in Chapter 4. The second option will compile your program directly into an executable file. The third option links the current .OBJ file and creates an .EXE file. The fourth option forces Turbo C to recompile and link all files in a project. (You will learn more about multifile projects in Part Three of this book.) The final option lets you specify a primary file that you want to compile. If you do specify a primary file, then any of the other **Compile** options or the **Run** command will use that file. If you do not specify a file, Turbo C will use the file currently loaded in the editor. Press ESC at this time to return to the main menu.

Project

You use the **Project** option on the main menu when you develop and maintain large, multifile programs.

Options

Select **Options** from the main menu at this time. As you can see, the options in the **Options** pull-down menu are

> **Compiler**
> **Linker**
> **Environment**
> **Args**
> **Retrieve options**
> **Store options**

Each of these options causes Turbo C to display a pull-down window that contains other options that relate to that particular option. You need not be concerned about most of these options at this time because Turbo C's default mode of operation is applicable to all of the examples in this book and to most programming projects. (Part Three will discuss several of the more important options.) However, one of the options found under the **Compiler** option concerns memory models, a topic that needs a few words of explanation.

Memory Models   If you have looked through the Turbo C user manual briefly, you have probably encountered the term *memory model* more than once. If you do not know what this term means, don't worry: Turbo C's default approach is fine for most applications, and is all that you will need for the examples in this book. In fact, to understand the impact of the various models fully requires an understanding of how the 8086 family of processors works. It is beyond the scope of this book to look at this subject in great detail; however; the short discussion that follows may help you understand the general differences among the memory models. (You can find a detailed explanation of memory models in *Advanced Turbo C* by Herbert Schildt [Borland-Osborne/McGraw-Hill, available Summer 1987].)

As you may know, the 8086 family of processors uses a *segment-offset memory architecture.* In this architecture, each segment is 64K long. The segment part of the address determines which segment a program selects, while the offset specifies the specific byte within that segment. Bluntly stated, this architecture is not the most elegant approach and can cause some rather difficult programming situations. The trouble is that, in order to allow a program to access memory outside the segment in which it resides, the program must use a 32-bit address. However, if the memory accessed is inside the program's segment, then the program only requires a 16-bit address. Furthermore, a program may need to access code, data, or both in each of these ways. Another complication is that 32-bit addressing is much slower than 16-bit addressing. Thus, it is desirable to use 16-bit addressing when possible. Although you can always use 32-bit addressing, it causes programs to execute very slowly and should be used only as a last resort.

As a result, Turbo C defines six different memory models from which you may choose to use for the compiled form of your program. These models are shown in Table 2-2. Generally Turbo C's default small model is sufficient for the majority of programming tasks.

Debug

The **Debug** option lets you set the way that Turbo C displays compiler-error and linker-error messages. The default settings for **Debug** are generally what you want to use; you do not need to worry about **Debug** further at this time.

The Edit Window

Just below the main menu is the *edit window.* You will edit your program inside this window. Although you will learn how to use the editor in the next chapter, select **Edit** now. Turbo C places the cursor in the upper-left corner of the window. The editor is ready for you to enter text at this time. Try

Table 2-2.   The Turbo C Memory Models

Model	Description
Tiny	All addresses are 16-bits and all code and data must fit in one 64K segment. Can be used to produce .COM files.
Small	Code and data have separate segments. All addresses are 16-bits long. Good for most applications.
Medium	Code may use multiple segments and requires 32-bit address. Data has one segment and uses 16-bit addresses. Best for large programs that do not have much data.
Compact	Complement of the medium model: data may use multiple segments. Code has one segment and uses 16-bit addresses. Best for average-size program with a lot of data.
Large	Both code and data may use multiple segments, and require 32-bit addresses. No single data item can exceed 64K. Best for large applications, but will run slowly.
Huge	Same as the large model, except single-data items may be larger than 64K. Runs the slowest of all models.

typing the line **This is a test** and then press RETURN. To leave the editor, press F10.

The Message Window

The message window lies beneath the edit window and is used to display various compiler or linker messages.

The Hot Keys

The Turbo C interactive environment supports a set of *hot keys* that you can use to activate the various menus or to perform a few common functions quickly. Table 2-3 shows the Turbo C hot keys. Because the hot keys are active at all times, you can instantly activate any menu—regardless of what

Figure 2-3.   The Turbo C Hot Keys

Hot Key	Meaning
F1	Activates the on-line help system
F2	Saves the file currently in the editor
F3	Loads a file
F5	Zooms the active window
F6	Switches the active window
F7	Allows you to go to previous error
F8	Allows you to go to next error
F9	Compiles and links your program
F10	Activates the main menu
ALT-F1	Brings back the last help screen
ALT-F3	Allows you to pick a file to load
ALT-F9	Compiles file in the editor to .OBJ
ALT-F10	Displays the version number
ALT-C	Activates the **Compile** menu
ALT-D	Activates the **Debug** menu
ALT-E	Activates the editor
ALT-F	Activates the **File** menu
ALT-O	Activates the **Options** menu
ALT-P	Activates the **Project** menu
ALT-R	Runs the current program
ALT-X	Quits Turbo C

you are currently doing. For example, you can compile a program without leaving the editor. At the bottom of the screen, Turbo C shows the hot keys that are the most relevant to what you are currently doing. But remember — all of the hot keys are always active.

One of the most important hot keys is F10, which activates the main menu. Other important hot keys are discussed here.

Help

You can activate the on-line help system by pressing F1. The help system is *context-sensitive*, which means that Turbo C will display information that is related to what you are currently doing. To see how the help system works, press F1 at this time. To leave the help system, press ESC.

Switching Windows and Using Zoom

By pressing F5 , you can enlarge either the edit window or the message window so that it covers the full size of the screen. The zoom feature is so named because it simulates the action of a zoom lens of a camera. The F5 is a toggle key, so pressing it again returns either the edit window or the message window to its regular size. Figure 2-3 shows the way that the screen looks when you zoom in on the edit window.

You press F6 to determine the window that you want to enlarge. The F6 is a toggle that switches between the edit and message windows. Pressing F6 once selects the message window. Pressing F6 again returns control to the edit window. You will select the message window when you want to examine the various messages the compiler generates.

Make

The Make key is F9. The **Make** option provides a simple way to compile programs that consist of multiple source files. You will see the use of the Make key later in this book.

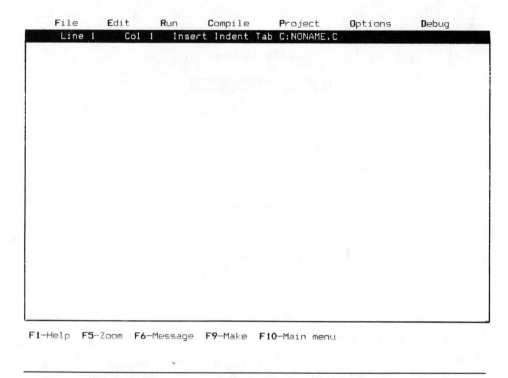

Figure 2-3. Zooming in on the edit window

The *TCINST* Program

Turbo C includes an installation program called TCINST, which you use to set several attributes and default settings of the Turbo C integrated environment. To execute this program, simply type **TCINST** from the command line. When the program begins to execute, you will see a display that is similar to the one in Figure 2-4. Each of the **TCINST** options is discussed here.

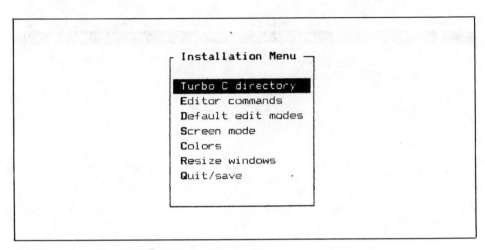

Figure 2-4.   The TCINST initial screen

Turbo C Directory

The **Turbo C Directory** option is an installation parameter that determines which directory will contain Turbo C's help and configuration files. If you do not enter anything, then Turbo C assumes that it should use the current working directory.

Editor commands

You can customize the Turbo C editor by selecting the **Editor commands** option. Doing so produces the screen shown in Figure 2-5. If you are familiar with another type of editor, you can make the Turbo C editor imitate it by changing the keystrokes that make up each command.

To change a command, first position the highlight on the command that you want to change and press ENTER. Turbo C only highlights the right side of the command because this is the side that you can change. It is not possible to change the left command. To clear the right-side sequence of the command, type **C**. To restore the original sequence, type **R**. To enter a new key-stroke sequence, simply type the proper characters. For example, to change the command for moving one word to the right to the keystroke sequence CTRL-F CTRL-W, first select the **Word Right** command. Next, type **C** to clear the old command. Now press CTRL-F, then CTRL-W, and then ENTER. Pressing ENTER terminates the command sequence. The screen will look like Figure 2-6. If you wish to use ENTER as part of the command, you must press SCROLL LOCK first. This causes Turbo C to treat ENTER literally, instead of as a signal of the end of the keystroke sequence.

===== Turbo C Installation Program =====		
↑-↓-scroll PgUp-PgDn-page ◄┘-modify R-restore factory defaults ESC-exit		
New Line	**\<Enter\>**	**\<Enter\>**
Cursor Left	\<Ctr1S\>	**\<Lft\>**
Cursor Right	\<Ctr1D\>	**\<Rgt\>**
Word Left	\<Ctr1A\>	**\<CtrlLft\>**
Word Right	\<Ctr1F\>	**\<CtrlRgt\>**
Cursor Up	\<Ctr1E\>	**\<Up\>**
Cursor Down	\<Ctr1X\>	**\<Dn\>**
Scroll Up	\<Ctr1W\>	
Scroll Down	\<Ctr1Z\>	
Page Up	\<Ctr1R\>	**\<PgUp\>**
Page Down	\<Ctr1C\>	**\<PgDn\>**
Left of Line	\<Ctr1Q\>\<Ctr1S\>	**\<Home\>**
Right of Line	\<Ctr1Q\>\<Ctr1D\>	**\<End\>**
Top of Screen	\<Ctr1Q\>\<Ctr1E\>	**\<CtrlHome\>**
Bottom of Screen	\<Ctr1Q\>\<Ctr1X\>	**\<CtrlEnd\>**
Top of File	\<Ctr1Q\>\<Ctr1R\>	**\<CtrlPgUp\>**
Bottom of File	\<Ctr1Q\>\<Ctr1C\>	**\<CtrlPgDn\>**
Move to Block Begin	\<Ctr1Q\>\<Ctr1B\>	
Move to Block End	\<Ctr1Q\>\<Ctr1K\>	
Move to Previous Position	\<Ctr1Q\>\<Ctr1P\>	
Move to Marker 0	\<Ctr1Q\>0	
Move to Marker 1	\<Ctr1Q\>1	

Figure 2-5.   The Editor Commands window of TCINST

```
================ Turbo C Installation Program ============Command====
      ←—backspace   C-clear   R-restore   ↵—accept edit   <Scroll Lock> literal
======================================================================

New Line                  <Enter>              <Enter>
Cursor Left               <Ctrl S>             <Lft>
Cursor Right              <Ctrl D>             <Rgt>
Word Left                 <Ctrl A>             <CtrlLft>
Word Right                <Ctrl F>             <CtrlF><CtrlW>
Cursor Up                 <Ctrl E>             <Up>
Cursor Down               <Ctrl X>             <Dn>
Scroll Up                 <Ctrl W>
Scroll Down               <Ctrl Z>
Page Up                   <Ctrl R>             <PgUp>
Page Down                 <Ctrl C>             <PgDn>
Left of Line              <Ctrl Q><Ctrl S>     <Home>
Right of Line             <Ctrl Q><Ctrl D>     <End>
Top of Screen             <Ctrl Q><Ctrl E>     <Ctrl Home>
Bottom of Screen          <Ctrl Q><Ctrl X>     <Ctrl End>
Top of File               <Ctrl Q><Ctrl R>     <Ctrl PgUp>
Bottom of File            <Ctrl Q><Ctrl C>     <Ctrl PgDn>
Move to Block Begin       <Ctrl Q><Ctrl B>
Move to Block End         <Ctrl Q><Ctrl K>
Move to Previous Position <Ctrl Q><Ctrl P>
Move to Marker 0          <Ctrl Q>0
Move to Marker 1          <Ctrl Q>1
```

Figure 2-6.   Changing the **Word Right** command

Default edit modes

You use the entries under the **Default edit modes** option to set the state of certain options in the default operation of the Turbo C editor. The next chapter will explain what these options do.

Screen mode

The **Screen mode** option determines how Turbo C communicates with the video controller in your computer. There are various ways to write the screen. Depending upon the setup of your system, you may experience "snow" on screen when you use the fastest method. The **Screen Mode** option allows you to test for snow, based upon the type of video adapter you have.

Colors

The **Colors** option lets you select the color scheme that Turbo C uses when running in a color environment. Turbo C has three built-in color options. In addition, you may define your own color scheme for every part of the Turbo C user interface. To do this, after you select the **Colors** option, select the **Customize Colors** option. Turbo C asks you what area you wish to modify. If you select the main menu, then Turbo C will show you another menu that lets you select what part of the main menu you wish to adjust the color of. Your screen will look like Figure 2-7. Once you have selected the part that you wish to change, then Turbo C will show you a table of color options. As you try each option, the partial view of the main menu will change to reflect the particular color scheme.

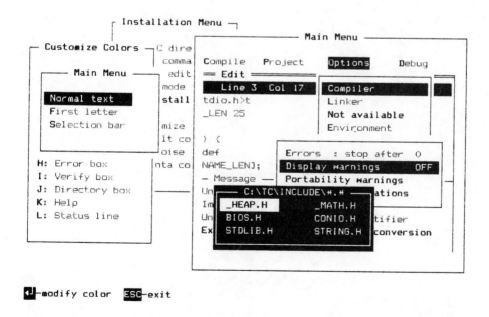

Figure 2-7.   Selecting the **Customize Colors** options with TCINST

Resize windows

You can use the **Resize windows** option to change the size of the edit and message windows in relation to each other. After selecting this option, you can use the up-arrow and down-arrow keys to move the line that separates the two windows.

Quit/save

The **Quit/save** option terminates the installation program. Turbo C will ask you whether you want to write into Turbo C the changes that you made while running the program; if you do, they will become the default mode of **Options**. If you do, answer **yes**. However, you probably should answer **no** at this time.

Now that you know your way around the basics of Turbo C's programming environment, you are ready to learn how to use the editor.

Using the Turbo C
Editor

CHAPTER 3

In this chapter, you will learn to use the editor that is built into Turbo C's integrated programming environment. The operation of this editor is similar to Micropro's WordStar program and the editors that are provided by Turbo Pascal, Turbo Prolog, and SideKick. If you already know how to use one of these editors, then skip to Chapter 4 at this time.

The Turbo C editor contains about 50 commands and is quite powerful. However, you will not have to learn all of its commands at once. The most important command types are insertion, deletion, block moves, searching, and searching with replacement. After you have mastered these basic command types, you will be able to learn the rest of the editor commands easily, and use them as you need them. Actually, learning to use the editor will be suprisingly simple because you will have Turbo C's on-line context-sensitive help system at your disposal.

Editor Commands

Before you begin, it is important to explain the way to give commands to the Turbo C editor. With few exceptions, all editor commands begin with a control character. In many commands, this character is then followed by another character. For example, the sequence CTRL-Q F is the command that tells the editor to find a string. (This chapter will use the abbreviation CTRL to stand for *control*.) This sequence indicates that you press CTRL-Q and then type **F** in either uppercase or lowercase.

Invoking the Editor and Entering Text

When Turbo C begins, it waits at the sign-on message until you press a key. When you do, Turbo C highlights the option **File** on the main menu. To invoke the editor, you either use the cursor keys to move the highlight to **Edit** or you simply type **e**. After doing that, the screen will look like the one in Figure 3-1. (The screens shown here reflect the way that Turbo C looks when you use a monochrome monitor. When you run Turbo C on a color system, the screens will look slightly different.) To leave the editor, you simply press F10.

The highlighted line is the *editor-status line* and tells you various things about the state of the editor and the file that you are editing. The first two items **Line** and **Col** display the line number and column number of the cursor. The **Insert** message indicates that the editor is in insert mode; that is, as you enter text, Turbo C will insert it in the middle of what (if anything) is already in the editor. The opposite mode is called *overwrite;* in this mode of operation, new text can overwrite existing text. You can toggle between these two modes by pressing INS. You will probably always use the default insert mode because it is the mode that is commonly used. The **Indent** message indicates that auto-indentation is on. You will see how this feature works shortly. You toggle the indentation mode by pressing CTRL-O I. The **Tab** message tells you that you may insert tabs by using TAB. You toggle the tab mode by pressing CTRL-O T. The final item on the editor-status line is the name of the file that you are editing. It is possible to tell Turbo C what file you want to edit when you invoke Turbo C from the command line, as you will see later. However, since you have not done so, Turbo C uses the default filename NONAME.C.

As soon as you invoke the editor, it is ready to accept text. So, to start, type the following lines:

>   **Roses are red**
>   **violets are blue**
>   **and so will you.**

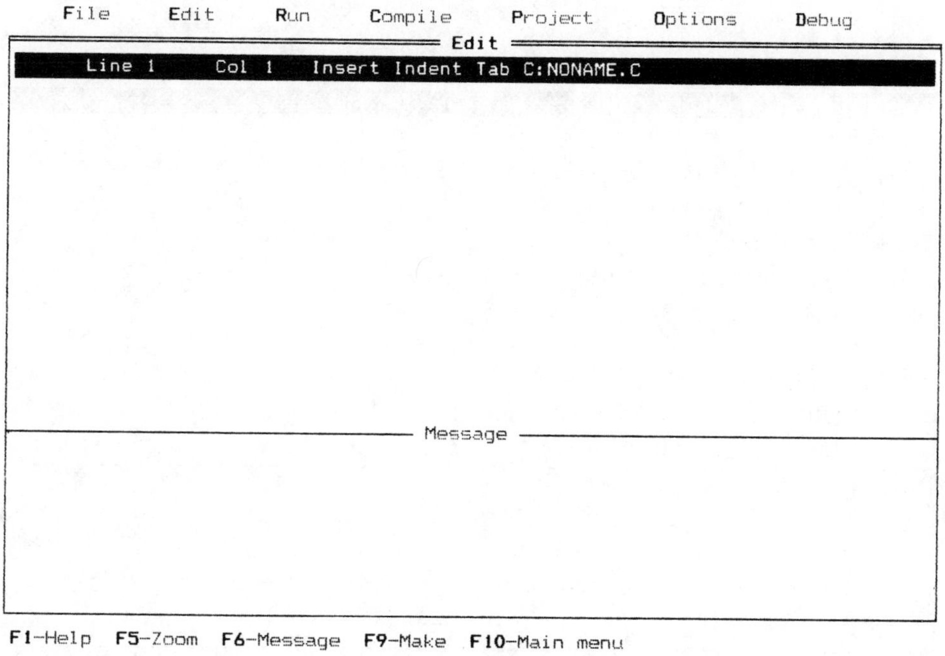

```
   File      Edit      Run      Compile      Project      Options      Debug
══════════════════════════════════════════ Edit ══════════════════════════════
    Line 1      Col 1     Insert Indent Tab C:NONAME.C





                                 ─── Message ───



F1─Help  F5─Zoom  F6─Message  F9─Make  F10─Main menu
```

Figure 3-1. The initial editor screen

Be sure to press ENTER after you type the last line. If you make mistakes, you can use the backspace key to correct them. Your screen will now look like the one in Figure 3-2. In the figure, notice the position of the cursor and the values that are associated with **Line** and **Col**.

You may use the arrow keys to move the cursor around in the file. At this time, use the keys to position the cursor at the far-left side of the line **and so will you**. Now, type the line **I like Turbo C** and press ENTER. As you type, watch the way that Turbo C moves the existing line to the right instead of overwriting it. This is what happens when the editor is in insert mode. If you had toggled the editor into overwrite mode, Turbo C would have overwritten the original line. The screen will now look like the one in Figure 3-3.

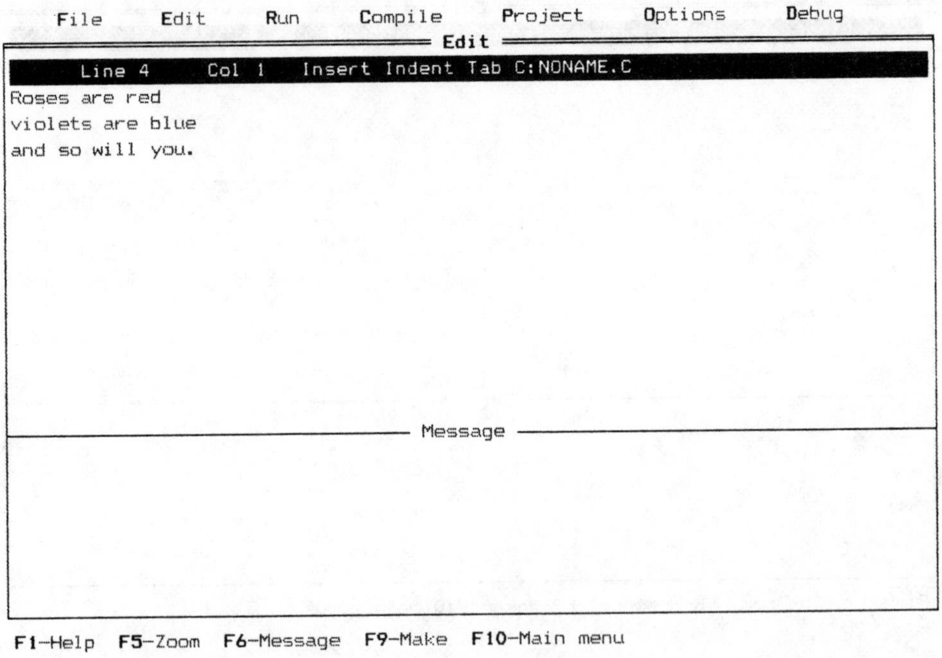

```
   File      Edit     Run     Compile    Project    Options    Debug
═══════════════════════════════════ Edit ═══════════════════════════════
      Line 4     Col 1    Insert Indent Tab C:NONAME.C
Roses are red
violets are blue
and so will you.

















──────────────────────────── Message ───────────────────────────────────








```

F1—Help F5—Zoom F6—Message F9—Make F10—Main menu

Figure 3-2. The editor screen with text entered

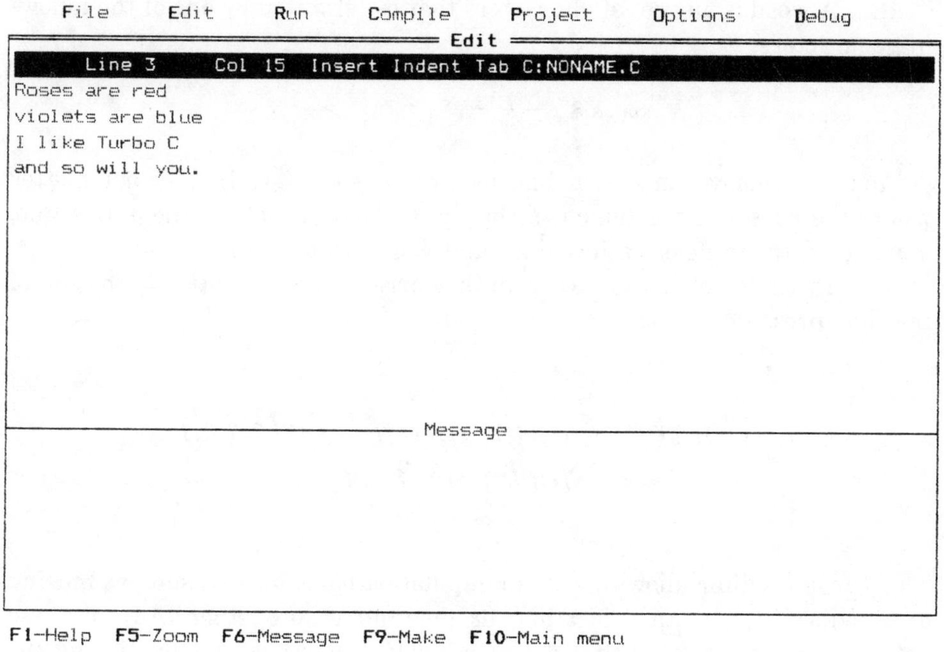

```
     File     Edit     Run     Compile     Project     Options     Debug
                              ═══ Edit ═══
      Line 3      Col 15   Insert Indent Tab C:NONAME.C
Roses are red
violets are blue
I like Turbo C
and so will you.




                           ─── Message ───




F1-Help  F5-Zoom  F6-Message  F9-Make  F10-Main menu
```

Figure 3-3. The editor screen after the insertion of a line

Deleting Characters, Words, and Lines

You can delete a single character in either of two ways: you can use the backspace key or DEL. The backspace key deletes the character immediately to the left of the cursor, while DEL deletes the character that the cursor is on.

You can delete an entire word that is to the right of the cursor by pressing

CTRL-T. A word is any set of characters that is delimited by one of the following characters:

$$\textit{space } \$ \ / - + * ' \wedge \ [\ ] \ (\ . \ ; \ , < >$$

You can remove an entire line by pressing CTRL-Y. It does not matter where the cursor is positioned in the line—Turbo C deletes the entire line. You should try to delete a few lines and words at this time.

If you wish to delete the text from the current cursor position to the end of the line, press CTRL-Q Y.

Moving, Copying, and Deleting Blocks of Text

The Turbo C editor allows you to manipulate a block of text, such as moving or copying it to another location, or deleting it altogether. Any of these actions requires that you first define a block. You can do this by moving the cursor to the beginning of the block and pressing CTRL-K B. Next, you move the cursor to the end of the block and press CTRL-K K. Turbo C will highlight the block that you have defined (or will display it in a different color if you have a color system). For example, move the cursor to the **I** at the beginning of the third line that you just entered and press CTRL-K B. Next, move the cursor to the end of the last line and press CTRL-K K. Your screen should look like the one in Figure 3-4.

To move a block of text, you move the cursor to the place where you want the text to go and then press CTRL-K V. This process causes Turbo C to delete the previously defined block of text from its current position and place it at the new location.

To copy a block, press CTRL-K C. For example, move the cursor to the top of the file and press CTRL-K C. Your screen will look like the one in Figure 3-5. You should experiment with these commands at this time.

To delete the currently marked block, press CTRL-K Y.

You may mark a single word by positioning the cursor on the first character in the word and pressing CTRL-K T.

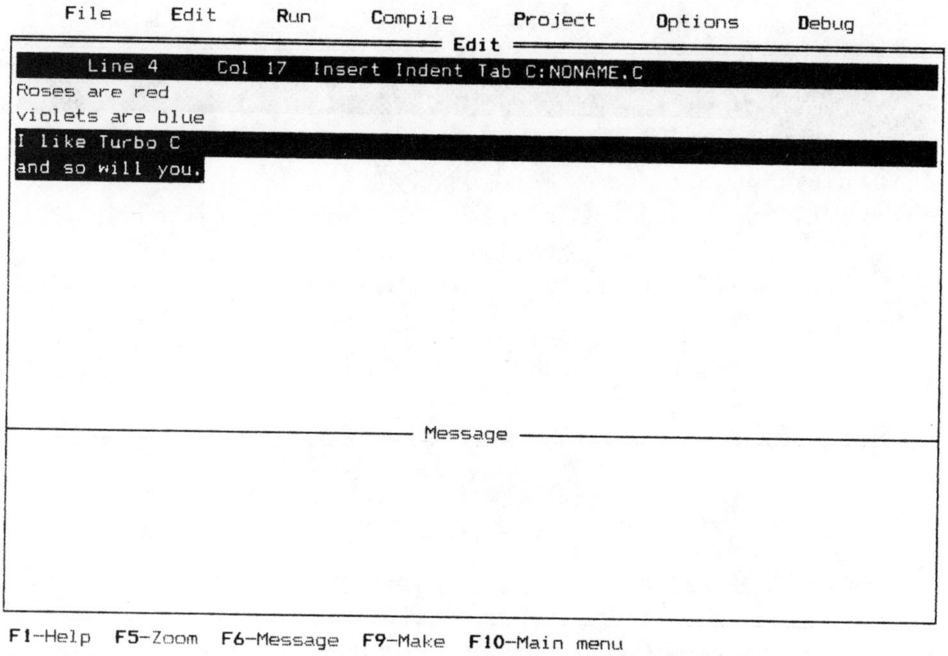
File Edit Run Compile Project Options Debug
Edit
Line 4 Col 17 Insert Indent Tab C:NONAME.C
Roses are red
violets are blue
I like Turbo C
and so will you.
Message
F1-Help F5-Zoom F6-Message F9-Make F10-Main menu

Figure 3-4. The editor screen after the definition of a block

More on Cursor Movement

The Turbo C editor has a number of special cursor commands, which are summarized in Table 3-1. Now, take the time to experiment with these commands.

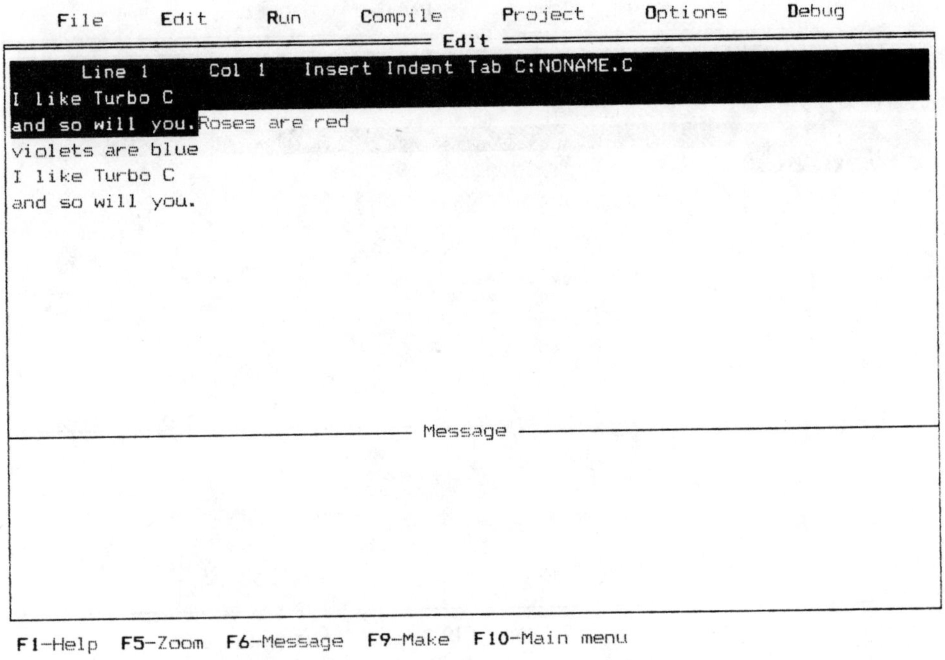

```
    File      Edit     Run     Compile     Project     Options     Debug
                                    = Edit =
     Line 1        Col 1    Insert Indent Tab C:NONAME.C
I like Turbo C
and so will you.Roses are red
violets are blue
I like Turbo C
and so will you.




                              — Message —




F1—Help  F5—Zoom  F6—Message  F9—Make  F10—Main menu
```

Figure 3-5.   The editor screen after a block copy

Find and
Find-and-Replace

To find a specific sequence of characters, you press CTRL-Q F. Turbo C will then prompt you at the status line for the string of characters that you wish to find. Type the string that you are looking for and then press ENTER. Turbo C will then prompt you, again at the status line, for search options. The search options modify the way that Turbo C conducts the search. The search

Table 3-1.   The Cursor Commands

Command	Action
CTRL-A	Moves to the start of the word that is to the left of the cursor.
CTRL-S	Moves left one character.
CTRL-D	Moves right one character.
CTRL-F	Moves to the start of the word that is to the right of the cursor.
CTRL-E	Moves the cursor up one line.
CTRL-R	Moves the cursor up one full screen.
CTRL-X	Moves the cursor down one line.
CTRL-C	Moves the cursor down one full screen.
CTRL-W	Scrolls the screen down.
CTRL-Z	Scrolls the screen up.
PGUP	Moves the cursor up one full screen.
PGDN	Moves the cursor down one full screen.
HOME	Moves the cursor to the start of the line.
END	Moves the cursor to the end of the line.
CTRL-QE	Moves the cursor to the top of the screen.
CTRL-QX	Moves the cursor to the bottom of the screen.
CTRL-QR	Moves the cursor to the top of the file.
CTRL-QC	Moves the cursor to the bottom of the file.

options are shown in Table 3-2. For example, typing **G2** will cause Turbo C to find the second occurrence of the string. No options need to be specified; you may simply press ENTER. If no options are present, then the search proceeds from the current cursor position forward, allowing case sensitivity and substring matches. You should try some searches at this time.

You can repeat a search by simply pressing CTRL-L. This feature is very convenient when you are looking for a specific string in the file.

To activate the find-and-replace command, press CTRL-Q A. Its operation is identical to the find command except that the find-and-replace command allows you to replace the string that you are looking for with another string. If you specify the **N** option, Turbo C will not ask you whether or not it should

Table 3-2.   The Search Options of the **Find** Commands

Option	Effect
B	Searches the file backwards starting from the current cursor position.
G	Searches the entire file, regardless of where the cursor is located.
N	Replaces without asking; for find-and-replace mode only.
U	Matches either uppercase or lowercase.
W	Matches only whole words—not substrings within words.
n	Causes the nth occurrence of the string to be found where **n** is an integer.

replace each occurrence of the search string with the replacement string. If you do not specify the **N** option, Turbo C will prompt you for a decision each time that a match occurs. You should try some find-and-replace examples now.

   You may enter control characters into the search string type by first pressing CTRL-P and then typing the control character that you want.

Setting and Finding Place-Markers

You can set up to four place-markers in your file by pressing CTRL-K and entering a number n, where n is the number of the place-marker (0 to 3). After you set a marker, pressing CTRL-Q n, where n is the marker number, causes the cursor to go to that marker.

Saving and Loading Your File

There are three methods to save your file. Two of them will save your file to a file that has the same name as that shown on the status line. The third method allows you to save your file to a disk file of a different name, and then makes that name the current name of your file. Let's look at how each method works.

At this time, exit the editor and return to the main menu by pressing F10. Select the **File** option. Your screen will look like the screen shown in Figure 3-6. The **Save** option saves what is currently in the editor into a disk file that uses the name shown on the status line. If you select the **Save** option now, you will create a file called NONAME.C. Although doing this won't hurt anything, you should probably use a different filename. To save under a different filename, you will use the **Write to** option, which allows you to enter the name of the file that you wish to write the current contents of the editor to. It also makes this name the default filename. Select the **Write to** option now. When Turbo C prompts you for the filename, type **test** and then press ENTER. This process causes Turbo C to save your file. You can also save your file while inside the editor by pressing F2.

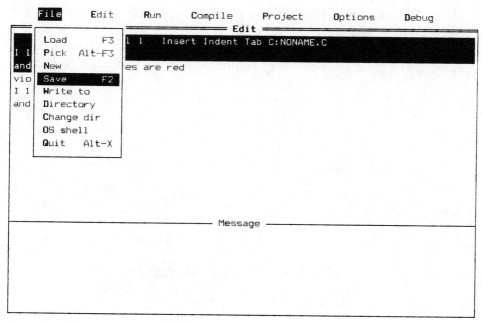

Figure 3-6. The **Save** option

To load a file, you may either press F3 while inside the editor, or select the **Load** option in the **File** menu. After you have loaded a file, Turbo C will prompt you for the name of the file that you wish to load. There are two ways that you can specify the filename. First, if you know the name, you can type it at this time. Second, if you are unsure of the name, do not type anything; Turbo C will display a list of all files with the .C extension, from which you may choose a file by using the arrow keys to position the highlight over it and then pressing ENTER.

Understanding Auto-indentation

Good programmers use indentation to help make the programs that they write clearer and easier to understand. To help assist in this practice, after you press ENTER, the Turbo C editor will automatically place the cursor at the same indentation level as the line that you just typed, assuming that the auto-indentation feature is on. (Remember that you toggle this feature by pressing CTRL-O I.) For example, make certain that the auto-indentation feature is on and enter the following few lines exactly as they are shown here.

> **This is an illustration**
> **of the autoindentation**
> **mechanism**
> **of the Turbo C**
> **editor.**

As you begin to write Turbo C programs, you will find this feature quite handy.

Moving Blocks of Text to and from Disk Files

It is possible to move a block of text into a disk file for later use. You can do this by first defining a block and then pressing CTRL-K W. After you have done so, Turbo C will prompt you for the name of the file that you wish to save the block in. Turbo C does not remove the original block of text from your program.

To read a block in, press CTRL-K R. Turbo C will prompt you for the filename, and then will read in the contents of that file at the current cursor location.

These two commands—CTRL-K W and CTRL-K R—are the most useful when you are moving text between two or more files, as is so often the case during program development.

Miscellaneous Commands

You can abort any command that requests input by pressing CTRL-U at the prompt. For example, if you execute the find command and then change your mind, simply press CTRL-U.

If you wish to enter a control character into the file, you first press CTRL-P and then type the control character that you want. Turbo C displays control characters in either low intensity or reverse video, depending on how your system is configured.

To undo changes that you made to a line before you move the cursor off that line, simply press CTRL-Q L. Remember that, once you have moved the cursor off the line, all changes are final.

If you wish to go to the beginning of a block, press CTRL-Q B. Pressing CTRL-Q K takes you to the end of a block.

One particularly useful command is CTRL-Q P, which puts the cursor back to its previous position. This command is handy if you want to search for something and then return to the position that you were at.

The Editor Command Summary

Table 3-3 shows all of the Turbo C editor commands.

Table 3-3. A Summary of Turbo C Editor Commands by Category

Cursor commands	
Command	**Action**
Left-arrow or CTRL-S	Left one character
Right-arrow or CTRL-D	Right one character
CTRL-A	Left one word
CTRL-F	Right one word
Up-arrow or CTRL-E	Up one line
Down-arrow or CTRL-X	Down one line
CTRL-W	Scroll up
CTRL-Z	Scroll down
PGUP or CTRL-R	Up one page
PGDN or CTRL-C	Down one page
HOME or CTRL-Q S	Go to the start of the line
END or CTRL-Q D	Go to the end of the line
CTRL-Q E	Go to the top of the screen
CTRL-Q X	Go to the bottom of the screen
CTRL-Q R	Go to the top of the file
CTRL-Q C	Go to the bottom of the file
CTRL-Q B	Go to the start of the block
CTRL-Q K	Go to the end of the block
CTRL-Q P	Go to the last cursor position
Insert commands	
INS or CTRL-V	Toggle insert mode
ENTER or CTRL-N	Insert a blank line
Delete commands	
CTRL-Y	Entire line
CTRL-Q Y	To end of the line
Backspace	Character to the left
DEL or CTRL-G	Character at the cursor
CTRL-T	Word to the right
Block commands	
CTRL-K B	Mark the beginning
CTRL-K K	Mark the end
CTRL-K T	Mark a word
CTRL-K C	Copy a block
CTRL-K Y	Delete a block
CTRL-K H	Hide or display a block
CTRL-K V	Move a block
CTRL-K R	Write a block to disk
CTRL-K W	Read a block from disk

Table 3-3. A Summary of Turbo C Editor Commands by Category (*continued*)

Find commands	
Command	**Action**
CTRL-Q F	Find
CTRL-Q A	Find-and-replace
CTRL-Q N	Find place-marker
CTRL-L	Repeat find
Miscellaneous commands	
CTRL-U	Abort
CTRL-O I	Toggle auto-indentation mode
CTRL-P	Control character prefix
F10	Exit the editor
F3	New file
CTRL-Q W	Restore the overwritten error message
F2	Save
CTRL-K N	Set a place-marker
CTRL-O T	Toggle tab mode
CTRL-Q L	Undo

Invoking Turbo C with a Filename

As mentioned earlier, you can specify the name of the file that you want to edit when you invoke Turbo C. To do this, simply type the name of the file after the **TC** on the command line. For example, typing **TC MYFILE** will execute Turbo C and cause it to load the file MYFILE.C into the editor. Turbo C automatically adds the extension .C. If MYFILE does not exist, Turbo C will create it.

Turbo C Essentials

C H A P T E R   4

When it comes to programming languages, the saying "You can't learn it if you don't know it already" has never been more true! The problem is that each element in a programming language does not exist in a void, but rather exists in relation to the other elements.

To solve this problem, this chapter develops and discusses a number of simple sample programs without going into a lot of detail. Also, the chapter presents a few essential aspects of Turbo C. This chapter is designed for either the novice programmer or the programmer who has never used a structured language before. Reading this chapter will give you a rough idea about how Turbo C works. Most of the material presented here will be examined more fully later, so if you already know a little about Turbo C, you may want to skip to Chapter 5 at this time.

Turbo C Is
Case-Sensitive

If you are familiar with languages such as Turbo Pascal or BASIC, one of the first differences that you will see in Turbo C is that it is *case-sensitive*. This means that it treats uppercase and lowercase letters as separate characters. For example, in Turbo Pascal, the variable names **count**, **Count**, and **COUNT** are three ways of specifying the same variable. However, in Turbo C, these names would represent three different variables. So, when you enter the sample programs shown in this book, be very careful to use the proper case.

A Simple
Turbo C Program

To begin, execute Turbo C and select the **Edit** option. Next, enter the following short program at this time.

```
/* Sample program #1 */

main()
{
   int age;

   age = 36;

   printf("My age is %d\n", age);
}
```

After you are finished editing, press F10 to return to the main menu. To compile and run this program, select **Run**. Turbo C will then compile the program, link it with the necessary library functions (libraries will be described shortly), and execute it.

As the compilation begins, Turbo C opens the *compiler/linker window*, which allows you to monitor the progress of the compilation. Your screen should look like the one in Figure 4-1 during compilation. When the compilation is complete, the screen will clear and Turbo C will display the line **My age is 36**, followed by a carriage-return-linefeed.

A Closer Look

Let's take a closer look at what each line in the sample program just presented does. The first line

```
/* Sample program #1 */
```

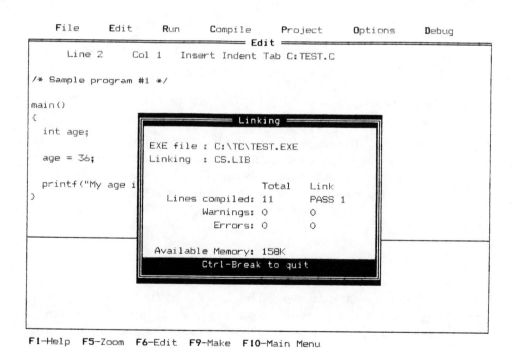

Figure 4-1.   The Turbo C compilation window

is a comment. In Turbo C, comments begin with the sequence /* and are terminated by the sequence */. The Turbo C compiler ignores anything that is between the beginning and ending comment symbols.

If you examine the sample program closely, you will notice that a blank line follows the comment line. In Turbo C, blank lines are permitted and have no effect upon the program.

The line

```
main()
```

specifies the name of a function. All Turbo C programs begin execution by calling the **main()** function. You will learn more about functions a little later.

The next line consists of a single curly brace

```
{
```

which signifies the start of the **main()** function.

The first line of code inside function **main()** is

```
int age;
```

This line declares a variable called **age** and tells the compiler that **age** is an integer. In Turbo C, you must declare all variables before you use them. The declaration process involves the specification of both the variable's name and its type. In this case, **age** is of type **int**, which is Turbo C's keyword for the integer type. Integers are whole numbers between -32768 and 32767.

The next line is

```
age = 36;
```

which is an assignment statement. This line places the value **36** into the variable **age**. Notice that Turbo C uses a single equal sign for assignment, unlike Turbo Pascal, which uses the := pair. Also notice that this statement ends with a semicolon. You terminate all statements in Turbo C with a semicolon.

The next line, which outputs information to the screen, is

```
printf("My age is %d\n", age);
```

This statement is important for two reasons. First, it is an example of a function call. Second, it illustrates the use of Turbo C's standard output function **printf()**. This line of code consists of two parts: the function name, which is **printf()**, and its two arguments: **"My age is %d \n"**, and **age**. As shown earlier, since this line is a Turbo C statement, it ends with a semicolon.

In Turbo C, there are no built-in I/O routines. Instead, these functions are provided by Turbo C's standard library and are called when needed. In fact, Turbo C's standard library contains many useful functions. Any program that you write will also contain functions that you create, in addition to the library functions. In either case, to call a function is quite easy: you simply write its name and supply the necessary arguments. Calling a function will be explained more completely shortly.

The **printf()** statement works in this way. The first argument is a string that may contain either characters or format codes. A format code begins with the percent sign. When Turbo C encounters the **%d**, it acts as a signal that an integer is to be displayed in decimal format. The second argument presents the value to be displayed—in this case, **age**. The **\n** is a special format code that tells **printf()** to issue a carriage-return-linefeed sequence. To understand the relationship between the normal characters and the format codes, change the line to read

```
printf("My %d age is\n", age);
```

and rerun the program. Turbo C now displays the message **My 36 age is**. Therefore, the position of the format command in the string determines when the second argument to **printf()** will be printed. As you will shortly see, **printf()** is substantially more powerful than this example shows.

The last line of the program is a closing curly brace, which signals the end of the **main()** function. When Turbo C reaches the end of **main()**, program execution is terminated.

Handling Errors

Invoke the editor and remove the opening parenthesis from the statement **main()** and the semicolon that terminates the line **int age;**. Try to compile the program. As you would expect, the program generates errors, which

Turbo C displays in the message window. Your screen will look like the one in Figure 4-2. Notice that Turbo C highlights the first error in the message window, as well as highlighting the line in the program in which the error was detected. Remember, Turbo C tries to make sense out of whatever you give it so the point at which Turbo C detects an error might be one line after the error occurred because that is the point at which Turbo C finally decided that you made a mistake!

One of the best features about the Turbo C integrated environment is that you can interactively fix the errors in your program. By pressing F8, you can advance to the next error. Pressing F7 causes you to go to the previous error. Pressing ENTER activates the editor. You should fix your program at this time. Don't worry about the third error message. Turbo C generated this message because the other two errors caused Turbo C to interpret the call to **printf( )** incorrectly.

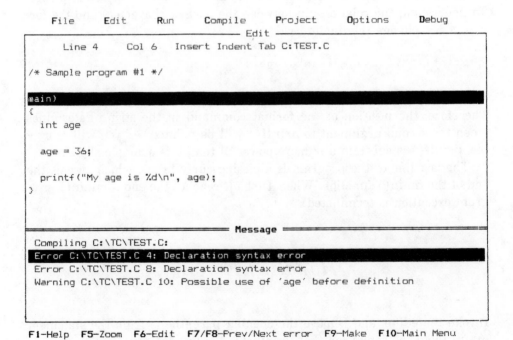

Figure 4-2.   A compilation with errors

Errors Versus Warnings

The third error message that Turbo C generated when you mangled the program actually is not an error message, but rather is a warning. As stated earlier, C was designed to be very forgiving and to allow the compilation of virtually anything that is syntactically correct. However, some things, even though syntactically correct, are highly suspicious. When encountering one of these, Turbo C prints a warning. You as the programmer then must decide whether Turbo C's suspicions are justified or not.

In the example, Turbo C generated the warning message as a side effect of the other errors, but you will undoubtedly encounter several real warnings as you continue to write Turbo C programs.

A Second Program

Although the first sample program illustrates some important aspects about Turbo C, it is fairly pointless. The second sample program does something that is useful: it converts from feet to meters. In doing so, it also illustrates a second library function called **scanf( )**, that is used to read an integer value entered by a user. Enter this program into your computer now:

```
/* Sample program #2 - feet to meters */

main()
{
   int feet;
   float meters;

   printf("Enter number of feet: ");

   scanf("%d", &feet);

   meters = feet * 0.3048; /* feet to meters conversion */

   printf("%d feet is %f meters\n", feet, meters);
}
```

The program introduces some important new features. First, it declares two variables: **feet** of type **int**; and **meters** of type **float**, which means that it can have a fractional component. (Type **float** corresponds to Turbo Pascal's type **REAL**.)

Second, the program uses the library function **scanf( )** to read an integer entered at the keyboard. The **%d** in the first argument tells **scanf( )** to read an integer and to place the results in the variable that follows. The **&** that precedes **feet** is necessary for **scanf( )** to work properly, but for now you will have to take this explanation on faith until you know more about the way that Turbo C works. (Don't leave the **&** out—if you do, it could cause a crash!)

Next, the program converts the number of feet to meters. Notice that, even though **feet** is an integer, it may be divided by a floating-point number and may be assigned to a floating-point variable. Unlike Turbo Pascal and many other modern languages, Turbo C allows you to use different types of data in an expression. As is the case in virtually all other programming languages, the * signifies multiplication.

The program displays the conversion by using a call to **printf( )**. As you can see, this time **printf( )** takes three arguments: the control string, and the variables **feet** and **meters**. The general rule for **printf( )** is that there are as many arguments that follow the control string as there are format codes in the control string. Since **printf( )** uses two percent commands, it needs two additional arguments. These arguments are matched in order, from left to right, with the format commands. If you look closely at the function, you will notice that it uses **%f** to print **meters**, and does not use **%d**. The reason for this is that **printf( )** must know precisely what type of data it is going to display. The **%f** indicates that a value of type **float** follows.

A Variation

One limitation to the second sample program is that it can only convert whole numbers of feet into meters. A more flexible program would be able to convert floating-point values into meters. You can accomplish this by changing the program, as shown here.

```
/* Sample program #2 version 2 - feet to meters */

main()
{
  float feet, meters;  /* make feet a float */

  printf("Enter number of feet: ");

  scanf("%f", &feet);  /* read a float */

  meters = feet * 0.3048; /* feet to meters conversion */

  printf("%f feet is %f meters\n", feet, meters);
}
```

As you can see, the first feature that has been changed is **feet**, which is now of type **float**. In Turbo C, you can declare several variables of the same type by using a comma-separated list. Next, this version calls the **scanf()** statement by using **%f**, instead of **%d**. This change causes **scanf()** to read a floating-point variable. (Do you notice the similarity between the **printf()** and **scanf()** format codes? You should—the codes are the same.) Finally, the **printf()** statement now needs a **%f** command to display **feet**.

A Quick Review

Before you proceed, let's review the most important Turbo C features that you have learned:

1. All Turbo C programs must have a **main()** function, which marks the point at which program execution begins.

2. A program must declare all variables before using them.

3. Turbo C supports a variety of data types, including integer and floating-point.

4. The **printf()** function outputs information to the screen.

5. The **scanf()** function reads information from the keyboard.

6. Program execution stops when the end of **main()** is encountered.

What Is a Turbo C Function?

The C language is based on the concept of *building blocks*. The building blocks are called *functions*. A C program is a collection of one or more functions. To write a program, you first create functions and then put them together.

In C, a function is a subroutine that contains one or more C statements, and that performs one or more tasks. In well-written C code, each function performs only one task. Each function has a name and a list of arguments that the function will receive. In general, you can give a function whatever name you please, with the exception of **main**, which C reserves for the function that begins execution of your program. If you are familiar with Turbo Pascal (or any other structured language), keep in mind that Turbo C functions are similar to Pascal procedures and functions.

When denoting functions, this book will use a notational convention that has become standard in texts about C. A function will have parentheses after the function name. For example, if a function's name is **max**, then this book will write the function as **max()**. This notation will help you distinguish variable names from function names in this book.

Here is the general form of a C function:

> *function-name (parameter list)*
> *parameter declarations;*
> {
>   *body of code*
> }

All Turbo C programs must have a **main()** function because it is the function that is first executed when your program begins to run. Furthermore, your program may have one and only one function called **main()**. (If you used more than one **main()**, Turbo C would not know which one to call first.)

You can create other functions in much the same way that you used to create **main()**, and you can call them from other parts of your program. For example, this program uses the function **hello()** to print **hello** on the screen:

```
/* A simple program with two functions */

main()
{
   hello(); /* call the hello function */
}

hello()
{
   printf("hello\n");
}
```

Functions with Arguments

A function argument is simply a value that is passed to the function at the time that the function is called. You have already seen two functions that take arguments: **printf( )** and **scanf( )**. You can create functions that take arguments, too. For example, the function **sqr( )** in this program takes an integer argument and displays the square of the integer:

```
/* A program that uses a function with an argument */
main()
{
  int num;

  printf("enter a number: ");

  scanf("%d", &num);

  sqr(num);  /* call sqr() with num */
}

sqr(x)   /* parameter name goes inside parentheses */
int x;   /* declaration of the parameter */
{
  printf("%d square is %d\n", num, num*num);
}
```

The declaration of **sqr( )** places the variable that will be receiving the value passed to **sqr( )** inside the parentheses that follow the function name. (Functions that do not take arguments do not need any variables, so the parentheses are empty.) Then, the program declares the variable because the function must know what type of data it will receive. You should enter this program and run it so that you can see that it does operate as expected.

It is important to keep two terms straight. First, the term *argument* refers to the value that is used to call a function. The term *formal parameter* refers to the variable in a function that receives the value of the arguments used in the function call. In fact, functions that can take arguments are called *parameterized functions*. The important distinction to understand is that the variable used as an argument in a function call has nothing to do with the formal parameter that receives its value.

Here is another simple example of a parameterized function. The function **mul( )** prints the product of its two integer arguments.

```
/* another example of function arguments */

main()
{
  mul(10, 11);
}

mul(a, b)
int a, b;
{
  printf("%d", a*b);
}
```

Chapter 9 will cover functions and their arguments later, but this short overview should give you the basic idea.

Functions that Return Values

Before you leave this discussion of functions, it is necessary to touch lightly upon *function return values*. Many of the Turbo C library functions that you will need use them. In Turbo C, a function may return a value to the calling routine by using the **return** keyword. To illustrate, you can rewrite the program given earlier that prints the product of two numbers as shown here:

```
/* A program that uses return */

main()
{
  int answer;

  answer = mul(10, 11); /* assign return value */

  printf("The answer is %d\n", answer);
}

/* This function returns a value */
mul(a, b)
int a, b;
{
  return a*b;
}
```

In this example, **mul( )** returns the value of **a∗b** by using the **return** statement. The program then assigns this value to **answer**; that is, the value returned by the **return** statement becomes the value of **mul( )** in the calling routine.

Be careful: just as there are different types of variables, there are different types of return values. The type that the **mul( )** routine returns is **int** by default. You will have to wait until Chapter 9 to see how to return values of different types.

You can cause a function to return by using the **return** statement without any values attached to it. In addition, you can use more than one **return** in a function.

Two Simple Commands

In order to understand the examples in the next chapters, you must understand, in their simplest form, two Turbo C commands: the **if** and the **for**. Later chapters will explore the capabilities of these commands completely.

The if Statement

The Turbo C **if** statement operates in much the same way that an IF statement operates in any other language. Its simplest form is

if(*condition*) *statement*;

where *condition* is an expression that evaluates to either true or false. In C, true is nonzero and false is zero. For example, this fragment prints the phrase **10 is less than 11** on screen:

```
if(10 < 11) printf("10 is less than 11");
```

The comparison operators in Turbo C are similar to those in other languages, such as < for less than, or >= for greater than or equal to. However, in C, the equality operator is ==. Therefore, this statement does not print the message **hello**:

```
if(10==11) printf("hello"):
```

The for Loop

The **for** loop in Turbo C can operate much like the FOR loop in other languages, including Turbo Pascal and BASIC. The simplest form of the **for** loop is

for(*initialization, condition, increment*) *statement;*

where *initialization* sets the loop-control variable to an initial value. The *condition* is an expression that Turbo C tests each time the loop repeats. As long as *condition* is true, the loop keeps running. The *increment* portion increments the loop-control variable. For example, this program prints the numbers 1 through 100 on screen:

```
/* A simple program that illustrates the for loop */

main()
{
  int count;

  for(count=1; count<=100; count++) printf("%d ", count);
}
```

Here, the program initializes **count** to 1. Each time that the loop repeats, the program tests the condition **count<=100**. If the condition is true, the program executes the **printf( )** statement and increases **count** by one, which is indicated by the two plus signs after **count**. When **count** is greater than 100, the condition is false and the loop stops.

Blocks of Code

Because C is a structured language, it supports the creation of blocks of code. A *code block* is a logically connected group of program statements that the computer treats as a unit. In Turbo C, you create a code block by placing a sequence of statements between opening and closing curly braces. For example, in

```
if(x<10) {
  printf("too low, try again");
  scanf("%d", &x);
}
```

Turbo C executes the two statements after **if** and between the curly braces if **x** is less than 10. These two statements and the braces represent a block of code. They are a logical unit: one statement cannot execute without the other also executing. In C, the target of most commands may be either a single statement or a code block. Not only do code blocks allow you to implement many algorithms with greater clarity, elegance, and efficiency, but also they help you conceptualize the true nature of the routine.

Characters and Strings

Another important data type in Turbo C is **char**, which stands for *character*. A character is a one-byte value that you can use to hold printable characters or integers in the range of −128 through 127. In a program, a character constant is enclosed between single quotes. For example, this program prints the letters **ABC** on screen. Notice that this program introduces a new **printf()** format code, which prints a single character.

```
/* A simple example of characters */

main()
{
  char ch;

  ch = 'A';
```

```
    printf("%c", ch);

    ch = 'B';
    printf("%c", ch);

    ch = 'C';
    printf("%c", ch);
}
```

Although you can use **scanf( )** to read a single character from the keyboard, a more common way is to use Turbo C's library function **getche( )**. The **getche( )** function waits until you press a key and then returns the result. For example, this program will print the message **you pressed my magic key** if you type an **H**:

```
main()
{
   char ch;

   ch = getche();   /* read one character from the keyboard */

   if(ch=='H') printf("you pressed my magic key\n");
}
```

This program also illustrates that you can use characters in **if** statements.

Strings

In Turbo C, a string is an array of characters that is terminated by a null. Turbo C does not have a "string" type. Instead, you must declare an array of characters and use the various string functions in the library to manipulate them. Although this book covers the subject of arrays later, here you will see the way to create a string and learn two basic principles. This chapter presents this material now because strings are so common and are useful in developing examples of other concepts.

An array is simply a list of variables of the same type. You create an array by placing the size of the array between angle brackets after the array name. The following fragment declares an 80-element single-dimension character array called **str**:

```
   char str[80];
```

To reference a specific element, you place the index of the element between square brackets after the array name. All arrays in Turbo C are indexed from zero. Therefore, **str[0]** is the first element, **str[1]** is the second element, and so on until **str[79]**, which is the eightieth and last element.

The single most important feature to remember about arrays in Turbo C—in fact, in C in general—is that Turbo C performs no bounds checking. This means that you can, if you are not careful, "run off the end" of an array. For now, the easiest way to prevent this problem is always to use an array that is large enough to hold whatever you will put into it. As mentioned earlier, all strings end in a null. A null in Turbo C is a 0 and is specified in a program as the character constant ' \0'. Therefore, in order for a character array to be large enough to hold the word **hello**, it must be at least six characters long: five characters for the string and one character for the null terminator, as shown here.

h	e	l	l	o	'\0'

To read a string from the keyboard, you first create a character array to hold the string and then use the library function **gets( )**. The **gets( )** function takes the name of the string as an argument and reads characters from the keyboard until you press ENTER. ENTER is not stored but is replaced by the null terminator. The following program illustrates the use of **gets( )**.

```
/* A simple string example */
main()
{
   char str[80];

   printf("enter your name: ");

   gets(str);

   printf("hello %s", str);
}
```

Notice that the program uses the format command %s to tell **printf( )** that it should print a string.

A Quick Review
of *print()*

In this book, nearly every program example that does console output will use the **printf()** function. You have already seen several examples in the preceding programs. Let's take a more formal look at **printf()** now.

The general form of **printf()** is

printf(*"control string",argument list*)

In the **printf()** function, the *control string* contains either characters that will be displayed on screen, format commands that tell **printf()** how to display the rest of the arguments, or both. The format codes that you have learned so far are shown here:

Code	Meaning
%d	Display an integer in decimal format
%f	Display a float in decimal format
%c	Display a character
%s	Display a string

There are several other format codes, which will be explained later.

You may embed format-control commands anywhere in the first string of characters. When you call **printf()**, it scans the control string. The **printf()** function simply prints on screen all regular characters as they appear. When encountering a format command, **printf()** remembers it and uses it when printing the appropriate argument. The function matches up format commands and arguments left to right. The number of format commands in the control string tells **printf()** how many subsequent arguments to expect.

The following examples will show you the **printf()** function in action.

```
printf("%s %d","this is a string ", 100);

        displays: this is a string 100

printf("this is a string %d",100);

        displays: this is a string 100

printf("number %d is decimal, %f is float.",10,110.789);
```

```
       displays: number 10 is decimal, 110.789 is float.
printf("%c %s %d-%x",'a'," number in decimal and hex: ",10,10);
       displays: a number in decimal and hex: 10-A
    printf("%s","HELLO\n");
       displays: HELLO  (same as the program)
```

You *must* have the same number of arguments as you do format commands in the control string. If you do not, the screen will display either garbage or no information at all.

A Quick Review of scanf()

The **scanf()** function is one of Turbo C's input functions. Although you can use it to read virtually any type of data entered at the keyboard, in the first few chapters of this book, you will be using it only to input integers or **floats**. The general form of **scanf()** is

scanf(*"control string"*, *argument list*);

For now, assume that the *control string* may only contain format codes. (In fact, until you study **scanf()** in detail later, don't put anything in the *control string* other than the format codes or you will probably confuse the function.) The two codes that you will need are **%d** and **%f**, which tell **scanf()** to read an integer and a floating-point number, respectively. The *argument list* must contain exactly the same number of arguments as the number of format codes in the *control string*. If this is not the case, various problems could occur—including a program crash.

In the *argument list*, an **&** must precede the variables that will receive the values read from the keyboard. The need for this format is too complicated to explain at this time; for now, it is sufficient to say that the **&** lets **scanf()** place a value into the argument.

Semicolons, Braces, and Comments

You may have been wondering why so many statements in C are terminated with a semicolon. In C, the semicolon is a *statement terminator;* thus, you must end each individual statement with a semicolon. The semicolon indicates the end of one logical entity. (If you are familiar with Pascal, *be careful.* The semicolon in Pascal is a statement *separator;* in C, it is a statement *terminator.*)

In C, a block is a set of logically connected statements, which is inside opening and closing braces. If you consider a block as a group of statements with a semicolon after each statement, it makes sense that the block is not followed by a semicolon.

Unlike BASIC, C does not recognize the end of the line as a terminator. This means C does not limit position, which makes it easier to group statements together visually for clarity, as shown by these two equivalent code fragments.

```
x=y;

y=y+1;

mul(x,y);
```

is the same as

```
x=y;   y=y+1;          mul(x,y);
```

You may place comments in C anywhere in a program. Comments are enclosed between two markers. The starting comment marker is /* and the ending comment marker is */. In ANSI standard C, you may not nest comments, as shown in the following comment within a comment, which will generate a compile-time error:

```
/* this is /* an error */ */
```

Turbo C does have an option that allows nested comments but using it will make your code nonportable.

Indentation
Practices

As you may notice, the earlier examples indented certain statements. The C language is *free-form* because C does not care where you place statements in relation to each other on a line.

However, over the years, a common and accepted indentation style has developed that creates readable programs. This book will follow that style and recommends that you do so as well. Using this style, you indent one level after each opening brace and back one level at each closing brace. There are certain statements that encourage some additional indenting and these will be covered later.

Sometimes, in a particularly complex routine, the indentation is so great that the lines of code begin to wrap around. To avoid wrapping, you can break a statement into two parts and put them on separate lines. For example, this statement is perfectly valid:

```
count = 10 * unit /
        amount_left;
```

In general, you can break a line wherever you can place a space. However, you should break lines only when necessary because it can confuse anyone reading the code.

The Turbo C
Library

The Turbo C library and its functions have been mentioned frequently in this chapter. Now it's time for you to learn about them. All C compilers have libraries that provide functions to perform most commonly needed tasks. The designers of Turbo C have implemented a library that exceeds that defined in the ANSI standard for C. This library contains most of the general-purpose functions that you will use. You should examine the section of the Turbo C user manual that describes these functions because they can help save you coding time. This book will introduce library functions as needed, with Chapter 16 discussing the most important ones.

When you use a function that is not part of the program you wrote, Turbo C "remembers" its name. When the *linker* takes over, it finds the missing function and adds it to your object code. The linker is a program that combines your program with the necessary library functions. The functions in the library are in *relocatable* format. This means that the functions do not define the absolute memory address for the various machine-code instructions, but rather keep only offset information. When your program links with the functions in the standard library, Turbo C uses these memory offsets to create the actual addresses used. Several technical manuals and books explain this process in more detail. However, you do not need any further explanation of the actual relocation process in order to program in Turbo C.

There are several versions of the Turbo C library, with one version for each memory model. Also, there is a separate mathematics library for 8087 emulation. You don't need to worry about any of the libraries now, however, because Turbo C automatically selects the correct library based upon the options that you set with the **Options** selection from the main menu.

The Turbo C Keywords

Like all other programming languages, Turbo C consists of keywords and syntax rules that apply to each keyword. A *keyword* is essentially a command and, to a great extent, the keywords of a language define what can be done and how it will be done.

As you know from Chapter 1, C is being standardized and Turbo C supports the entire set of keywords that the proposed ANSI standard specifies. These keywords are shown in Table 4-1.

In addition, Turbo C adds eight additional keywords that you can use to take advantage of the memory organization of the 8088/8086 family of processors, and three keywords that support interlanguage programming and interrupts. The extended keywords are shown in Table 4-2.

Table 4-1. The 32 Keywords, as Defined by the Proposed ANSI Standard

auto	double	int	struct
break	else	long	switch
case	enum	register	typedef
char	extern	return	union
const	float	short	unsigned
continue	for	signed	void
default	goto	sizeof	volatile
do	if	static	while

Table 4-2. The Turbo C Extended Keywords

asm	_cs	_ds	_es
_ss	cdecl	far	huge
interrupt	near	pascal	

All Turbo C keywords are lowercase. As stated earlier, C is case-sensitive; hence, **else** is a keyword, while **ELSE** is not. You may not use a keyword for any other purpose in a Turbo C program. For example, you cannot use a keyword as the name of a variable.

A Review of Terms

Before you go on to the next chapter, you should review these terms:

Compile-time. The events that occur while your program is being compiled. A common compile-time occurrence is a syntax error.

Library. The file containing the standard functions that your program may use. These functions include all I/O operations, as well as other useful routines.

Linker. A program that links separately compiled functions together into one program; used to combine the functions in the standard C library with the code that you write.

Object code. The code that the computer can read and execute directly, and that has been translated from the source code of a program.

Run-time. The events that occur while your program is executing.

Source code. The text of a program that a user can read; commonly thought of as "the program."

Turbo C Basics

P A R T   T W O

▲

Now that you have installed Turbo C on your computer, know how to use the editor, are familiar with the Turbo C programming environment, and have run a few C programs, you are ready to learn the language in a somewhat more formal way. In Part Two, you will learn the essentials of Turbo C programming, including variables, operators, expressions, program-control statements, functions, strings, and basic I/O.

The following notational conventions will be observed. Any word that is part of the Turbo C language will be printed in boldface. In addition, any variable or function name used in a program will be in boldface when referred to in the text. Descriptive words that are not part of the Turbo C language but that are used to form a general description will be displayed in italics.

▼

Variables,
Constants,
Operators, and
Expressions

C H A P T E R   5

Operators manipulate variables and constants to form expressions. These four—variables, constants, operators, and expressions—are the underpinnings of the C language. Before you can study Turbo C much further, you should understand the concepts presented in this chapter. Unlike some computer languages—notably BASIC—that have a simple (and limited) approach to variables, operators, and expressions, C gives much greater power and importance to these elements. Although you might feel tempted to skip ahead to later chapters that present the "meat" of the language, you are urged not to do so because this chapter presents some important principles.

Identifiers

The C language defines *identifiers* as the names that are used to refer to variables, functions, labels, and various other user-defined objects. In C, an identifier can vary from one character to several characters. The first character must be a letter or an underscore, with subsequent characters being either letters, numbers, or an underscore. Turbo C also allows you to use a dollar sign ($) within an identifier — but not as the beginning character. Here are some examples of correct and incorrect identifiers.

Correct	Incorrect
count	1count
test23	hi!there
high—balance	high..balance

In Turbo C, the first 32 characters of an identifier are significant. This means that if two variables have the first 32 characters in common and differ only on the thirty-third, Turbo C will not be able to tell them apart. For example, these two identifiers

> **this_is_a_very_long_name_used_as_an_example**

and

> **this_is_a_very_long_name_used_as_an_example_too**

will appear like this to Turbo C:

> **this_is_a_very_long_name_used_as**

The C language treats uppercase and lowercase letters as being different and distinct. For example, **count**, **Count**, and **COUNT** are three separate identifiers.

An identifier may not be the same as a Turbo C keyword, and it should not have the same name as functions either that you wrote or that are in the Turbo C library.

Data Types

As you saw in Chapter 4, all variables in C must be declared prior to their use. This is necessary because Turbo C must know what type of data a variable is before it can properly compile any statement that that variable is used in. In C, there are five basic data types: *character, integer, floating-point, double-floating-point,* and *valueless.* The keywords used to declare variables of these types are **char, int, float, double,** and **void,** respectively. Table 5-1 presents the size and range of each data type of Turbo C for the IBM PC.

You use variables of type **char** to hold 8-bit ASCII characters such as **A, B,** or **C** or any other 8-bit quantity. Variables of type **int** can hold integer quantities that do not require a fractional component. You often use variables of this type to control loops and conditional statements. You include variables of the types **float** and **double** in your programs either when you need a fractional component or when your application requires very large numbers. The difference between a **float** variable and a **double** variable is the magnitude of the largest (and smallest) number that they can hold. As Table 5-1 shows, a **double** in Turbo C can store a number approximately ten times larger than a **float.** You use the **void** type to help enhance type checking; it will be discussed later in this book.

Table 5-1. Size and Range of Turbo C's Basic Data Types

Type	Bit width	Range
char	8	0 to 255
int	16	−32768 to 32767
float	32	3.4E−38 to 3.4E+38
double	64	1.7E−308 to 1.7E+308
void	0	valueless

Type Modifiers

Except for **void**, the basic data types may have various *modifiers* that precede them. You use a modifier to alter the meaning of the base type to fit the needs of various situations more precisely. Here is a list of the modifiers:

signed
unsigned
long
short

You may apply the modifiers **signed**, **unsigned**, **long**, and **short** to character and integer base types. However, you may also apply **long** to **double**. Table 5-2 presents all allowed combinations of the basic types and the type modifiers. Although allowed, the use of **signed** on integers is redundant because the default integer declaration assumes a signed number.

The difference between signed and unsigned integers is in the way that the computer interprets the high-order bit of the integer. If you specify a signed integer, then the Turbo C compiler will generate code that assumes that it should use the high-order bit of an integer as a *sign flag*. If the sign flag is zero, then the number is positive; if it is one, then the number is negative. Here are two examples:

```
 127 in binary is  0 0 0 0 0 0 0 0  0 1 1 1 1 1 1 1
-127 in binary is  1 0 0 0 0 0 0 0  0 1 1 1 1 1 1 1
                   ↑
                 Sign bit
```

Be aware that most computers will use *two's complement arithmetic*, which will cause the representation of −127 to appear differently. However, the use of the sign bit is the same as was just shown. To create a negative number in two's complement, reverse all of the bits and add one. For example, −127 in two's complement will look like this:

```
1 1 1 1 1 1 1 1  1 0 0 0 0 0 0 1
```

Signed integers are important for many algorithms, but they only have half of the absolute magnitude of their unsigned counterparts. For example, here is 32767:

```
0 1 1 1 1 1 1 1  1 1 1 1 1 1 1 1
```

Table 5-2. All Possible Combinations of Turbo C's Basic Types and Modifiers

Type	Bit width	Range
char	8	−128 to 127
unsigned char	8	0 to 255
signed char	8	−128 to 127
int	16	−32768 to 32767
unsigned int	16	0 to 65535
signed int	16	−32768 to 32767
short int	16	−32768 to 32767
unsigned short int	16	0 to 65535
signed short int	16	−32768 to 32767
long int	32	−2147483648 to 2147483647
signed long int	32	−2147483648 to 2147483647
unsigned long int	32	0 to 4294967295
float	32	3.4E−38 to 3.4E+38
double	64	1.7E−308 to 1.7E+308
long double	64	1.7E−308 to 1.7E+308

If the high-order were set to 1, the computer would then interpret the number as −32768. However, if you had declared this number to be an **unsigned int**, then the number becomes 65535 when the high-order bit is set to 1.

To understand the difference between the way that Turbo C interprets signed and unsigned integers, run this short program now:

```
/* Show the difference between signed and unsigned
    integers.
*/
main()
{
  int i;   /* a signed integer */
  unsigned int j; /* an unsigned integer */

  j = 60000;
  i = j;
  printf("%d %u", i, j);
}
```

When you run this program, the output is **−5536 60000**. The reason for this output is that the computer interprets the bit pattern that represents 60000 in an unsigned integer as −5536 as a signed integer. As you know, the **%d** in the program tells **printf( )** to display an integer in decimal form. The **%u** is another format code that tells **printf( )** that you want to display an **unsigned int**.

Turbo C allows you to use a shorthand notation to declare **unsigned** or **long** integers: you may simply use the word **unsigned** or **long** without **int**. For example,

```
unsigned x;
unsigned int y;
```

both declare unsigned integer variables.

You may use variables of type **char** to hold values other than just the ASCII character set. In addition, you can use a **char** variable both as a "small" integer with the range −128 through 127, and in place of an integer when the situation does not require larger numbers. The main advantage of using a character variable over an integer when the situation allows it is that the computer requires less time to load or store a byte than a word value. To prove this fact, enter the following program into your computer at this time. (This program uses nested **for** loops that do nothing except increment their control variables. These loops may look odd at this time but the program nicely illustrates the difference between the access time of characters and integers. You will learn more about loops in Chapter 6.)

```
/*   This program shows the difference between
     integers and characters for loop control.
*/
main()
{
  int i, j, k;
  char c, d, e;
  long tm;

  tm = time(0);
  for(i=0; i<100; i++)
    for(j=0; j<100; j++)   /* do nothing */
      for(k=0; k<100; k++) ;
  printf("Time for integer loops: %ld\n", time(0)-tm);

  tm = time(0);
```

```
    for(c=0; c<100; c++)
      for(d=0; d<100; d++)   /* do nothing */
        for(e=0; e<100; e++) ;
    printf("Time for character loops: %ld\n", time(0)-tm);
  }
```

This program uses the function **time( )**, which is supplied in Turbo C's library, to time the execution of the loops. When the program calls **time( )** with an argument of zero, it returns the current system time in seconds. Since this number is large it must be of type **long**. For this same reason, the program uses l in the format **%ld** to tell **printf( )** that a long integer is coming. Later, you will see the way to use **printf( )** with any type of data. When the timer program is run with an 8MHz AT-compatible computer, the integer loops run in 8 seconds and the character loops run in 6 seconds — a very respectable increase over integers.

Declaring Variables

Here is the general form of a variable declaration statement:

type variable—list;

Here, *type* must be a valid Turbo C data type and *variable—list* may consist of one or more identifiers with comma separators. Here are some sample declarations:

```
int i,j,l;

short int si;

unsigned int ui;

double balance, profit, loss;
```

Unlike some other computer languages, the name of a variable in C has nothing to do with its type.

Where Variables Are Declared

Where a variable is declared greatly affects the way that the other parts of your program can use that variable. The rules that determine how a variable can be used based upon where its declaration is in the program are called the *scope rules* of the language. A complete discussion of these rules and their ramifications will have to wait until you know more about Turbo C, but the basics of the rules will be covered here.

There are three places in a C program where you can declare variables. The first place is outside of all functions, including the **main()** function. The variable that you declare in this way is called *global*, and may be used by any part of your program. The second place where you can declare a variable is inside a function. Variables declared in this way are called *local* variables, and may be used only by statements that are in the same function. In essence, a local variable is known only to the code inside its function and is unknown outside that function. The last place where variables can be declared is in the declaration of the formal parameters of a function. (As described in Chapter 4, you use the formal parameters to receive the arguments when that function is called). Aside from being used to receive the information that is passed to the function, these parameters act like any other local variables. Figure 5-1 shows a short program that declares variables at each place and produces the following output:

```
..........the current sum is 0
..........the current sum is 1
..........the current sum is 3
..........the current sum is 6
..........the current sum is 10
..........the current sum is 15
..........the current sum is 21
..........the current sum is 28
..........the current sum is 36
..........the current sum is 45
```

As you can see in Figure 5-1, any function in the program may access the global variable **sum**. However, **total ()** cannot directly access the local variable **count** in **main()**, which must pass **count** as an argument. This is necessary because a local variable can only be used by code that is in the same function in which the variable is declared. Note that the **count** in **display()** is completely separate from the **count** in **main()**, again, because a local variable is known only to the function in which it is declared.

```
/* sum the numbers 0 through 9 */

int sum;  ◄─────────────────────────── Global Variable

main()
{
  int count;  ◄─────────────────────── Local Variable

  sum = 0;  /* initialize */

  for(count=0; count<10; count++) {
    total(count);
    display();
  }
}

/* add to running total */
total(x)
int x;  ◄─────────────────────────── Formal Parameter
{
  sum = x + sum;
}


display()
{                                    ─── Local Variable
  int count;  /* this count is different from
                 the one in main()
              */

  for(count=0; count<10; count++) printf(".");
  printf("the current sum is %d\n", sum);
}
```

Figure 5-1.   Using global and local variables

You must understand two important aspects of variables. First, no two global variables may have the same name. If they did, the compiler would not know which variable to use. Second, a local variable in one function may have the same name as a local variable in another function without conflict. The reason for this is that the code and data inside one function are completely separate from those in another function. Simply stated, the statements inside one function have no knowledge about the statements inside another function. However, remember that no two variables within the same function should have the same name. Later, after you know more about functions, this book will explain and elaborate these basic concepts.

Constants

In C, constants refer to fixed values that the program may not alter. For the most part, constants and their usage are so intuitive that all of the preceding programs in this book have used them in one form or another. However, you are now ready to study them formally.

Turbo C constants can be of any of the basic data types. The way that you represent each constant depends upon its type. You enclose character constants in single quotes. For example 'a' and '%' are both character constants.

You specify integer constants as numbers without fractional components. For example, **10** and **−100** are integer constants. Floating-point constants require the use of the decimal point followed by the number's fractional component. For example, **11.123** is a floating-point constant. Here are some other examples:

Data type	Constant examples			
char	'a' '\n' '9'			
int	1 123 21000 −234			
long int	35000 −34			
short int	10 −12 90			
unsigned int	10000 987 40000			
float	123.23 4.34e−3			
double	123.23 12312333 −0.9876324 1.0E100			

Hexadecimal and Octal Constants

As you probably know, it is sometimes easier in programming to use a number system that is based on 8 or 16, instead of 10. The number system that is based on 8 is called *octal* and uses the digits 0 through 7. In octal, the number 10 is the same as the number 8 in decimal. The number system that is based on 16 is called *hexadecimal*. It uses the digits 0 through 9 and the letters A through F, which stand for the numbers 10 through 15, respectively. For example, the number 10 in hexadecimal is the number 16 in decimal. Because of the frequency with which these two number systems are used, Turbo C allows you to specify integer constants in hexadecimal or octal instead of decimal if you prefer. A constant in hexadecimal form must begin with a **0x** (a zero followed by an **x**). An octal constant begins with a zero. Here are some examples:

```
int hex = 0xFF;    /* 255 in decimal */

int oct = 011;     /* 9 in decimal */
```

String Constants

Turbo C supports another type of constant in addition to those constants of the predefined data types: the *string*. A string is a set of characters that is enclosed with double quotes. For example, "this is a test" is a string. You have seen examples of strings in some of the **printf( )** statements in the programs given so far in this book.

Do not confuse the strings with characters. You enclose a single-character constant with single quotes; for example, 'a'. However, "a" is a string that contains only one letter.

Backslash Character Constants

Using single quotes to enclose all character constants works for most printing characters, but a few, such as the carriage return, are impossible to enter from the keyboard. For this reason, C provides the special backslash character constants, which are shown in Table 5-3.

Table 5-3. Backslash Codes

Code	Meaning
\b	backspace
\f	form feed
\n	newline
\r	carriage return
\t	horizontal tab
\"	double quote
\'	single quote
\0	null
\ \	backslash
\v	vertical tab
\a	alert
\o	octal constant
\x	hexadecimal constant

You use a backslash code in exactly the same way as you would any other character. For example,

```
ch='\t';

printf("this is a test\n");
```

first assigns a tab to **ch**, and then prints **this is a test** on screen followed by a newline. You will see more examples of the backslash codes later in this book.

Variable Initializations

In C, you can give values to most variables at the same time that you declare them by placing an equals sign and a constant after the variable name. The general form of initialization is

$$type\ variable\_name = constant;$$

Some examples are as follows:

```
char ch = 'a';

int first = 0;

float balance = 123.23
```

Global variables can be initialized only at the start of the program. However, local variables will be initialized each time that the function in which they are declared is entered. Turbo C initializes all global variables to zero if you do not specify another initializer. Local variables that are not initialized will have unknown values before you make the first assignment to them.

The main advantage of initializing variables is that it slightly reduces the amount of code in the program. For a simple example of variable initialization, here is a reworked version of the running total program developed earlier in Figure 5-1:

```
/* An example using variable initialization */

main()
{
```

```
  int t;

  printf("enter a number: ");
  scanf("%d", &t);
  total(t);
}

total(x)
int x;
{
  int sum=0, i;

  for(i=0; i<x; i++) {
    sum = sum + i;
    for(count=0; count<10; count++) printf(".");
    printf("the current sum is %d\n", sum);
  }
}
```

Operators

Turbo C is rich in built-in operators. An *operator* is a symbol that tells the compiler to perform specific mathematical or logical manipulations. C has three general classes of operators: *arithmetic, relational and logical,* and *bitwise.* In addition, C has some special operators for particular tasks.

This chapter will examine only the arithmetic, relational and logical, assignment, and **sizeof** operators. This book will discuss the other operators as needed or later in Part Three.

Arithmetic Operators

Table 5-4 lists the C arithmetic operators. The operators +, −, *, and / all work in the same way in C as they do in most other computer languages. You can apply the operators to almost any built-in data type that C allows. When you apply / to an integer or character, the computer will truncate any remainder; for example, **10/3** will equal 3 in integer division.

The modulo division operator % yields the remainder of an integer division. However, as such, you cannot use % on type **float** or **double.** The following program illustrates both integer division and the % operator:

```
main()
{
  int x, y;

  x = 10;
  y = 3;

  printf("%d", x/y);    /* will display 3 */
  printf("%d", x%y);    /* will display 1, the remainder of
                           the integer division */

  x = 1;
  y = 2;

  printf("%d %d", x/y, x%y); /*  will display 0 1 */

}
```

The reason that the last line prints **0** and **1** is that **1/2** in integer division is 0 with a remainder of 1.

The unary minus multiplies its single operand by −1. Thus, any number preceded by a minus sign switches the sign of the number.

Increment and Decrement

C allows two useful operators that are not generally found in other computer languages. These are the increment and decrement operators: ++ and −−. The operator ++ adds 1 to its operand, and the operator −− subtracts one.

Table 5-4.   Arithmetic Operators

Operator	Action
−	subtraction, also unary minus
+	addition
*	multiplication
/	division
%	modulo division
−−	decrement
++	increment

Therefore, the following are equivalent operations:

```
x++;
x--;
```

are the same as

```
x = x+1;
x = x-1;
```

Both the increment and decrement operators may either begin or follow the operand. For example, you can write

```
x=x+1;
```

either as

```
++x;
```

or as

```
x++;
```

However, there is a difference when you use them in an expression. When an increment or decrement operator precedes its operand, C then performs the increment or decrement operation before using the operand's value. When the operator follows its operand, C then uses the operand's value before incrementing or decrementing it. Consider the following:

```
x = 10;
y = ++x;
```

In this case, C sets **y** to **11** because C first increments **x** and then assigns it to **y**. However, if the code had been written as

```
x=10;
y=x++;
```

C would have set **y** to 10 and then would have incremented **x**. In both cases, **x**

Table 5-5. Relational and Logical Operators

Relational Operators

Operator	Action
>	greater than
>=	greater than or equal
<	less than
<=	less than or equal
==	equal
!=	not equal

Logical Operators

Operator	Action
&&	AND
||	OR
!	NOT

is still set to 11; the difference is when it is set. There are significant advantages in being able to control when the increment or decrement operation takes place, as you will see later in this book.

Here is the precedence of the arithmetic operators:

Highest	++ --
	−
	* / %
Lowest	+ −

The computer evaluates operators on the same precedence level from left to right. Of course, you may use parentheses to alter the order of evaluation. The C language treats parentheses in the same way as virtually all other computer languages treat them: they force an operation, or a set of operations, to have a higher precedence level.

Relational and Logical Operators

In the terms *relational operator* and *logical operator*, *relational* refers to the relationships that values can have with one another, and *logical* refers to the ways that these relationships can be connected together. The key to the concepts of relational and logical operators is the idea of true and false. In C, true is any value other than zero, while false is zero. Expressions that use relational or logical operators will return 0 for false and 1 for true. Table 5-5 shows the relational and logical operators.

You use the relational operators to determine the relationship of one quantity to another. They always return a 1 or a 0, depending upon the outcome of the test. The following program illustrates the outcome of each operation and displays the reults of each operation as either a 0 or a 1:

```
/* This program illustrates the relational operators. */
main()
{
    int i, j;

    printf("enter two numbers: ");
    scanf("%d%d", &i, &j);

    printf("%d == %d is %d\n", i, j, i==j);
    printf("%d != %d is %d\n", i, j, i!=j);
    printf("%d <= %d is %d\n", i, j, i<=j);
    printf("%d >= %d is %d\n", i, j, i>=j);
    printf("%d < %d is %d\n", i, j, i <j);
    printf("%d > %d is %d\n", i, j, i>j);

}
```

Enter this program now and experiment by using various combinations of numbers.

You may apply the relational operators to any of the basic data types. For example, this fragment displays the message **greater than** because a 'B' is greater than an 'A' in the ASCII collating sequence.

```
ch1 = 'A';
ch2 = 'B';
if(ch2>ch1) printf("greater than");
```

Later, this book will show you many more uses of the relational operators.

The logical operators are used to support the basic logical operations of AND, OR, and NOT according to the following truth table, which uses 1 for true and 0 for false.

p	q	p AND q	p OR q	NOT p
0	0	0	0	1
0	1	0	1	1
1	1	1	1	0
1	0	0	1	0

This program illustrates the operation of the logical operators:

```
/* This program illustrates the logical operators. */
main()
{
   int i, j;

   printf("enter two numbers (each being either 0 or 1): ");
   scanf("%d%d", &i, &j);
   printf("%d AND %d is %d\n", i, j, i && j);
   printf("%d OR %d is %d\n", i, j, i || j);
   printf("NOT %d is %d\n", i, !i);
}
```

Now enter this program, and experiment with various combinations of true and false until you are comfortable with the operations.

Both the relational and logical operators are lower in precedence than the arithmetic operators. This means that C evaluates an expression such as **10 > 1+12** as if you wrote **10 > (1+12)**. The result of the expression is false.

The C language allows you to combine several operations into one expression, as shown here. This expression

```
10>5 && !(10<9) || 3<=4
```

will evaluate true.

The following shows the relative precedence of the relational and logical operators:

```
Highest          !
                 > >= < <=
                 == !=
                 &&
Lowest           ||
```

As with arithmetic expressions, you can use parentheses to alter the natural order of evaluation in a relational or logical expression. For example,

```
1 && !0 || 1
```

will be true because C evaluates the ! first, which makes the AND true. However, if you use parentheses in the same expression, as shown here, the result is false:

```
1 && !(0 || 1)
```

Because **(0 || 1)** evaluates to true, the NOT changes the result to false and, thus, causes the AND to be false.

Remember that all relational and logical expressions produce a result of either 0 or 1. Therefore, the following program is not only correct, but will also print the number 1 on screen:

```
main()
{
  int x;

  x = 100;
  printf("%d", x>10);
}
```

You use the relational and logical operators to support the program-control statements, which include all loops and the **if** statement. For example, this program uses an **if** statement to print the even numbers between 1 and 99:

```
/* print the even numbers between 1 and 99 */
main()
{
  int i;

  for(i=1; i<=100; i++)
    if(!i%2) printf("%d ",i);
}
```

Here, the modulus operation will produce a zero result (false) if you use it on an even number. The NOT then inverts this result.

The Assignment Operator

The assignment operator in Turbo C is the equal sign (=). Unlike many computer languages, Turbo C allows you to use the assignment operator in expressions that also involve other operators. For example, consider the expression in the **if** statement of this program:

```
main()
{
  int x, y, product;

  printf("enter two numbers: ");
  scanf("%d%d", &x, &y);

  if( (product=x*y) < 0 )
    printf("one number is negative\n");
}
```

First, C assigns the value of **x*y** to **product**. Next, C tests the parenthesized assignment expression against zero. This code in the **if** statement is perfectly valid. In fact, statements of this type are common in professionally written C code. Let's take a close look at how and why this statement works.

You can think of the assignment operator in Turbo C as doing two things. First, the operator assigns the value of the right side to the variable on the left. However, when you use the assignment operator as part of a larger expression, it produces the value of the right side of the expression. Therefore the **(product=x*y)** part of the expression assigns the value of **x*y** to **product** and returns that value. It is this value that is then tested against zero in the **if**. The parentheses are necessary because the assignment operator is lower in precedence than the arithmetic operators.

The *sizeof* Operator

Turbo C includes the compile-time operator called **sizeof** that returns the size of the variable or type that is its operand. The keyword **sizeof** precedes the operand's variable or type name. If **sizeof** operates on a data type, then the type must appear in parentheses. For example, this evaluates to 2:

```
sizeof (int)
```

You will see many uses of this operator in this book.

Expressions

Operators, constants, and variables are the constituents of *expressions*. An expression in C is any valid combination of those pieces. Because most expressions tend to follow the general rules of algebra, they are often taken for granted. However, expressions have a few aspects that relate specifically to C. This section will discuss these aspects.

Type Conversion in Expressions

When you mix constants and variables of different types in an expression, C converts them to the same type. The C compiler will convert all operands "up" to the type of the largest operand on an operation by operation basis, as described in these type-conversion rules:

1. All **char**s and **short int**s are converted to **int**s. All **float**s are converted to **double**s.

2. For all operand pairs, the following occurs in sequence. If one of the operands is a **long double**, the other operand is converted to **long double**. If one of the operands is **double**, the other operand is converted to **double**. If one of the operands is **long**, the other operand is converted to **long**. If one of the operands is **unsigned**, the other is converted to **unsigned**.

After the compiler applies these conversion rules, each pair of operands will be of the same type, and the result of each operation will be the same as the type of both operands. Note that the second rule has several conditions that must be applied in sequence.

For example, consider the type conversions that occur in Figure 5-2. First, the computer converts the character **ch** to an **int** and **float f** to **double**. Then the computer converts the outcome of **ch/i** to a **double** because **f*d** is **double**. The final result is **double** because, by this time, both operands are **double**.

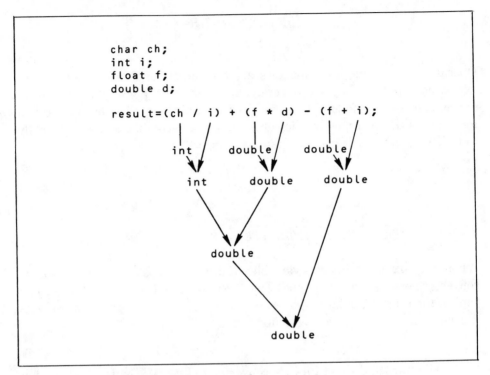

Figure 5-2.   A type-conversion example

Casts

You can force an expression to be of a specific type by using a construction called a *cast*. The general form of a cast is

(*type*) *expression*

where *type* is one of the standard C data types. For example, if **x** is an integer and you wished to make sure that the computer would evaluate the expression **x/2** to type **float** in order to guarantee a fractional component, you could write

```
(float) x / 2
```

Here, the cast **(float)** is associated with **x**, which causes the computer to elevate 2 to type **float** and the outcome to be **float**. However, be careful—if you try to write the cast in this way, the computer will not evaluate a fractional component:

```
(float) (x /2)
```

In this case, the computer carries out an integer division, and elevates the result of that to **float**.

Casts are often considered operators. As an operator, a cast is unary and has the same precedence as any other unary operator.

Sometimes, casts can be very useful. For example, suppose that you want to use an integer for loop control, but that performing a computation on the integer requires a fractional part, as in this program:

```
main() /* print i and i/3 with fractions */
{
   int i;

   for(i=1; i<=100; ++t )
      printf("%d / 2 is: %f",i,(float) i/3);
}
```

Without the cast **(float)**, the computer would have performed only an integer division; but the cast ensures that the fractional part of the answer will be displayed on the screen.

Spacing and Parentheses

At your discretion, you may place spaces in an expression to aid readability. For example, the following two expressions are the same:

```
x=10/y*(127/x);

x = 10 / y * (127/x);
```

The use of redundant or additional parentheses will not cause errors or slow down the execution of the expression. Try to use parentheses to make clear the exact order of evaluation, both for yourself and for others who may have to understand your program later. For example, study the following expressions:

```
x=y/2-34*temp-127;
x=(y/2) - ((34*temp) - 127);
```

Which one is easier to read?

Program-Control Statements

C H A P T E R 6

In a sense, the program-control statements are the essence of any computer language because they govern the flow of program execution. The way that they are implemented affects the language's personality and feel. Turbo C's program-control statements are rich and powerful, and help explain the language's popularity.

You can divide the program-control statements into three categories. The first consists of the conditional instructions **if** and **switch**. The second is the loop-control statements **while**, **for**, and **do-while**. The third category contains the unconditional branch instruction **goto**.

Before you begin to read this chapter, remember that a statement may consist of one of the following: a single statement, a block of statements, or no statement, which is called an *empty statement*. The descriptions presented in this chapter use the term *statement* to mean all of these possibilities.

The *if* Statement

Although you had a short introduction to the **if** statement in Chapter 4, you are now ready to look at it in depth. The general form of the **if** statement is

> **if**(*condition*) *statement*;
> **else** *statement*;

The **else** clause is optional. If *condition* evaluates to true (anything other than 0), the computer will execute the *statement* or block that forms the target of the **if**; otherwise, if the **else** exists, the computer will execute the statement or block that is the target of the **else**. Remember that only the code that is associated with **if** or the code that is associated with **else** will execute—never both.

For example, consider the following program that plays a simple version of the "guess the magic number" game. The program prints the message **** Right **** when you guess the magic number, and uses the Turbo C library function **rand()** to generate the magic number. The **rand()** function returns a random integer in the range of 0 through 32767.

```
/* magic number program */

main()
{
  int magic;   /* magic number */
  int guess;

  magic = rand(); /* generate a number */

  printf("guess: ");
  scanf("%d", &guess);

  if(guess == magic) printf("** Right **\n");
}
```

This program uses the equality operator (==) to determine whether the player's guess matches the magic number. If the guess does match, the program prints the message on screen.

Taking the magic number program further, this next version uses the **else** statement to print a message when the player tries a wrong number.

```
/* magic number program - improvement 1 */

main()
{
  int magic;  /* magic number */
  int guess;

  magic = rand(); /* generate a number */

  printf("guess: ");
  scanf("%d", &guess);

  if(guess == magic) printf("** Right **\n");
  else printf(".. Wrong ..\n");
}
```

Nested ifs

One of the most confusing aspects of **if** statements in any programming language is the *nested if*. A nested **if** is an **if** statement that is the object of either an **if** or an **else**. The reason that nested **ifs** are so troublesome is that you may have difficulty telling what **else** associates with what **if**. Consider this example:

```
if(x)
  if(y) printf("1");
  else printf("2");
```

To which **if** does the **else** refer? Fortunately, C provides a simple rule for resolving this question. In C, the **else** is linked to the closest **if** that does not already have an **else** statement associated with it. Both the **if** and the **else** must be inside the same code block. In this case, the **else** is associated with the **if(y)** statement. To make the **else** associate with the **if(x)**, you must use braces to override its normal association, as shown here:

```
if(x) {
  if(y) printf("1");
}
else printf("2");
```

The **else** is now associated with the **if(x)** because it is no longer part of the **if(y)** code block.

Here is another version of the magic number program:

```
/* magic number program improvement 2 */

main()
{
  int magic;  /* magic number */
  int guess;

  magic = rand(); /* generate a number */

  printf("guess: ");
  scanf("%d", &guess);

  if(guess == magic) {
    printf("** Right ** ");
    printf("%d is the magic number\n", magic);
  }
  else {
    printf(".. Wrong .. ");
    if(guess > magic) printf("Too high\n");
    else printf("Too low\n");
  }
}
```

This version uses a nested **if** to provide the player with feedback on how close each guess is.

The *if-else-if* Ladder

A common programming construct is the *if-else-if ladder*. It looks like this:

if (*condition*)
  statement;
else if (*condition*)
  statement;

>   **else if** (*condition*)
>   *statement*;
>   .
>   .
>   .
>   **else**
>   *statement*;

The computer evaluates the conditional expressions from the top downward. As soon as the computer finds a true condition, it executes the associated statement and bypasses the rest of the ladder. If none of the conditions are true, then the computer will execute the final **else**. The final **else** often acts as a *default condition;* that is, if all other conditional tests fail, then the computer performs the last **else** statement. If the final **else** is not present and all other conditions are false, then no action will take place.

Using an **if-else-if** ladder, the magic number program becomes

```
/* magic number program improvement 3 */

main()
{
  int magic;  /* magic number */
  int guess;

  magic = rand(); /* generate a number */

  printf("guess: ");
  scanf("%d", &guess);

  if(guess == magic) {
    printf("** Right ** ");
    printf("%d is the magic number\n", magic);
  }
  else if(guess > magic)
    printf(".. Wrong .. Too High\n");
  else printf(".. Wrong .. Too Low\n");

}
```

The Conditional Expression

Sometimes newcomers to C are confused by the fact that they can use any valid C expression to control the **if**; that is, you do not need to restrict the type of expression to only those that involve the relational and logical operators (as is the case in a language like BASIC). All that is required is that the expression evaluate to either a zero or nonzero value. For example, this program reads two integers from the keyboard and displays the quotient. In order to avoid a divide-by-zero error the program uses an **if** statement, which the second number controls.

```
/* divide the first number by the second */

main()
{
  int a, b;

  printf("enter two numbers: ");
  scanf("%d%d", &a, &b);

  if(b) printf("%d\n", a/b);
  else printf("cannot divide by zero\n");
}
```

This approach works because if **b** is zero, then the condition that controls the **if** is false and the **else** executes. If **b** is nonzero, the condition is true and the division takes place. It is unnecessary (and is considered extremely bad style) to write the **if** like this

```
if(b != 0) printf("%d\n", a/b);
```

because it is redundant and inefficient.

The *switch* Statement

Although the **if-else-if** ladder can perform multiway tests, it is hardly elegant. The code can be difficult to follow and can confuse even its author at a later date. For these reasons, C has a built-in multiple-branch decision

Program-Control Statements **101**

statement called **switch**. In the **switch**, the computer tests a variable successively against a list of integer or character constants. After finding a match, the computer executes the statement or block of statements that is associated with that constant. The general form of the **switch** statement is

```
switch(variable) {
    case constant1:
    statement sequence
    break;
    case constant2:
    statement sequence
    break;
    case constant3:
    statement sequence
    break;
    .
    .
    .
    default:
    statement sequence
}
```

where the computer executes the **default** statement if it finds no matches. The **default** is optional; if **default** is not present, no action takes place if all matches fail. When finding a match, the computer executes the statements associated with that **case** until it reaches the **break** or, in the case of the **default** (or last **case**, if no **default** is present) the end of the **switch** statement. (The **switch** statement is somewhat similar to BASIC's **ON-GOTO** statement or Turbo Pascal's **CASE** statement.)

There are two important things to know about the **switch** statement:

1. The **switch** differs from the **if** in that **switch** can only test for equality, whereas the **if** conditional expression can be of any type.

2. No two **case** constants in the same **switch** can have identical values. Of course, a **switch** statement that is enclosed by an outer **switch** may have **case** constants that are the same.

Often, you will use the **switch** statement to process keyboard commands, such as menu selection. As shown here, the function **menu()** displays a menu for a spelling-checker program, and will call the proper procedures based upon user input:

```
menu()
{
  char ch;

  printf("1. Check Spelling\n");
  printf("2. Correct Spelling errors\n");
  printf("3. Display Spelling Errors\n");
  printf("Strike Any Other Key to Skip\n");
  printf("       Enter your choice: ");

  ch=getchar();  /* read the selection from
                    the keyboard */

  switch(ch) {
    case '1':
      check_spelling();
      break;
    case '2':
      correct_errors();
      break;
    case '3':
      display_errors();
      break;
    default :
      printf("No option selected");
  }
}
```

Technically, the **break** statements are optional inside the **switch** statement. You use **break** statements to terminate the statement sequence that is associated with each constant. If you omit the **break** statement, execution will continue into the statements of the next **case** until the computer reaches either a **break** or the end of the **switch**. Think of the **cases** as labels. Execution will start at the label that matches the control variable and will continue until the computer finds a **break** statement, or the **switch** ends. Pay special attention to the **switch** statement in this program:

```
/* A very silly program */

main()
{
  int t;

  for(t=0; t<10; t++)
    switch(t) {
      case 1:
        printf("Now");
        break;
      case 2:
        printf(" is ");
      case 3:
        printf("the");
        printf(" time for all good men\n");
        break;
      case 5:
      case 6:
        printf("to ");
        break;
    case 7:
    case 8:
    case 9:
        printf(".");
    }

}
```

When run, this program produces the following output:

```
Now is the time for all good men
the time for all good men
to to ...
```

This program illustrates the fact that you can have empty **case** statements. Using empty **case** statements is helpful when several conditions use the same piece of code. As you can probably guess, the ability of the **cases** to run together when no **break** statement is present enables you to write efficient code by avoiding unwarranted duplication.

You must understand that the statements associated with each label are not code blocks, but rather are *statement sequences*. (Of course, the entire **switch** statement does define a block.) Usually, this technical distinction is not important except in certain special situations.

Nested *switch* Statements

You can have a **switch** that is part of the statement sequence of an outer **switch**. Even if the **case** constants of the inner **switch** and the outer **switch** contain common values, no conflicts will arise. For example, the following code fragment is perfectly acceptable:

```
switch(x) {
  case 1:
    switch(y) {
      case 0: printf("divide by zero error");
              break;
      case 1: process(x,y);
    }
    break;
  case 2:
    .
    .
    .
```

Here is another example. The simple database program shown next illustrates the way that you might use a nested **switch** statement. This program asks the user for the region and the salesperson, and then displays the current sales figure for that person. The program must use nested **switch** statements because several salespeople have similar first initials. Notice that the program introduces the use of the standard library function **toupper()**. This function returns the uppercase equivalent of its character argument. This allows the user to enter responses in either uppercase or lowercase. (The complement of **toupper()** is **tolower()**, which converts uppercase characters to lowercase.)

```
/* A simple regional salesperson database */
main()
{
  char division, salesperson;

  printf("Divisions are: East, Midwest, and West\n");
```

```
printf("Enter first letter of division: ");
division = getche();
division = toupper(division); /* make uppercase */
printf("\n");

switch(division) {
  case 'E':
    printf("Salespersons are: Ralph, Jerry, and Mary\n");
    printf("Enter the first letter of salesperson: ");
    salesperson = toupper(getche());
    printf("\n");

    switch(salesperson) {
      case 'R': printf("Sales: $%d\n", 10000);
        break;
      case 'J': printf("Sales: $%d\n", 12000);
        break;
      case 'M': printf("Sales: $%d\n", 14000);
        break;
    }
    break;

  case 'M':
    printf("Salespersons are: Ron, Linda, and Harry\n");
    printf("Enter the first letter of salesperson: ");
    salesperson = toupper(getche());
    printf("\n");
    switch(salesperson) {
      case 'R': printf("Sales: $%d\n", 10000);
        break;
      case 'L': printf("Sales: $%d\n", 9500);
        break;
      case 'H': printf("Sales: $%d\n", 13000);
        break;
    }
    break;

  case 'W':
    printf("Salespersons are: Tom, Jerry, and Rachel\n");
    printf("Enter the first letter of salesperson: ");
    salesperson = toupper(getche());
    printf("\n");

    switch(salesperson) {
      case 'R': printf("Sales: $%d\n", 5000);
        break;
      case 'J': printf("Sales: $%d\n", 9000);
        break;
      case 'T': printf("Sales: $%d\n", 14000);
        break;
    }
    break;
}

}
```

To see how the program works, select the Midwest region by typing **M**. This causes the outer **switch** statement to select **case** 'M'. To see Harry's total sales, type **H** to cause the program to display the value **13000**.

Note that a **break** statement in a nested **switch** has no effect on the outer **switch**.

Loops

Loops allow the computer to repeat a set of instructions until it reaches a certain condition. Turbo C supports the same type of loops as other modern, structured languages. The C loops are the **for**, the **while**, and the **do-while**.

The for Loop

Although Chapter 4 introduced the simple form of the **for** loop, you may be surprised in this chapter to see just how powerful and flexible the **for** is. Let's review what you have learned about it so far.

The Basics of the for Loop

You are probably familiar with the general format of C's **for** loop because it is found in some form in all procedural programming languages. The general form of the **for** statement is

for(*initialization; condition; increment) statement*;

In its simplest form, the *initialization* is an assignment statement that the compiler uses to set the loop-control variable. The *condition* is a relational expression that tests the loop-control variable against some value to determine when the loop will exit. The *increment* defines the way that the loop-control variable will change each time that the computer repeats the loop. You must separate these three major sections by using semicolons. The **for** loop will continue to execute as long as the condition is true. Once the condition becomes false, program execution will resume on the statement that follows the **for**.

As a simple example, the following program prints the numbers 1 through 100 on the screen:

```
main()
{
   int x;

   for(x=1; x<=100; x++) printf("%d ", x);
}
```

This program initially sets **x** to 1. Since **x** is less than 100, the program calls **printf()**. After **printf()** returns, the program increases **x** by 1, and tests it to see if it is still less than or equal to 100. This process repeats until **x** is greater than 100, at which point the loop terminates. In this example, **x** is the loop-control variable, which is changed and checked each time that the loop repeats.

The **for** loop need not always run in a forward direction. You can create a negative running loop by decrementing, rather than incrementing, the value of the loop-control variable. For example, this program prints the numbers 100 through 1 on screen:

```
main()
{
   int x;

   for(x=100; x>0; x--) printf("%d ", x);
}
```

However, C does not restrict you to incrementing or decrementing the value of the loop-control variable. Instead, you may use any type of assignment statement that you like. For example, the following loop prints the numbers 0 through 95 by fives (5, 10, 15, and so on).

```
main()
{
  int x;

  for(x=0; x<=100; x=x+5) printf("%d ", x);
}
```

By using a code block, you can have a **for** statement repeat multiple statements, as shown here. This example prints the squares of the numbers 0 through 99:

```
main()
{
  int i;

  for(i=0; i<100; i++) {
    printf("this is i: %d", i);
    printf(" and i squared: %d\n", i*i);
  }
}
```

An important point about **for** loops is that you must always perform the conditional test at the top of the loop. This means that the computer may not execute the code inside the loop at all if the condition is false. In this example,

```
x = 10;

for(y=10; y!=x; ++y) printf("%d", y);

printf("%d", y);
```

the loop will never execute because **x** and **y** are in fact equal when the computer enters the loop. Because this causes the conditional expression to evaluate to false, the computer will execute neither the body of the loop nor the increment portion of the loop. Hence, **y** will still have the value 10 assigned to it, and the output will be only the number **10** printed once on screen.

Variations of the *for* Loop

The discussion so far described the most common form of the **for** loop. However, C allows several variations that increase the **for** loop's power, flexibility, and applicability to certain programming situations.

One of the most common variations is the use of two or more loop-control variables. Here is an example, in which the variables **x** and **y** both control the loop:

```
main()
{

  int x,y;

  for(x=0, y=0; x+y<100; ++x, y++)
    printf("%d ", x+y);

}
```

This program prints the numbers from 0 to 98 by increments of 2. Notice that commas separate the initialization and increment sections. The comma is actually a C operator that means essentially "do this and this," and this book will discuss it more fully later. During each time through the loop, the computer increments both **x** and **y**. Both **x** and **y** must be at the correct value for the loop to terminate.

The conditional expression does not necessarily have to involve testing the loop-control variable against some target value. In fact, the condition may be any valid C expression. This means that you can test for several possible terminating conditions. For example, this program helps to drill a child on addition. However, if the child tires and wants to stop, he or she simply types **N** when asked for more. Pay special attention to the condition portion of the **for** loop.

```
/* Drill on addition */
main()
{
  int i, j, answer;
  char done = ' ';

  for(i=1; i<100 && done!='N'; i++) {
    for(j=1; j<10; j++) {
      printf("what is %d + %d? ", i, j);
      scanf("%d", &answer);
      if(answer != i+j) printf("wrong\n");
      else printf("right\n");
    }
    printf("more? ");
    done = getche();
  }
}
```

You can create another interesting variation of the **for** loop because, in actuality, each of its three sections may consist of any valid C expression. The expressions do not need to have anything to do with what the section is actually used for in the simplest case. With this in mind, consider the following program:

```
/* an unusual use of the for */

main()
{
  int t;

  for(prompt(); t=readnum(); prompt())
    sqrnum(t);
}

prompt()
{
  printf("enter an integer: ");
}

readnum()
{
  int t;

  scanf("%d", &t);
  return t;
}

sqrnum(num)
int num;
{
  printf("%d\n", num*num);
}
```

This program first displays a prompt and then waits for input. When you enter a number, the program displays its square and prompts you again for input. This process continues until you enter a 0.

If you look closely at the **for** loop in **main()**, you will see that each part of the **for** contains function calls that prompt the user and read the number that is entered from the keyboard. If the number entered is zero, the loop terminates because the conditional expression will be false; if the number is not zero, the program squares the number. Thus, this **for** loop uses the initialization and increment portions in a "nontraditional," but completely valid, sense. Enter this program into your computer and try to modify it to behave in different ways.

Another interesting trait of the **for** loop is that it does not require all pieces of the loop definition to be defined. In fact, the **for** loop does not need an expression for any of the sections—the expressions are optional. For example, this loop will run until you enter the number 123:

```
for(x=0; x!=123; ) scanf("%d", &x);
```

Notice that the increment portion of the **for** definition is blank. Thus, each time that the loop repeats, the program tests **x** to see if it equals 123, but does not change **x** in any way. However, if you type **123** at the keyboard, the loop condition becomes false and the loop terminates.

The Infinite Loop

One of the most interesting uses of the **for** loop is to create the infinite loop. Since none of the three expressions that form the **for** loop are required, you can make an endless loop by leaving the conditional expression empty, as shown in this example:

```
for(;;) printf(" this loop will run forever.\n");
```

Breaking Out of a *for* Loop

The **for(;;)** construct does not necessarily create an infinite loop because C's **break** statement, when encountered anywhere inside the body of a loop, causes immediate termination. Program control would then pick up at the code that follows the loop, as shown here:

```
for(;;) {
  ch = getche();  /* get a character */
  if(ch=='A') break;  /* exit the loop */
}

printf("you typed an A");
```

This loop will run until you type **A** at the keyboard. (This chapter will examine the **break** more closely later.)

Using *for* Loops with No Bodies

As defined by the C syntax, a statement may be empty. This means that the body of the **for** (or any other loop, for that matter) may also be empty. You can use this fact to improve the efficiency of certain algorithms, as well as to create time-delay loops. The following shows the way to create a time delay by using **for**:

```
for(t=0;t<SOME_VALUE;t++) ;
```

The *while* Loop

The second loop available in C is the **while**. Its general form is

while(*condition*) *statement*;

where *statement*, as stated earlier, can be either an empty statement, a single statement, or a block of statements that will be repeated. The *condition* may be any valid expression. The loop iterates as long as the *condition* is true. When the *condition* becomes false, program control passes to the line that follows the loop.

This example shows a keyboard-input routine that simply loops until you press **A**:

```
wait_for_char()
{
  char ch;

  ch = '\0';  /* initialize ch */
  while(ch!='A')  ch = getche();
}
```

First, the routine initializes **ch** to null. Since **ch** is a local variable, its value is unknown when the computer executes **wait_for_char( )**. The **while** loop then begins by checking to see if **ch** is not equal to 'A'. Because the routine initialized **ch** to null beforehand, the test is true and the loop begins. Each time that you press a key on the keyboard, the program tries the test again. After you press **A**, the condition becomes false because **ch** equals 'A', and the loop terminates.

As with the **for** loop, **while** loops check the test condition at the top of the loop, which means that the loop code may not execute at all. In the example just given, this is the reason that **ch** had to be initialized to prevent it from accidentally containing 'A'. Because the **while** performs the conditional test at the top, the **while** is good for those situations when you may not want the loop to execute. The position of the test eliminates the need to perform a separate conditional test before the loop. For example, the function **center( )** in the program that follows uses a **while** loop to output the correct number of spaces needed to center a line of text on an 80-column screen. If **len** equals zero, as it would if the line to be centered is 80 characters long, the loop will not execute.

```c
/* A program that centers text on the screen */
main()
{
  char str[255];

  printf("enter a string: ");
  gets(str);

  center(strlen(str));
  printf(str);
}

/* Compute and output proper number of spaces to
   center a string of len length.
*/
center(len)
int len;
{
  len = (80-len)/2;

  while(len>0) {
    printf(" ");
    len--;
  }
}
```

Where several separate conditions may be needed to terminate a **while** loop, you can use a single variable as the conditional expression, setting the value of this variable at various points throughout the loop. For example, study this function:

```
func1()
{
  int working;

  working = 1;    /* i.e., true */

  while(working) {
    working=process1();
    if(working)
      working=process2();
    if(working)
      working=process3();
  }
}
```

Here, any of the three routines may return false and may cause the loop to exit.

You do not need to include any statements at all in the body of the **while** loop. For example,

```
while((ch=getche()) != 'A') ;
```

will simply loop until you type **A** at the keyboard. If you feel uncomfortable placing the assignment inside the **while** conditional expression, remember that the equal sign is simply an operator that evaluates to the value of the operand on the right.

The *do/while* Loop

Unlike the **for** loop and the **while** loop that test the loop condition at the top of the loop, the **do/while** loop checks the loop condition at the bottom of the loop. This characteristic causes a **do/while** loop always to execute at least once. The general form of the **do/while** loop is

```
do {
    statement;
} while(condition);
```

Although the braces are not necessary when only one statement is present, you usually use them to improve readability and to avoid confusion (on the part of the reader, and not the compiler) with the **while**.

This program uses a **do/while** to read numbers from the keyboard until one of the numbers is less than 100:

```
main()
{
    int num;

    do {
        scanf("%d", &num);
    } while(num>100);
}
```

Perhaps the most common use of the **do/while** is in a menu-selection routine, which should always execute at least once. When you type a valid response, the routine returns the response as the value of the function. Invalid responses will cause the routine to prompt again for input. The following shows an improved version of the spelling-checker menu that was developed earlier in this chapter:

```
menu()
{

    char ch;

    printf("1. Check Spelling\n");
    printf("2. Correct Spelling Errors\n");
    printf("3. Display Spelling Errors\n");

    do {
        printf("        Enter your choice: ");
        ch = getche();  /* read the selection from
                            the keyboard */
    switch(ch) {
      case '1':
```

```
        check_spelling();
        break;
      case '2':
        correct_errors();
        break;
      case '3':
        display_errors();
        break;
    }
  } while(ch!='1' && ch!='2' && ch!='3');
}
```

After displaying the options, the program will loop until you select a valid option.

As another example of the **do/while** loop in action, here is a final improvement to the magic number program:

```
/* magic number program improvement final version */

main()
{
  int magic;  /* magic number */
  int guess, tries = 0;

  magic = rand(); /* generate a number */
  do {
    printf("guess: ");
    scanf("%d", &guess);

    if(guess == magic) {
      printf("** Right ** ");
      printf("%d is the magic number\n", magic);
    }
    else if(guess > magic)
      printf(".. Wrong .. Too High\n");
    else printf(".. Wrong .. Too Low\n");
    tries++;
  } while. (guess != magic);
  printf("You took %d tries.\n", tries);
}
```

Now, instead of simply giving the player one chance, the program loops until the player guesses the number. It also reports the number of tries the player needed to guess correctly.

Nested Loops

When one loop is inside of another loop, the inner loop is said to be *nested*. Nested loops allow you to solve some interesting programming problems. For example, this short program displays the first four integer powers of the numbers 1 through 9:

```
/* Display a table of the even powers of the
   numbers 1 to 9.
*/
main()
{
  int i, j, k, temp;

  printf("       i        i^2      i^3      i^4\n");
  for(i=1; i<10; i++) {   /* outer loop */
    for(j=1; j<5; j++) {   /* 1st level of nesting */
      temp = 1;
      for(k=0; k<j; k++) /* innermost loop */
        temp = temp*i;
      printf("%9d", temp);
    }
    printf("\n");
  }
}
```

When you run this program, it produces the results shown in Figure 6-2. Notice that all of the numbers in the column are aligned. This alignment is due to the use of a *minimum field-width specifier* in the **printf()** statement that prints the numbers. If you place a number between the percent sign and the **d**, the number tells **printf()** to add spaces as necessary up to the width specified. In this way, you can make the program line up the numbers in the columns.

It is sometimes important to determine how many iterations an inner loop executes. You determine this number of iterations by multiplying the number of times that the outer loop iterates by the number of times that the

```
A:\>power
            i          i^2        i^3        i^4
            1          1          1            1
            2          4          8           16
            3          9         27           81
            4         16         64          256
            5         25        125          625
            6         36        216         1296
            7         49        343         2401
            8         64        512         4096
            9         81        729         6561

A:\>
```

Figure 6-1.   Output from the integer powers program

inner loop repeats each time it is executed. In the power program just given, the outer loop repeats 9 times and the second loop repeats 4 times each time that they are executed; thus, the second loop actually iterates 36 times. The innermost loop executes an average of two times, which means that its total number of iterations is 72.

Loop Breaking

The **break** statement has two uses. The first use is to terminate a **case** in the **switch** statement. The section on the **switch** presented earlier in this chapter covered this use. The second use is to force immediate termination of a loop, bypassing the normal loop conditional test.

When encountering the **break** statement inside a loop, the computer immediately terminates the loop and program control resumes at the next statement that follows the loop. For example, study this program:

```
main()
{
  int t;
  for(t=0; t<100; t++) {
    printf("%d ", t);
    if(t==10) break;
  }
}
```

This program prints the numbers 0 through 10 on the screen and then terminates because the **break** causes immediate exit from the loop. The **break** overrides the conditional test **t<100** built into the loop.

The **break** is especially useful when an external event controls a loop, as the following program illustrates. This simple program tests your sense of time: it asks you to wait five seconds between the time that you start and the time that you end. To begin, press RETURN. When you think five seconds are up, press any key. If your sense of time is accurate, you win. (But, no cheating with a watch!)

```
/* How's your timer? */
main()
{
  int x,y;
  long tm;

  printf("This program tests your sense of time!");
  printf("When ready, press return, wait five seconds\n"),
  printf("and strike any key: ");
  getche();
  printf("\n");

  tm = time(0);
  for(;;)
    if(kbhit()) break;
  if(time(0)-tm==5) printf("You win!!!");
  else printf("Your timing is off");
}
```

This program uses Turbo C's **time()** function to read the current system time. The current system time is given in seconds and represents the elapsed time since 00:00:00, Greenwich time, January 1, 1970. Because the number of seconds exceeds that which can be held by an integer, the program must use a **long int** variable. (The zero used as an argument to **time()** causes the function to return the time. Do not use any other values as arguments until you understand the use of pointers.) This program introduces another library function, **kbhit()**. It checks to see if the user has pressed a key on the keyboard. If the user has pressed a key, the function returns true; if not, it returns false.

It is important to understand that a **break** will cause an exit from only the innermost loop. For example,

```
for(t=0; t<100; ++t) {
  count=1;
  for(;;) {
    printf("%d ", count);
    count++;
    if(count==10) break;
  }
}
```

will print the numbers 1 through 10 on the screen 100 times. Each time that the computer encounters the **break**, the program passes control back to the outer **for** loop.

A **break** that is used in a **switch** statement will affect only that **switch**, and not any loop that the **switch** happens to be in.

The *continue* Statement

The **continue** statement works in a way somewhat similar to the **break** statement. However, instead of forcing termination, **continue** forces the next iteration of the loop to take place, and skips any code in between. For example, the following program will display only even numbers:

```
main()
{
  int x;

  for(x=0; x<100; x++) {
    if(x%2) continue;
    printf("%d ", x);
  }
}
```

Each time that the program generates an odd number, the **if** statement executes because an odd number modulus 2 always equals 1, which is true. Thus, an odd number causes the **continue** to execute, which causes the next iteration to occur, bypassing the **printf()** statement.

In **while** and **do/while** loops, a **continue** statement causes program control to go directly to the conditional test and then continue the looping process. In the case of the **for**, the computer first performs the increment part of the loop and then the conditional test, before, finally, the loop continues.

You can use **continue** to expedite the termination of a loop by forcing the computer to perform the conditional test as soon as it encounters some terminating condition. Consider this program that acts like a simple code machine:

```
/* A simple code machine */
main()
{
  printf("enter the letters you want coded.\n");
  printf("Type a $ when you are done.\n");

  code();
}

/* code the letters */
code()
{
  char done, ch;

  done = 0;
  while(!done) {
    ch = getche();
    if(ch=='$') {
```

```
        done = 1;
        continue;
    }
    printf("%c", ch+1);   /* shift the alphabet one
                             position */
    }
}
```

You could use **code()** to code a message by shifting each character to one letter higher; for example, an **a** would become a **b**. The function will terminate when it reads a $. No further output will occur because the conditional test, brought into effect by **continue**, will find **done** to be true and will cause the loop to exit.

Labels and *goto*

Although the **goto** fell out of favor with the programming community some years ago, it has managed to polish its tarnished image a bit recently. This book will not judge its validity as a form of program control. However, it should be stated that there are no programming situations that require the use of **goto** — it is not a necessary item to make the language complete. Rather, **goto** is a convenience that, if used wisely, can be beneficial in certain programming situations. As such, this book does not use the **goto** extensively outside of this section. (In a language like Turbo C, which has a rich set of control structures and allows additional control through the use of **break** and **continue**, there is little need for **goto**.) The chief concern that most programmers have about the **goto** is its tendency to confuse and render a program nearly unreadable. However, sometimes the use of the **goto** will actually clarify program flow, rather than confuse it.

The **goto** requires a *label* for operation. A label is a valid C identifier that is followed by a colon. Furthermore, the label must be in the same function as the **goto** that uses it. For example, you could write a loop from 1 to 100 by using a **goto** and a label, as shown here:

```
x=1;

loop1:
  x++;
  if(x<100) goto loop1;
```

One good time to use the **goto** is when you want to exit from several layers of nesting. For example, consider the following code fragment:

```
for(...) {
  for(...) {
    while(...) {
      if(...) goto stop;
       .
       .
       .
    }
  }
}

stop:
  printf("error in program\n");
```

Eliminating the **goto** would force the code to perform a number of additional tests. Using a simple **break** statement would not work here because it would cause only the exit from the innermost loop. If you substituted checks at each loop, the code would then look like

```
done = 0;
for(...) {
  for(...) {
    while(...) {
      if(...) {
        done = 1;
        break;
```

```
      }
        .
        .
        .
    }
    if(done) break;
  }
  if(done) break;
}
```

You should use the **goto** sparingly — if at all. However, if the code would be much more difficult to read, or if execution speed of the code is critical, then by all means use the **goto**.

Now that your study of the program-control statements is complete, you are ready to move on to the study of arrays and strings.

Arrays and Strings

CHAPTER 7

An array is a collection of variables of the same type that are referenced by a common name. In Turbo C, an array consists of contiguous memory locations. The lowest address corresponds to the first element, and the highest address corresponds to the last element. An array may have from one dimension to several dimensions. You access a specific element in an array by using an index.

The array that you will most often use is the character array. Because C has no built-in string data type, C uses arrays of characters. As you will shortly see, this approach to strings allows greater power and flexibility than are available in languages that use special string types.

Singly Dimensioned Arrays

The general form of a single-dimension array declaration is

type var__name[size];

Here, *type* declares the *base type* of the array. The base type determines the data type of each element of the array. The *size* defines how many elements the array will hold. For example, the following declares an integer array named **sample** that is 10 elements long:

```
int sample[10];
```

In C, all arrays use zero as the index of their first element. Therefore, the above example declares an integer array that has 10 elements: **sample[0]** through **sample[9]**. For example, the following program loads an integer array with the numbers 0 through 9:

```
main()
{
  int x[10];   /* this reserves 10 integer elements */
  int t;

  for(t=0;t<10;++t)  x[t]=t;
}
```

For a singly dimensioned array, you compute the total size of an array in bytes as shown here:

Total bytes = **sizeof**(type) ∗ length of array

Arrays are common in programming because they allow you to deal easily with many related variables. For example, the use of arrays makes it easy to compute the average of a list of numbers, as shown in this program:

```
/* find the average of ten numbers */

main()
{
  int sample[10], i, avg;
```

```
for(i=0; i<10; i++) {
  printf("enter number %d: ", i);
  scanf("%d", &sample[i]);
}

avg = 0;

/* now, add up the numbers */
for(i=0; i<10; i++) avg = avg+sample[i];
printf("The average is %d\n", avg/10);
}
```

No Bounds Checking

The C language performs no bounds checking on arrays: thus, nothing stops you from overrunning the end of an array. If you overrun the end of an array during an assignment operation, then you will assign values to some other variable's data or even into a piece of the program's code. Here is another way to view this problem: you can index an array of size N beyond N without causing any compile-time or run-time error messages, even though doing so will probably cause your program to crash. As a programmer, you are responsible for ensuring that all arrays are large enough to hold whatever the program will put in them, and for providing bounds checking when necessary. For example, Turbo C will compile and run this program even though it overruns the array **crash**:

```
/* an incorrect program */

main()
{
  int crash[10], i;

  for(i=0; i<100; i++) crash[i]=i;
}
```

In this case, the loop will still iterate 100 times even though **crash** is only 10 elements long!

You may wonder why Turbo C, or the C language in general, does not provide boundary checks on arrays. The answer is that C was designed to replace assembly language coding in most situations. In order to do this, C includes virtually no error checking because it slows (often dramatically) the execution of a program. Instead, C expects you the programmer to be responsible enough to prevent array overruns in the first place.

One-Dimensional Arrays Are Lists

Single-dimension arrays are essentially lists of information of the same type. For example, after you run this program

```
char ch[7];

main()
{
  int i;

  for(i=0; i<7; i++) ch[i] = 'A'+i;
}
```

ch looks like this:

ch[0]	ch[1]	ch[2]	ch[3]	ch[4]	ch[5]	ch[6]
A	B	C	D	E	F	G

Strings

By far, the most common use for one-dimensional arrays is to create character strings. In C, a string consists of a character array that is terminated by a null. A null is specified as ' \0' and is generally zero. For this reason, you must declare character arrays to be one character longer than the largest string that you want them to hold. For example, if you want to declare an array **str** that will hold a ten-character string, you would write

```
char str[11];
```

This declaration makes room for the null at the end of the string.

As you saw in Chapter 5, while C does not have a string data type, it still allows string constants. Remember that a string constant is a list of characters that is enclosed between double quotes. Here are two examples:

"hello there"
"this is a test"

You do not need to add the null manually onto the end of string constants—the Turbo C compiler does this automatically. Thus, the string **"hello"** will look like this in memory:

h	e	l	l	o	'\0'

Reading a String from the Keyboard

The best way to input a string from the keyboard is by using the **gets( )** library function. The general form of **gets( )** is

gets(array-name**);**

To read a string, you call **gets( )** with the name of the array, without any index, as its argument. Upon return from **gets( )**, the array will hold the string that was entered from the keyboard. The **gets( )** function will continue to read characters until you enter a carriage return.

For example, this program simply repeats the string that you typed at the keyboard:

```
/* A simple string example */

main()
{
  char str[80];

  gets(str); /* read a string from the keyboard */

  printf("%s", str);
}
```

Notice that you can use **str** as an argument to **printf( )**. Also notice that the program uses the array name without an index. For reasons that will be clear after you read a few more chapters, you can use the name of a character array, without an index, that holds a string anywhere that you can use a string constant.

Keep in mind that **gets( )** does not perform any bounds checking on the array that it is called with. Therefore, if you enter a string longer than the size of the array, the array will be overwritten.

Some String Library Functions

Turbo C supports a wide range of string-manipulation functions. The most common functions are

strcpy( )
strcat( )
strcmp( )
strlen( )

Let's take a look at them now.

The strcpy( ) Function

A call to **strcpy( )** takes this general form:

strcpy(*to, from*);

You use the **strcpy( )** function to copy the contents of the string *from* into *to*. Remember that the array that forms *to* must be large enough to hold the string in *from*. If *to* is not large enough, the array will be overrun and will probably damage your program.

For example, study this program:

```
main()
{

    char str[80];
```

```
    strcpy(str, "hello");
}
```

This program will copy **"hello"** into string **str**.

The strcat() Function

A call to **strcat( )** takes this form:

strcat(*s1*, *s2*);

The **strcat( )** function appends *s2* to the end of *s1; s2* is unchanged. Both strings must have been null-terminated, and the result is null-terminated. Here is an example:

```
main()
{
  char first[20], second[10];
  strcpy(first, "hello");
  strcpy(second, " there");
  strcat(s1, s2);
  printf("%s", s1);
}
```

This program will print **hello there** on screen.

The strcmp() Function

A call to **strcmp( )** takes this general form:

strcmp(*s1*, *s2*);

The **strcmp( )** function compares two strings and returns 0 if they are equal.

If *s1* is lexicographically greater than *s2*, then the function returns a positive number; if *s1* is less than *s2*, the function returns a negative number.

You can use the following function as a password-verification routine:

```
/* return true if password accepted; false otherwise */
password()
{
   char s[80];

   printf("enter password: ");

   gets(s);

   if(strcmp(s, "password")) {
     printf("invalid password\n");
     return 0;
   }

   return 1;

}
```

Remember that **strcmp()** returns false when the strings match. Therefore, you must use the NOT operator if you wish something to occur when the strings are equal. For example,

```
main()
{
   char s[80];

   for(;;) {
     printf(": ");
     gets(s);
     if(!strcmp("quit", s)) break;
   }
}
```

continues to request input until you type **quit**.

The ***strlen()*** *Function*

The general form of a call to **strlen( )** is

strlen(*s*);

where *s* is a string. The **strlen( )** function returns the length of the string that *s* points to.

This program prints the length of the string that you enter at the keyboard:

```
main()
{
   char str[80];

   printf("enter a string: ");

   gets(str);

   printf("%d", strlen(s));

}
```

For example, if you enter the string **hi there**, this program would display **8**. The **strlen( )** function does not count the null terminator.

This program prints the reverse of the string that you enter at the keyboard. For example, entering hello causes the program to print **olleh**. Remember that strings are simply character arrays; thus, you may refer to each character individually.

```
/* Print a string backwards */
main()
{
   char str[80];
   int i;
```

```
   gets(str);

   for(i=strlen(str)-1; i>=0; i--) printf("%c", str[i]);
}
```

As a final example, the following program illustrates the use of all four string functions:

```
main()
{
   char s1[80], s2[80];

   gets(s1); gets(s2);

   printf("lengths: %d %d\n",strlen(s1),strlen(s2));

   if(!strcmp(s1, s2)) printf("The strings are equal\n");

   strcat(s1, s2);
   printf("%s\n", s1);
}
```

If you run this program, and enter the strings **hello** and **hello**, then the output will be

```
lengths: 5 5
The strings are equal
hellohello
```

It is important to remember that **strcmp( )** returns false if the strings are equal. Be sure to use the ! to reverse the condition, as the program just given shows, if you are testing for equality.

Using the Null Terminator

You can often put the fact that all strings are null-terminated to good use in order to simplify various operations on strings. For example, look at how little code is required to make every character in a string uppercase:

```
/* convert a string to uppercase */
main()
{
   char str[80];
   int i;

   strcpy(str, "this is a test");

   for(i=0; str[i]; i++) str[i] = toupper(str[i]);

   printf("%s", str);
}
```

This program will print **THIS IS A TEST**. To convert each character in the string, the program uses the library function **toupper()**, which returns the uppercase equivalent of its character argument. Notice that the test condition of the **for** loop is simply the array that the control variable indexes. The reason that this program works is that true is any nonzero value. Therefore, the loop runs until it encounters the null terminator, which is zero. As you progress, you will see many situations that are similar to this example.

A Variation of printf()

So far, to display the string held in a character array by using **printf()**, this book has used this basic format:

> **printf("%s"**, *array-name*);

However, remember that the first argument to **printf()** is a string, and that **printf()** prints all characters that are not format commands. Therefore, if you only want to print one string, you can use this form:

> **printf(***array-name***)**;

The following example demonstrates this form.

```
main()
{
  char str[80];

  strcpy(str, "Hello Tom");

  printf(str);
}
```

This program prints **Hello Tom** on the screen.

Two-Dimensional Arrays

C allows multidimensional arrays. The simplest form of the multidimensional array is the two-dimensional array. In essence, a two-dimensional array is an array of one-dimensional arrays. To declare a two-dimensional integer array **twod** of size 10,20, you would write

```
int twod[10][20];
```

Pay careful attention to the declaration: unlike most other computer languages, which use commas to separate the array dimensions, C places each dimension in its own set of brackets.

Similarly, to access point 3,5 of array **twod**, you would use **twod[3][5]**. This program loads a two-dimensional array with the numbers 1 through 12:

```
main()
{
  int t,i, num[3][4];

  for(t=0;t<3;++t)
    for(i=0;i<4;++i)
      num[t][i]=(t*4)+i+1;
}
```

In this example, **num[0][0]** will have the value 1, **num[0][1]** will have the value 2, **num[0][2]** will have the value 3, and so on. The value of **num[2][3]** will be 12.

The C language stores two-dimensional arrays in a row-column matrix, where the first index indicates the row and the second index indicates the column. This structure means that the rightmost index changes faster than the leftmost when you are accessing the array elements in the order that C actually stores them in memory. Figure 7-1 presents a graphic representation of a two-dimensional array in memory. You can think of the first index as being a "pointer" to the correct row.

Remember that C allocates storage for all array elements permanently. In the case of a two-dimensional array, you can use the following formula to find the number of bytes of memory:

$$bytes = row * column * \textbf{sizeof}(data\ type)$$

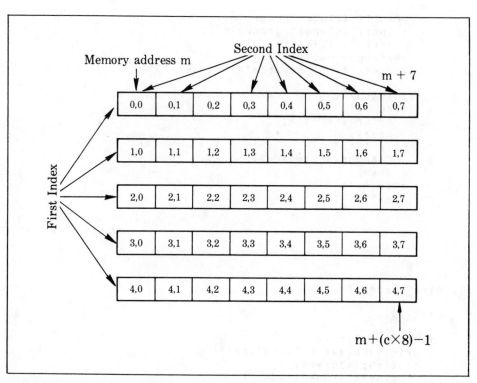

Figure 7-1. A two-dimensional array in memory

Therefore, an integer array with dimensions 10,5 would have

$$10 \times 5 \times 2$$

or 100 bytes allocated.

The short program shown here uses a two-dimensional array to store the numeric grade of each student in each class of a teacher:

```c
/* class grades program */

int grade[3][30];

main()
{
  char ch;

  for(;;) {
    do {
      printf("(E)nter grades\n");
      printf("(R)eport grades\n");
      printf("(Q)uit\n");
      ch=toupper(getche());
    } while(ch!='E' && ch!='R' && ch!='Q');

    switch(ch) {
      case 'E':
        enter_grades();
        break;
      case 'R':
        disp_grades(grade);
        break;
      case 'Q':
        exit(0);
    }
  }

}

/* enter the grades */
enter_grades()
{
  int t,i;

  for(t=0;t<3;t++) {
    printf("Class # %d:\n",t+1);
    for(i=0;i<30;++i) {
      printf("student %d: ");
      scanf("%d", &grade[t][i]);
    }
  }
}
```

```
/* display the grades */
disp_grades()
{
  int t,i;
  for(t=0;t<3;++t) {
    printf("Class # %d:\n",t+1);
    for(i=0;i<30;++i)
      printf("student #%d is %d\n", i+1, grade[t][i]);
  }
}
```

The program assumes that the teacher has 3 classes and a maximum of 30 students per class. Notice the way that each function accesses the array **grade.**

Arrays of Strings

In programming it is not uncommon to use an array of strings. For example, the input processor to a database may verify user commands against a string array of valid commands. To create an array of strings, you use a two-dimensional character array, in which the size of the left index determines the number of strings and the size of the right index specifies the maximum length of each string. For example, this declares an array of 30 strings, with each string having a maximum length of 80 characters:

```
char str_array[30][80];
```

Accessing an individual string is quite easy: you simply specify only the left index. For example, this statement calls **gets( )** with the third string in **str_array**:

```
gets(str_array[2]);
```

This statement is functionally equivalent to

```
gets(&str_array[2][0]);
```

However, the first form is much more common in professionally written C code.

To understand the way that string arrays work, study the following short program.

```
/* enter and display lines */
main()
{
  register int t, i, j;
  char text[100][80]

  for(t=0; t<100; t++) {
    printf("%d: ", t);
    gets(text[t]);
    if(!*text[t]) break; /* quit on blank line */
  }

  for(i=0; i<t; i++)
    printf("%s\n", text[i]);
}
```

This program inputs lines of text until the user enters a blank line. The program then redisplays each line.

Multidimensional Arrays

As stated earlier, C allows arrays with more than two dimensions. The general form of a multidimensional-array declaration is

$$type\ name[size1][size2]\dots[sizeN];$$

For example, this statement creates a $4 \times 10 \times 3$ integer array:

```
int threed[4][10][3];
```

You do not use arrays of three or more dimensions often because of the amount of memory that is required to hold them. As stated before, C allocates storage for all array elements. For example, a 4-dimensional character array with the dimensions 10,6,9,4 would require

$$10 \times 6 \times 9 \times 4$$

or 2160 bytes. If the array contained 2-byte integers, it would need 4320 bytes. If the array were **double** (8 bytes long), then it would require 34560 bytes. The required storage increases exponentially with the number of dimensions.

Array Initialization

C allows the initialization of global arrays. You cannot initialize local arrays. (Actually, you can initialize local variables, including arrays, if you declare them as **static**. You will learn about this process later in Part Three of this book.) The general form of array initialization is similar to that of other variables, as shown here:

type-specifier array_name[size1]...[sizeN] = { *value-list* };

The *value-list* is a comma-separated list of constants that are type compatible with the base type of the array. This statement will place the first constant in the first position of the array, the second constant in the second position, and so on. Note that a semicolon follows the }. The following example initializes a 10-element integer array with the numbers 1 through 10:

```
int i[10] = {1,2,3,4,5,6,7,8,9,10};
```

This statement indicates that **i[0]** will have the value 1 and **i[9]** will have the value 10.

Character arrays that will hold strings allow a shorthand initialization that takes the form

char *array_name[size]* = *"string"*;

For example, this code fragment initializes **str** to "hello":

```
char str[6] = "hello";
```

This code is the same as this fragment:

```
char str[6] = {'h','e','l','l','o','\0'};
```

Because strings in C must end with a null, make sure that the array that you declare is long enough to hold it. This is the reason that **str** must be six characters long, even though **hello** is only five characters long. When you use the string constant, the compiler automatically supplies the null terminator.

You initialize multidimensional arrays in the same way that you initialize singly dimensioned ones. For example, the following initializes **sqrs** with the numbers 1 through 10 and their squares:

```
int sqrs[10][2] = {
  1,1,
  2,4,
  3,9,
  4,16,
  5,25,
  6,36,
  7,49,
  8,64,
  9,81,
  10,100
};
```

Unsized-Array Initializations

Imagine that you are using array initialization to build a table of error messages, as shown here:

```
char e1[12] = "read error\n";
char e2[13] = "write error\n";
char e3[18] = "cannot open file\n";
```

As you might guess, it is tedious to count the characters in each message manually in order to determine the correct array dimension. You can let Turbo C automatically dimension the arrays in this example by using *unsized arrays*. In an array-initialization statement, if you do not specify the size of the array, then Turbo C will automatically create an array big enough to hold all of the initializers present. If you use this approach, the message table becomes

```
char e1[] = "read error\n";
char e2[] = "write error\n";
char e3[] = "cannot open file\n";
```

Given these initializations, the statement

```
printf("%s has length %d\n",e2,sizeof e2);
```

will print

```
write error
has length 13
```

Besides being less tedious, the unsized-array initialization method allows you to change any of the messages without having to worry about accidentally miscounting.

The C language does not restrict unsized-array initializations to only singly dimensioned arrays. For multidimensioned arrays, you must specify all but the leftmost dimensions in order to allow Turbo C to index the array properly. In this way, you may build tables of varying lengths while the compiler automatically allocates enough storage for them. For example, here is the declaration of **sqrs** as an unsized array:

```
int sqrs[][2] = {
  1,1,
  2,4,
  3,9,
  4,16,
  5,25,
  6,36,
  7,49,
  8,64,
  9,81,
  10,100
};
```

The advantage of this declaration over the sized version is that you may lengthen or shorten the table without changing the array dimensions.

A Tic Tac Toe Example

This chapter concludes with a longer example that illustrates many of the ways that you can manipulate arrays by using C. You commonly use two-dimensional arrays to simulate board-game matrices, such as those found in chess and checkers. While it is beyond the scope of this book to present a program for chess or checkers, this section will develop a simple Tic Tac Toe program.

The program will represent the Tic Tac Toe matrix by using a 3-by-3-character array. You are always **X** and the computer is always **O**. When you move, the program will place the **X** into the specified position of the game matrix. When it is the computer's turn to move, it scans the matrix and puts its **O** in the first empty location of the matrix. (This makes for a fairly dull game—you might find it fun to spice the program up a bit!) If the computer cannot find an empty location, it reports a draw game and exits. The program initializes the game matrix to contain spaces at the start of the game. Here is the global array **matrix**, **main()**, and **get—player—move()**, which is the function that inputs your move:

```
char matrix[3][3] = {  /* the tic tac toe matrix */
  ' ', ' ', ' ',
  ' ', ' ', ' ',
  ' ', ' ', ' '
};


main()
{
  char done;

  printf("This is the game of Tic Tac Toe.\n");
  printf("You will be playing against the computer.\n");

  done=' ';
  do {
    disp_matrix();
    get_player_move();
    done=check(); /* see if winner */
    if(done!=' ') break; /* winner!*/
    get_computer_move();
    done=check(); /* see if winner */
  } while(done==' ');
```

```
   if(done=='X') printf("You won!\n");
   else printf("I won!!!!\n");
   disp_matrix(); /* show final positions */
}

get_player_move()
{
   int x, y;
   int ok=0;

   printf("Enter coordinates for your X: ");
   do {
     scanf("%d%d", &x, &y);
     x--; y--;
     if(matrix[x][y]!=' ')
       printf("Invalid move, try again.\n");
     else {
       matrix[x][y] = 'X';
       ok = 1;  /* input ok */
     }
   }while(!ok);
}
```

The function **get—computer—move( )**, shown next, puts an **O** in the first open location. The function also reports a draw game if it cannot find an open location.

```
get_computer_move()
{
   register int t, i;

   /* look for an unused location */
   for(t=0; t<3; ++t) {
     for(i=0; i<3; ++i)
       if(matrix[t][i]==' ') break;
     if(matrix[`][i]==' ') break;
   }

   /* product will be 9 if no open spot found
   if(t*i==9)  {
     printf("draw\n");
     exit(0); /* terminate the program */
   }
   else matrix[t][i] = '0';
}
```

This function introduces a new library function. If a draw game occurs, get_computer_move() terminates the program through a call to **exit()**. The function **exit()**, which you can find in the standard library, causes immediate termination of the program. You traditionally call **exit()** with an argument of 0 to indicate that termination is normal. You can use other arguments to indicate some sort of error to the operating system. A common use of **exit()** occurs when a mandatory condition for the program's execution is not satisfied.

Here is the routine that displays the game matrix:

```
disp_matrix()
{
  int t,i;

  for(t=0; t<3; t++) {
    printf(" %c | %c | %c ", matrix[t][0],
      matrix[t][1], matrix [t][2]);
    if(t!=2) printf("\n---|---|---\n");
  }
  printf("\n");
}
```

This routine initializes the array to contain spaces because a space is used to indicate to **get_player_move()** and **get_computer_move()** that a matrix position is vacant. The fact that the routine uses spaces instead of nulls, for example, simplifies the matrix display function, **disp_matrix()**, by allowing the contents of the array to be printed on screen without any translations.

In the main loop, each time that you enter a move, the function **check()** is called. This function determines if the game has been won and by whom. The **check()** function will return an **X** if you have won, or an **O** if the computer has won. If no one has won yet, **check()** returns a space. The **check()** function works by scanning first the rows, then the columns, and finally the diagonals to look for a winning configuration.

All of the routines in this example access the array **matrix** differently. You should study the routines to make sure that you understand each array operation. Here is the complete program:

```
/* A simple tic tac toe game. */

char matrix[3][3] = {  /* the tic tac toe matrix */
  ' ',' ',' ',
  ' ',' ',' ',
  ' ',' ',' '
};
```

```
main()
{
  char done;

  printf("This is the game of Tic Tac Toe.\n");
  printf("You will be playing against the computer.\n");

  done = ' ';
  do {
    disp_matrix();
    get_player_move();
    done=check(); /* see if winner */
    if(done!=' ') break; /* winner!*/
    get_computer_move();
    done=check(); /* see if winner */
    } while(done==' ');
    if(done=='X') printf("You won!\n");
    else printf("I won!!!!\n");
    disp_matrix(); /* show final positions */
}

get_player_move()
{
  int x,y;
  int ok=0;

  printf("Enter coordinates for your X: ");
  do {
    scanf("%d%d", &x, &y);
    x--; y--;
    if(matrix[x][y]!=' ')
      printf("Invalid move, try again.\n");
    else {
      matrix[x][y] = 'X';
      ok = 1;   /* input ok */
    }
  }while(!ok);
}

get_computer_move()
{
  register int t, i;

  /* look for an unused location */
  for(t=0; t<3; ++t) {
    for(i=0; i<3; ++i)
      if(matrix[t][i]==' ') break;
    if(matrix[t][i]==' ') break;
  }

  /* product will be 9 if no open spot found */
  if(t*i==9) {
    printf("draw\n");
```

```
     exit(0); /* terminate the program */
   }
   else matrix[t][i] = '0';
}

disp_matrix()
{
  int t, i;

  for(t=0; t<3; t++) {
    printf(" %c | %c | %c ",matrix[t][0],
      matrix[t][1], matrix [t][2]);
    if(t!=2) printf("\n---|---|---\n");
  }
  printf("\n");
}

/* see if there is a winner */
check()
{
  int t;
  char *p;

  for(t=0; t<3; t++) { /* check rows */
    p=&matrix[t][0];
    if(*p==*(p+1) && *(p+1)==*(p+2)) return *p;
  }

  for(t=0; t<3; t++) /* check columns */
    if(matrix[0][t]==matrix[1][t] &&
      matrix[1][t]==matrix[2][t]) return matrix[0][t];

  for(t=0; t<3; t++) /* check columns */
    if(matrix[t][0]==matrix[t][1] &&
      matrix[t][1]==matrix[t][2]) return matrix[t][0];

  /* test diagonals */
  if(matrix[0][0]==matrix[1][1] && matrix[1][1]==matrix[2][2])
    return matrix[0][0];

  if(matrix[0][2]==matrix[1][1] && matrix[1][1]==matrix[2][0])
    return matrix[0][2];

  return ' ';
}
```

Enter this program now and experiment with it. With a little thought, you should be able to make it play a better game.

Now that you have studied arrays, it is time to move on to one of C's most important features: pointers.

Pointers

C H A P T E R   8

The understanding and correct use of pointers is critical to the creation of most successful C programs. There are three reasons for this: First, pointers provide the means by which functions can modify their calling arguments. Second, you can use them to support C's dynamic-allocation routines. Third, you can substitute them for arrays in many situations in order to increase efficiency.

In addition to being one of C's strongest features, pointers are also its most dangerous. For example, using uninitialized or wild pointers can cause a system crash. Perhaps worse, it is easy to use pointers incorrectly, which causes bugs that are difficult to find.

Because of the importance of pointers and their potential for abuse, this chapter examines them in detail.

Pointers Are
Addresses

A *pointer* is a variable that holds a memory address. Most commonly, this address is the location of another variable in memory. If one variable contains the address of another variable, then the first variable is said to *point* to the second. Figure 8-1 illustrates this situation.

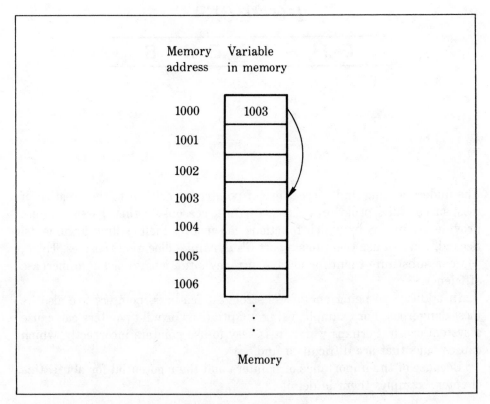

Figure 8-1.   One variable that points to another

Pointer Variables

If a variable is going to hold a pointer, then you must declare it as such. The general form for declaring a pointer variable is

type *var-name*;

where *type* may be any valid base type in C and *var-name* is the name of the pointer variable. The base type of the pointer defines what type of variables the pointer can point to. For example, these statements declare pointers to integers and characters:

```
char *p;

int *temp, *start;
```

The Pointer Operators

There are two special pointer operators: * and **&**. The **&** is a unary operator that returns the memory address of its operand. (A unary operator requires only one operand.) For example,

```
count_addr = &count;
```

places into **count_addr** the memory address of the variable **count**. This address is the computer's internal location of the variable. The address has *nothing* to do with the *value* of **count**. You can remember the operation of **&** as returning "the address of" to the variable that it precedes. Therefore, you can read the assignment statement just given as "**count_addr** receives the address of **count**."

To understand this assignment more clearly, assume that the variable **count** is located at address 2000. After the assignment just given, **count_addr** will have the value 2000.

The second operator, ∗, is the complement of the **&**. It is a unary operator that returns the *value of the variable located at the address that follows.* For example, if **count_addr** contains the memory address of the variable **count**, then

```
val = *count_addr;
```

will place the value of **count** into **val**. For example, if **count** originally had the value 100, then, after this assignment, **val** will have the value 100 because it is the value stored at location 2000, which is the memory address that was assigned to **count_value**. Remember the operation of the ∗ as "at address." Thus, in this case, you could read the statement just given as "**val** receives the value at address **count_addr**."

Unfortunately, in C, the multiplication sign and the "at address" sign are the same. As you write your programs, keep in mind that these operators have no relationship to each other. Both **&** and ∗ have a higher precedence than all other arithmetic operators except the unary minus, with which they are equal.

Here is a program that uses the two assignment statements just given to print the number 100 on screen:

```
main()
{
   int *count_addr, count, val;

   count = 100;

   count_addr = &count;  /* get count's address */
   val = *count_addr; /* get the value at that address */
   printf("%d", val); /* displays 100 */
}
```

The Importance of the Base Type

In the preceding discussion, you saw that you can assign to **val** the value of **count** indirectly by using a pointer to **count**. At this point, you may have asked an important question: How does Turbo C know how many bytes to copy into **val** from the address that is pointed to by **count_addr**? More generally, how does the compiler transfer the proper number of bytes for any assignment that uses a pointer? The answer to both questions is that the base type of the pointer determines the type of data that the compiler will assume the pointer is pointing to. In this case, because **count_addr** is an integer pointer, Turbo C copies two bytes of information into **val** from the address that **count_addr** points to. If **count_addr** had been a **double** pointer, then the compiler would have copied eight bytes.

Make sure that your pointer variables always point to the correct type of data. For example, when you declare a pointer to be of type **int**, the compiler assumes that any address that the pointer holds will point to an integer variable. Because C allows you to assign any address to a pointer variable, the following code fragment will compile, showing only a warning message:

```
/* this program will not work right */
main()
{
   float x=10.1, y;

   int  *p;

   p = &x;
   y = *p;
   printf("%f", y);
}
```

This program *will not* assign the value of **x** to **y**. Because the program declares **p** to be an integer pointer, the compiler will transfer only two bytes of information to **y**, and not the four bytes that normally make up a floating-point number.

Pointer Expressions

In general, expressions that involve pointers conform to the same rules as any other C expression. This section examines a few special aspects of pointer expressions.

Pointer Assignments

As with any variable, you may use a pointer in the right side of assignment statements to assign the value of the pointer to another pointer, as in this example:

```
main()
{
  int x;
  int *p1, *p2;

  p1 = &x;
  p2 = p1;
  printf(" %p", p2); /* print the hexadecimal value of the
                        address of x - - not x's value!*/

}
```

This program displays the address, in hexadecimal, of **x** by using another format code of **printf()**. The %p specifies that a pointer address will be displayed.

Pointer Arithmetic

In C, you may use only two arithmetic operations on pointers: + and −. To understand what occurs in pointer arithmetic, let **p1** be a pointer to an integer with a current value of 2000. After the expression

```
p1++;
```

the contents of **p1** will be 2002, and not 2001! Each time that the computer increments **p1**, it will point to the *next integer*. The same is true of decrements. For example,

```
p1--;
```

will cause **p1** to have the value 1998, if it previously was 2000.

Each time that the computer increments a pointer, it will point to the memory location of the next element of its base type. Each time that the computer decrements it, it will point to the location of the previous element. In the case of pointers to characters, pointer arithmetic will often appear as "normal" arithmetic. However, all other pointers will increase or decrease according to the length of the data type that they point to. For example, if you assume one-byte characters and two-byte integers, when the computer increments a character pointer, its value increases by one; however, when the computer increments an integer pointer, its value increases by two. Figure 8-2 illustrates this concept.

The C language does not limit you to only increments and decrements, however. You also may add or subtract integers to or from pointers. The expression

```
p1 = p1 + 9;
```

will make **p1** point to the ninth element of the base type of **p1** beyond the one that it is currently pointing to.

Beyond addition and subtraction of a pointer and an integer, you may perform no other arithmetic operations on pointers: specifically, you may not

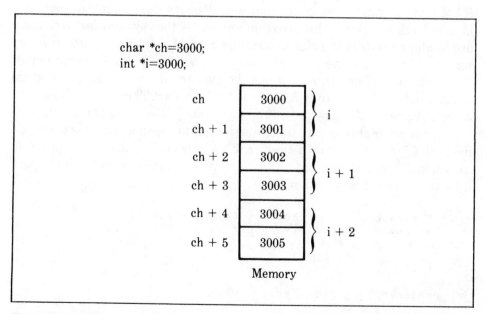

Figure 8-2.   The relation of pointer arithmetic to the base type of the pointer

multiply or divide pointers; you may not add or subtract two pointers; you may not apply the bitwise shift and mask operators to pointers; and you may not add or subtract type **float** or **double** to or from pointers.

Pointer Comparisons

It is possible to compare two pointers in a relational expression. For instance, given two pointers **p** and **q**, the following statement is perfectly valid:

```
if(p<q) printf("p points to lower memory than q\n");
```

Generally, you use pointer comparisons when two or more pointers are pointing to a common object.

A Memory Dump Example

An interesting use of pointers is for examining the contents of the computer's memory. The following program lets you enter the starting address of the RAM that you want to examine, and then displays the contents of each byte in hexadecimal format. This program introduces the keyword **far**, which you use to allow pointers to refer to locations that are not in the same memory segment that the pointer is in. The program uses **far** to allow **dump( )** to examine any part of memory — not just the memory segment that the program uses for data. You will study **far** more closely in Part Three, which discusses advanced topics — for now, take it on faith that you can use **far** like this.

The program also uses an **unsigned long int** to read an address because a memory address may exceed the size of an integer. Notice that the program calls **scanf( )** with the format code **%lu**, which means "read an unsigned long integer." Here is the program:

```
/* A simple program that displays the contents of
   memory at a specified address.
*/

main()
{
  unsigned long int start;
```

```
   printf("enter starting address: ");
   scanf("%ld", &start);
   dump(start);
}

dump(start)
unsigned int start;
{
  char far *p;
  int t;

  p = (char far *) start; /* convert to a pointer */

  for(t=0; ; t++, p++) {
    if(!(t%16))   printf("\n");
    printf("%2X ", *p); /* display in hex */
    if(kbhit()) return; /* stop when any key is hit */
  }
}
```

Notice that this program introduces the new **printf( )** format code **%X**, which tells the computer to display the argument in hexadecimal notation, and in uppercase letters. A **%x** displays in hexadecimal with lowercase letters.

In addition, note that the program uses an explicit type cast to transfer the unsigned integer value that you entered to a pointer. This step is necessary in order to avoid a warning message, and it is a good practice in programming.

Pointers and Arrays

There is a close relationship between pointers and arrays. Consider this fragment:

```
char str[80], *p1;

char *p1;
p1 = str;
```

This fragment sets **p1** to the address of the first array element in **str**. In C, an array name without an index is the address to the start of the array. In essence, the array name is a pointer to the array. To access the fifth element in **str**, you could write

```
str[4]
```

or

```
*(p1+4)
```

Both statements will return the fifth element. Remember that arrays start at zero, so these two statements use the number **4** to index **str**. You could also add 4 to the pointer **p1** to get the fifth element, because **p1** currently points to the first element of **str**.

The C language essentially allows two methods of accessing array elements, array indexing and pointer arithmetic. This fact is important because pointer arithmetic can be faster than array indexing. Since speed is often a consideration in programming, the use of pointers to access array elements is common in C programs.

To see an example of the way that you can use pointers in place of array indexing, consider these programs—one that uses array indexing and one that uses pointers—that display the contents of a string in lowercase:

```
/* array version */
main()
{
  char str[80];
  int i;

  printf("enter a string in uppercase: ");
  gets(str);

  printf("here's the string in lowercase: ");

  for(i=0; str[i]; i++) printf("%c", tolower(str[i]));
}


/* pointer version */
main()
{
  char str[80], *p;
```

```
   printf("enter a string in uppercase: ");
   gets(str);

   printf("here's the string in lowercase: ");

   p = str;   /* get the addres of str */
   while(*p) printf("%c", tolower(*p++));
}
```

The reason that the array version is slower than the pointer version is that C takes longer to index an array than it does to use the * operator.

Sometimes, novice C programmers mistakenly believe that they should never use array indexing because pointers are much more efficient. However, this is not the case. If you want to access the array strictly in either ascending or descending order, then pointers are faster and easier to use. However, if you want to access the array randomly, then array indexing is better because it generally will be as fast as evaluating a complex pointer expression, and because it is easier to program and understand. In addition, when you use array indexing, you are letting the compiler do some of the work for you.

Indexing a Pointer

In C, you can index a pointer as if it were an array. This ability further indicates the close relationship between pointers and arrays. For example, this fragment is perfectly valid and prints the numbers 1 through 5 on screen:

```
/* indexing a pointer */
main()
{
  int i[5] = {1, 2, 3, 4, 5};
  int *p, t;

  p = i;

  for(t=0; t<5; t++) printf("%d ", p[t]);
}
```

In C, the statement **p[t]** is identical to **p+t**.

Although programmers often do not index a pointer as an array, doing so can occasionally simplify certain algorithms. (You will see some examples of this in the next chapter.)

A Stack Example

The following stack routines present an interesting example of the way that you can mix arrays and pointers. A *stack* is a list that uses "first-in-last-out" accessing. It is often compared to a stack of plates on a table: the first plate set down on the table is the last one to be used. Stacks are used frequently in compilers, interpreters, spreadsheets, and other system-related software.

To create a stack, you would need two routines: **push()** and **pop()**. You use **push()** to place values on the stack, and **pop()** to take them off. The computer holds the stack in an array, but the stack routines will manipulate the stack by using pointers. Since the stack routines developed here are for integer quantities, the routines use an integer array. The variable **tos** will hold the memory address of the top of the stack, and will be used to prevent stack underflows. After the stack has been initialized, you may use **push()** and **pop()** to store and retrieve integers from it.

These stack routines use a simple **main()** to drive them. The **main()** reads numbers that you enter at the keyboard and stores them in the stack if they are nonzero. When you enter a zero, **pop()** pops a value from the stack. Here are the routines:

```
int stack[50]; /* get some memory for the stack */

int *p1, *tos;

main()
{
  int value;

  p1 = stack;
  tos = p1;  /* let tos hold top of stack */
  do {
    scanf("%d",&value);
    if(value!=0) push(value);
    else printf("this is it %d\n",pop());
```

```
   } while(value!=-1);
}

push(i)
int i;
{
   p1++;
   if(p1==(tos+50)) {
     printf("stack overflow");
     exit();
   }
   *p1=i;
}

pop()
{
   if((p1)==tos) {
     printf("stack underflow");
     exit();
   }
   p1--;
   return *(p1+1);
}
```

Both **push( )** and **pop( )** perform a relational test on the pointer **p1** to detect limit errors. The **push( )** tests **p1** against the end of stack by adding 50 (the size of the stack) to **tos**. The **pop( )** checks **p1** against **tos** to make certain that a stack underflow has not occurred.

In **pop( )**, the parentheses are necessary in the **return** statement. Without them, the statement would look like

```
   return *p1 +1;
```

which would return the value at location **p1** plus one, and not the value of the location **p1+1**. Be very careful to use parentheses to ensure the correct order of evaluation when you use pointers.

Pointers and Strings

Since an array name without an index is a pointer to the first element of that array, when you use the string functions that were discussed in the previous chapter, what actually happens is that the computer only passes a pointer to the strings to the functions, and not the actual string itself. To see how this works, here is one way that you could write **strcmp( )**:

```
strcmp(s1, s2)
char *s1, *s2;
{
  while(*s1)
    if(*s1-*s2) /* if not equal then return */
      return *s1-*s2;  /* the difference */
    else {
      s1++;
      s2++;
    }
  return '\0'; /* equal */
}
```

Remember that a null, which is a false value, terminates all strings in C. Therefore, a statement such as

```
while (*s1)
```

is true until the computer reaches the end of the string. Here, **strcmp()** will return zero if s1 is equal to s2. The **strcmp()** returns a value less than zero if s1 is less than s2; and it returns a value greater than zero if s1 is greater than s2.

At this point, you are probably wondering how you can call **strcmp()** with a string constant as an argument. For example, you may wonder how this fragment works.

```
if(!strcmp("hello", str)) printf("str contains hello");
```

The answer is that when you use a string constant, the computer only passes a pointer to the constant to **strcmp()**. More generally, when you use a string constant in any type of expression, the computer treats the constant as a pointer to the first character in the string. For example, this valid program prints the phrase **this program works** on screen:

```
main()
{
  char *s;
```

```
  s = "this program works";

  printf(s);
}
```

Getting the Address of an Array Element

So far, this chapter has simply been concerned with assigning the address of the first element of an array to a pointer. However, you can assign the address of a specific element of an array by applying the **&** to an indexed array. For example, this fragment places the address of the third element of **x** into **p**:

```
  p = &x[2];
```

One place that this practice is especially useful is in finding a substring. For example, this program prints the remainder of a string, that was entered at the keyboard, from the point that the computer finds the first space:

```
/* display the string after the first space */
main()
{
  char s[80];
  char *p;
  int i;

  printf("enter a string: ");
  gets(s);

  /* find first space or end of string */
  for(i=0; s[i] && s[i]!=' '; i++) ;

  p = &s[i];

  printf(p);
}
```

This program works because **p** will be pointing to either a space if one exists or a null if there are no spaces in the string. If **p** is pointing to a space, the program will print the space and then the remainder of the string. For example, if you entered **hi there**, then **print(f)** prints first a space and then **there**. If **p** is pointing to a null, then **printf( )** prints nothing.

Arrays of Pointers

You can make arrays of pointers just like any other data type. The declaration for an **int** pointer array of size 10 is

```
int *x[10];
```

To assign the address of an integer variable called **var** to the third element of the pointer array, you would write

```
x[2] = &var;
```

To find the value of **var**, you would write

```
*x[2]
```

A common usage of a pointer array is as a holder of pointers to error messages. You can create a function that will output a message, given its code number, as is shown here in **serror( )**:

```
char *err[] = {
  "cannot open file\n",
  "read error\n",
  "write error\n",
  "media failure\n"
};

serror(num)
int num;
{
  printf("%s",err[num]);
}
```

As you can see, the code calls **printf( )** inside **serror( )** with a character pointer that points to one of the various error messages indexed by the error number, which is passed to the function. For example, if the computer passes a 2 to **num**, then the code causes the computer to display the message **write error**.

Pointers to Pointers

An array of pointers is the same as *pointers to pointers*. The concept of arrays of pointers is straightforward because indexing the array keeps its meaning clear. However, pointers to pointers can be confusing.

A pointer to a pointer is a form of *multiple indirection*, or a chain of pointers. As you can see in Figure 8-3, in the case of a normal pointer, the value of the pointer is the address of the variable that contains the desired value. In the case of a pointer to a pointer, the first pointer contains the address of the second pointer, which points to the variable that contains the desired value.

You can carry multiple indirection to whatever extent desired, but there are few cases where more than a pointer to a pointer is necessary, or even wise to use. Excessive indirection is difficult to follow and prone to conceptual errors. (Do not confuse multiple indirection with *linked lists*, which are used in such applications as databases.)

You must declare a variable that is a pointer to a pointer as such. You can do this by placing an additional asterisk in front of the variable name. For

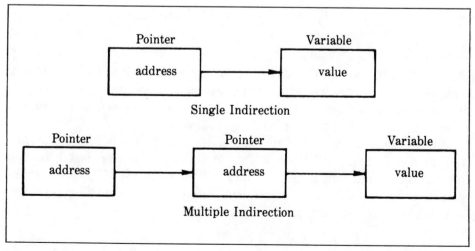

Figure 8-3.   Single and multiple indirection

example, this declaration tells the compiler that **newbalance** is a pointer to a pointer of type **float**:

```
float **newbalance;
```

It is important to understand that **newbalance** is not a pointer to a floating-point number, but rather is a pointer to a **float** pointer.

Accessing the target value that a pointer to a pointer indirectly points to requires you to apply the asterisk operator twice as is shown in this short example:

```
main()
{
  int x, *p, **q;

  x = 10;
  p = &x;
  q = &p;

  printf("%d", **q); /* print the value of x */
}
```

Here, this code declares **p** as a pointer to an integer, and **q** as a pointer to a pointer to an integer. The call to **printf()** will print the number 10 on screen.

Initializing Pointers

After you declare a pointer, but before you assign it a value, it will contain an unknown value. If you try to use the pointer prior to assigning it a value, you will probably crash not only your program, but also the operating system of your computer—an extremely nasty type of error!

By convention, you should give a pointer that points nowhere the value null to signify that the pointer points to nothing. However, just because a pointer has a null value does not make it "safe" to use. If you use a null pointer on the left side of an assignment statement, you will still run the risk of crashing your program or operating system.

Because Turbo C assumes that a null pointer is unused, you can use the null pointer to make many of your pointer routines easier to code and more efficient. For example, you could use a null pointer to mark the end of a pointer array. Doing this causes a routine that accesses that array to know that it has reached the end when it encounters the null value. The **for** loop shown here illustrates this approach:

```
/* look up a name */
  for(t=0;p[t];++t)
    if(!strcmp(p[t],name)) break;
```

The loop will run until the routine either finds a match or encounters a null pointer. Because the end of the array is marked with a null, the condition that controls the loop will fail when the routine reaches the null.

It is common practice in professionally written C programs to initialize strings. You saw an example of this in the **serror( )** function in the previous section. Another variation of initializing strings is this type of string declaration:

```
char *p="hello world\n";
```

As you can see, the pointer **p** is not an array. The reason that this type of initialization works has to do with the way that the compiler operates: Turbo C creates what is called a *string table* that is used internally to store the string constants of a program. Therefore, this declaration statement places the address of the string "**hello world**", as stored in the string table, into the pointer **p**. Throughout the program, **p** can be used like any other string. For example, the following program is valid:

```
char *p="hello world";

main()
{
  register int t;

  /* print the string forward and backwards */
  printf(p);
  for(t=strlen(p)-1;t>-1;t--) printf("%c",p[t]);
}
```

Problems with Pointers

Nothing will get you into more trouble than a "wild" pointer. Pointers are a mixed blessing. They offer tremendous power, and are necessary for many programs. But if a pointer accidentally contains a wrong value, it can be the most difficult bug to track down.

A pointer bug is difficult to find because the pointer itself is not the problem; the problem is that, each time you perform an operation that uses the pointer, you are reading or writing to some unknown piece of memory. If you read that piece of memory, the worst that can happen is that you get garbage. However, if you write to the area of memory, you will be writing over other pieces of your code or data. This error may not show up until later in the execution of your program, and may lead you to look for the bug in the wrong place. At that time, there may be little or no evidence to suggest that the pointer is the problem. This type of bug has caused programmers to lose sleep time and time again. Because pointer errors are such nightmares, you should do your best never to generate one.

Here are a few of the more common errors. First is the classic pointer error, the *uninitialized pointer*. Consider this program:

```
main()  /* this program is wrong */
{
   int x, *p;

   x = 10;
   *p = x;
}
```

This program assigns the value 10 to some unknown memory location. The program never gives a value to the pointer **p**; therefore, it contains a garbage value. This type of problem often goes unnoticed when your program is small because the odds are in favor of **p** containing a "safe" address—one that is not in your code, data area, or operating system. However, as your program grows, the probability of **p** having a pointer into something vital increases. Eventually, your program stops working. The solution to this type of pointer problem is always to make sure that a pointer is pointing at something valid before you use it.

A second common error is caused by a simple misunderstanding of the way to use a pointer. Study this program:

```
main()   /* this program is wrong */
{
   int x, *p;

   x = 10;
   p = x;
   printf("%d", *p);

}
```

The call to **printf( )** will not print the value of **x**, which is 10, but it will print some unknown value. The reason is that the assignment

```
p = x;
```

is wrong. The statement assigns the value 10 to the pointer **p**, which is supposed to contain an address and not a value. To correct the program, you should write

```
p = &x;
```

Just because pointers used incorrectly can cause tricky bugs is not a reason to avoid their use. Simply be careful and make sure that you know where each pointer is pointing before you use it.

Dynamic Allocation

Before you leave the subject of pointers, it is necessary to discuss Turbo C's dynamic-allocation system, which depends upon pointers for its operation.

There are two primary methods through which a C program can store information in the main memory of the computer. The first method uses global and local variables that C defines. In the case of global variables, the storage is fixed throughout the run-time of your program. For local variables, the program allocates storage from the stack space of the computer.

Although local variables are efficiently implemented in Turbo C, they require you to know, in advance, the amount of storage that is needed for every situation.

The second method that the program can use to store information is through Turbo C's dynamic allocation functions **malloc()** and **free()**. In this method, a program allocates storage for information from the free memory area called the *heap* that lies between your program with its permanent storage area and the stack. Figure 8-4 shows conceptually how a Turbo C program would appear in memory. The stack grows downward as the program uses it, so the design of the program determines the amount of memory that it needs. For example, a program with many recursive functions will make much greater demands on stack memory than a program that does not have recursive functions because local variables and return addresses are stored on the stack. Remember that the computer permanently allocates the memory required for the program and global data during the execution of the program. The computer takes the memory to satisfy a **malloc()** request

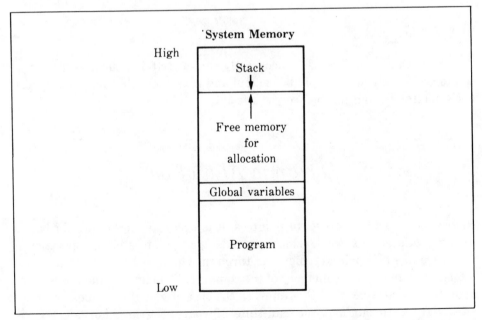

Figure 8-4.   A conceptual view of a Turbo C program's memory usage

from the free memory area, by starting just above the global variables and growing towards the stack. As you might guess, in fairly extreme cases, it is possible for the stack to run into allocated memory.

Let's begin the discussion of dynamic allocation with **malloc()** and **free()**.

The *malloc()* and *free()* Functions

The functions **malloc()** and **free()** form Turbo C's dynamic-allocation system and are part of its library. (Actually, Turbo C has several other dynamic allocation functions that add flexibility, but **malloc()** and **free()** are the most important.) They work together by using the free memory region that lies between your program and the top of the stack in order to establish and maintain a list of available storage. Each time that you make a **malloc()** memory request, it allocates a portion of the remaining free memory. Each time that you make a **free()** memory release call, it returns memory to the system.

The **malloc()** function is C's general-purpose memory-allocation function. You declare **malloc()** as follows:

$$\text{void *malloc(int } number\_of\_bytes);$$

It returns a pointer of type **void**, which means that you must use an explicit type cast when you assign the pointer returned by **malloc()** to a pointer of the type you want. After a successful call, **malloc()** will return a pointer to the first byte of the region of memory that was allocated from the heap. If not enough available memory exists to satisfy the **malloc()** request, an allocation failure occurs and **malloc()** returns a null. You can use **sizeof** to determine the exact number of bytes that each type of data needs. By doing this, you can make your programs portable to a variety of systems.

The opposite of **malloc()**, **free()**, returns previously allocated memory to the system. After you use **free()** to free memory, you can reuse it by using a subsequent call to **malloc()**. You declare the function **free()** as

$$\text{free(void *p);}$$

The only important aspect about **free()** to remember is that you must *never* call **free( )** with an invalid argument because doing so would cause the computer to destroy the free list.

The following short program will allocate enough storage for 40 integers, print their values, and then release the memory back to the system:

```
main()   /* short allocation example */
{
  int *p, t;

  p = (int *) malloc(40*sizeof(int));
  if(!p) /* make sure its a valid pointer */
    printf("out of memory\n");
  else {
    for(t=0; t<40; ++t) *(p+t) = t;
    for(t=0; t<40; ++t) printf("%d ",*(p+t));
    free(p);
  }
}
```

Remember: before you use the pointer that **malloc( )** returns, always make sure that your allocation request succeeds by testing the return value against zero. Do not use a pointer of value zero because it will most likely cause your system to crash.

Dynamic allocation is useful when you do not know in advance how many items of data you will be dealing with. (In *Advanced Turbo C*, this book's sequel [Borland-Osborne/McGraw-Hill, available Summer 1987], you will see how to use the dynamic-allocation system to support linked lists.) Now that you have a basic understanding of pointers, you are ready to unlock the power of C's functions.

A Closer Look
at Functions

CHAPTER 9

In C, functions are the building blocks in which all program activity occurs. With only a brief overview in Chapter 4, you have been using functions in a more or less intuitive way. In this chapter, you will study them in detail, learning such things as the way to make a function modify its arguments, the scope rules and lifetime of variables, the way to create recursive functions, and some special properties of the **main( )** function.

The General Form of a Function

The general form of a function is

> *type-specifier function__name(parameter-list)*
> *parameter declarations*
> {
>   *body of the function*
> }

The *type-specifier* specifies the type of value that the function will return through the use of **return**. The value may be of any valid type. If you do not specify a type, then by default the computer assumes that the function will return an integer result. The programs that you have been using so far have made use of this fact. If you review them, you will see that all of the functions returned either integer values or no value at all (which is legal). The *parameter list* is a comma-separated list of variable names that will receive the values of the arguments when the function is called. You do not have to include parameters in a function, in which case the parameter list will be empty. However, even if you do not include parameters, the parentheses are still required. You use the section that contains the *parameter declarations* to define the type of the parameters in the list.

The *return* Statement

Although Chapter 4 introduced the **return** statement as a means of returning a value from a function, this section will examine **return** more fully.

The **return** statement has two important uses. First, you can use it to cause an immediate exit from the function that it is in; that is, **return** will cause program execution to return back to the calling code as soon as the computer encounters it. Second, you may use **return** to return a value.

Returning from a Function

There are two ways that a function terminates execution and returns to the calling code. In the first way, the computer executes the last statement in the function and then, conceptually, encounters the function's ending }. (The final curly brace is not actually present in the object code, but you can think of the brace in this way.) For example, this function simply prints a string backwards:

```
pr_reverse(s)
char *s;
{
  register int t;

  for(t=strlen(s)-1; t; t--) printf("%c", s[t]);
}
```

After the function displays the string, there is nothing left for the function to do, so it returns to the place in the program that it was called from.

The second way that a function can return is through the use of the **return** statement. You can use the **return** statement without any value associated with it. For example, this function prints the outcome of one number raised to a positive integer power:

```
power(base, exp)
int base, exp;
{
  int i;

  if(exp<0) return; /* can't do negative exponents */

  i = 1;

  for( ; exp; exp--) i = base * i;
  printf("The answer is: %d: ", i);
}
```

If the exponent is negative, the **return** statement causes the function to terminate before the computer reaches the final curly brace but no value is returned.

A function may have several **return** statements in it. These may simplify certain algorithms. For example, the function shown here returns either the starting position of a substring within a string, or −1 if no match is found:

```
find_substr(sub,str)
char *sub,*str;
{
  register int t;
  char *p,*p2;

  for(t=0; str[t]; t++) {  /* get starting point */
    p=&str[t];
    p2=sub;
    while(*p2 && *p2==*p) { /* while equal advance */
      p++;                  /* through the string */
      p2++;
    }
    if(!*p2) return t;  /* if at the end of sub then match */
                        /* has been found */
  }
  return -1;
}
```

In this function, the use of two **return** statements simplifies the algorithm.

However, be careful: having too many **return** statements can muddy the operation of a routine and confuse its meaning. So, it is best to use multiple **return** statements only when they help to clarify a function.

Return Values

All functions, except those that you declare to be of type **void**, return a value. This value either is explicitly specified by the **return** statement, or is 0 if you do not use a **return** statement. Thus, as long as you do not declare a function as **void**, you may use it as an operand in any valid C expression. Therefore, each of the following expressions is valid in C.

```
x = abs(y);

if(max(x,y) > 100) printf("greater");

for(ch=getchar();isdigit(ch);) ... ;
```

However, a function cannot be the target of an assignment. A statement such as

```
swap(x,y)=100;   /* incorrect statement */
```

is wrong. Turbo C will flag it as an error and will not compile a program that contains such a statement.

Although all functions that are not of type **void** have return values, the functions that you write generally will be of three types. The first is simply computational. You design this function specifically to perform operations on its arguments and return a value based on that operation — in essence, it is a "pure" function. Examples of this type of function are the library functions **sqrt()** and **sin()** that return the square root of a number and its sine, respectively.

The second type of function manipulates information and returns a value that simply indicates the success or failure of that manipulation. An example is **fwrite()**, which you can use to write information to a disk file. If the write operation is successful, then **fwrite()** returns the number of bytes that you requested to be written; any other value indicates an error has occurred. (You will learn about file I/O in the next chapter.)

The last type of function has no explicit return value. In essence, the function is strictly procedural and produces no value. For murky, historical reasons, often functions that do not produce an interesting result will return something anyway. For example, **printf()** returns the number of characters written; however, it would be unusual to find a program that actually checked the return value. Therefore, although all functions, except those of type **void**, return values, you do not necessarily have any use for the values. A common question about function return values is, "Don't I have to assign this value to some variable since the function is returning a value?" The answer is no. If you do not specify an assignment, then the computer simply discards the return value. Consider the following program that uses **mul()**:

```
main()
{
  int x, y, z;

  x = 10;   y = 20;
  z = mul(x, y);                /* 1 */
  printf("%d", mul(x, y));      /* 2 */
```

```
    mul(x, y);                      /* 3 */
}

mul(a, b)
int a, b;
{
    return a*b;
}
```

Line 1 assigns the return value of **mul()** to **z**. In line 2, the return value is not actually assigned, but it is used by **printf()**. Finally, in line 3, the return value is lost because the line neither assigns it to another variable nor uses it as part of an expression.

Scope Rules of Functions

The *scope rules* of a language govern whether or not a piece of code knows about, or has access to, another piece of code or data. Chapter 4 lightly touched on this subject; now, this section will examine it more closely.

In C, each function is a discrete block of code. A function's code is private to that function, and cannot be accessed by any statement in any other function except through a call to that function. (For example, you cannot use **goto** to jump into the middle of another function.) The code that comprises the body of a function is hidden from the rest of the program and—unless the code uses global variables or data—it can neither affect nor be affected by other parts of the program. Here is another way to view this: the code and data that are defined within one function cannot interact with the code or data that is defined in another function because the two functions have a different scope.

There are three types of variables: *local variables, formal parameters,* and *global variables.* The scope rules govern how other parts of your program may access each of these types, and establish the lifetimes of the variables.

Local Variables

As you know, variables that are declared inside a function are called *local variables*. However, C supports a broader concept of the local variable than you have previously seen. A variable may be declared inside a block of code and is local to that block. In reality, variables that are local to a function are simply a special case of the general concept. Local variables may be referenced only by statements that are inside the block in which those variables are declared. Thus, local variables are not known outside their own code block, and their scope is limited to the block within which they are declared. Remember that a block of code begins when the computer encounters an opening curly brace, and terminates when the computer finds a closing curly brace.

One of the most important aspects of local variables that you should understand is that they exist only during the execution of the block of code in which they are declared; that is, a local variable is created upon entry into its block and destroyed upon exit.

The most common code block in which you declare local variables is the function. For example, consider these two functions:

```
func1()
{
  int x;

  x=10;
}
func2()
{
  int x;

  x=-199;
}
```

Here, the integer variable **x** is declared twice, once in **func1()** and once in **func2()**. The **x** in **func1()** has no bearing on, or relationship to, the **x** in **func2()** because each **x** is known only to the code that is within the same block as the variable's declaration.

The C language contains the keyword **auto**, which you can use to declare local variables. However, since C assumes that all nonglobal variables are, by default, **auto**, it is virtually never used. Hence, you will not see **auto** used in any of the examples in this book.

It is common practice to declare all variables that are needed within a function at the start of that function's code block. You should follow this practice primarily to make it easy for anyone who reads the code to know what variables the function is using. However, you do not need to do this because you may declare local variables within any block of code. Consider the following function:

```
f()
{
   char ch;

   printf("continue (y/n)? :");
   ch = getche();

   /* enter this block only if answer is yes */
   if(ch == 'y') {
     char s[80];  /* this is created only upon
                      entry into this block */
     printf("enter name:");
     gets(s);
     process_it(s);  /* do something */
   }
}
```

Here, **f()** creates the local variable s upon entry in the **if** code block and destroys it upon exit. Furthermore, s is known only within the **if** block and may not be referenced elsewhere—even in other parts of the function that contains it.

The main advantage of declaring a local variable within a conditional block is that the computer will allocate memory for the variable only if needed. The reason for this is that local variables do not come into existence until the computer enters the block in which they are declared. Although memory for a local variable is allocated but is not generally important in most situations, it can really matter when you are writing code for dedicated controllers (such as a garage door opener that responds to a digital security code) where RAM is in short supply.

Because the computer creates and destroys local variables with each entry and exit from the block in which they are declared, their content is lost once the computer leaves the block. This fact is especially important to remember when you are writing a function call. When a function is called, the computer creates its local variables and, upon its return, destroys them. Thus, local variables cannot retain their values between calls. (There is an exception to this rule, which Part Three will explain.)

Unless otherwise specified, storage for local variables is on the stack. The fact that the stack is a dynamic region of memory explains why local variables cannot, in general, hold their values between function calls.

Formal Parameters

If a function will use arguments, then it must declare variables that will accept the values of the arguments. These variables are called the *formal parameters* of the function. The formal parameters behave like any other local variables inside the function. As shown in the following program fragment, their parameter declaration occurs after the function name and before the function's opening brace:

```
/* return 1 if c is part of string s; 0 otherwise */
is_in(s,c)
char *s;
char c;
{
  while(*s)
    if(*s==c) return 1;
    else s++;

  return 0;
}
```

The function **is—in()** has two parameters: s and c. This function returns 1 if the character c is part of the string s; the function returns 0 if not. You must tell C what type of variables these are by declaring them as just shown in the fragment. After you do this, you may use them inside the function as normal local variables. Keep in mind that, as local variables, they are also dynamic and are destroyed upon the computer's exit from the function.

Remember to make sure that the formal parameters you declare are the same type as the arguments that you will use to call the function. In addition, even though these variables perform the special task of receiving the value of the arguments that are passed to the function, you can use them like any other local variable.

A Second Way to Declare Parameters

The ANSI standard (and Turbo C) allows a variation in the way that you may declare parameters to functions. You may place the entire declaration for each parameter inside the parentheses that are associated with the function. For example, you can code the declaration portion for the **is_in()** function shown earlier like this:

```
is_in(char *s, char c)
```

This book will continue to use the more traditional approach shown earlier because it is the one that virtually all existing C code uses. However, you may use whatever method best suits your needs.

Global Variables

Unlike local variables, global variables are known throughout the entire program and may be used by any piece of code. In essence, their scope is global to the program. Global variables will also hold their values during the entire execution of the program. You create global variables by declaring them outside of any function. Any expression may access them regardless of what function that expression is in.

As you can see, the following program fragment declares the variable **count** outside of all functions. Its declaration occurs before the **main()** function. However, you could place it anywhere, as long as it is not in a function, prior to its first use. Common practice dictates that it is best to declare global variables at the top of the program.

```
int count;  /* count is global  */

main()
{
   count=100;
   func1();
}
```

```
func1()
{
  int temp;

  temp=count;
  func2();
  printf("count is %d",count); /* will print 100 */
}

func2()
{
  int count;

  for(count=1;count<10;count++)
    printf(".");
}
```

If you study this program fragment carefully, it should be clear that, although neither **main()** nor **func1()** has declared the variable **count**, both functions may use it. However, **func2()** has declared a local variable called **count**. When referencing **count**, **func2()** will be referencing only its local variable, and not the global one. Remember that, if a global variable and a local variable have the same name, all references to that variable name inside the function in which the local variable is declared will refer to that local variable and have no effect on the global variable. This fact is a convenient benefit. However, forgetting this can cause your program to act strangely—even though it "looks" correct.

Storage for global variables is in a fixed region of memory that Turbo C sets aside for this purpose. Global variables are helpful when you use the same data in many functions in your program. However, you should avoid using unnecessary global variables, for three reasons: first, they take up memory during the entire execution of your program and not just when they are needed; second, using a global variable where a local variable will do makes a function less general because it relies on a variable that must be defined outside of itself; and, third, using a large number of global variables can lead to program errors because of unknown, and unwanted, side effects. You can see evidence of this third problem in BASIC, where all variables are global. A major problem in developing large programs is the accidental changing of a variable's value because you used it elsewhere in the program.

This problem can occur in C if you use too many global variables in your programs.

One of the principal features of a structured language is the compartmentalization of code and data. In C, you build compartmentalization by using local variables and functions. For example, here are two ways to write **mul()**, which is a simple function that computes the product of two integers.

General	Specific
	int x,y;
mul(x,y)	mul()
int x,y;	{
{	
return(x*y);	return(x*y);
}	}

Both functions will return the product of the variables **x** and **y**. However, you can use the generalized, or *parameterized*, version to return the product of *any* two numbers, whereas you can use the specific version to find only the product of the global variables **x** and **y**.

A Final Scope Example

Figure 9-1 presents the various scopes of view in the following short program. In the figure, code that is contained in an inner scope has knowledge of the outer scopes. However, the code in outer scopes has no effect on, or knowledge of, the code in inner scopes.

```
/* SCOPE: A program with various scopes */

int count; /* global to entire program */

main()
{
  char str[80];  /* local to main() */

  printf("enter a string: ");
  gets(str);
  play(str);
}
```

```
play(p)
char *p; /* local to play */
{

  if(!strcmp(p, "add")) {
    int a, b;   /* local to if block inside play */
    scanf("%d%d", &a, &b);
    printf("%d\n", a+b);
  }
  /* int a, b not known or existent here */
  else if (!strcmp(p, "beep")) printf("%c", 7);
}
```

You should be able to understand the various scopes in this example if you study Figure 9-1 closely. You may want to experiment to see how various changes affect the program.

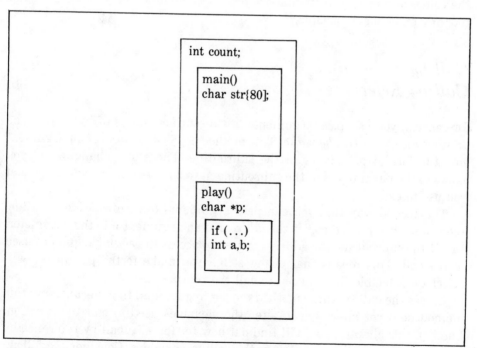

Figure 9-1. The scopes of the SCOPE program

Function Arguments

As you have seen earlier, you must make sure that the function's formal parameters are of the same type as the arguments that you use to call the function. If there is a type mismatch, the compiler will not issue an error message but unexpected results will occur. Unlike many other languages, C is very robust and generally will do something—even if it is not what you want. For example, if a function expects an integer argument but is called with a **float**, then the compiler will use the first two bytes of the **float** as the integer value! It is your responsibility as the programmer to make sure that such errors do not occur.

As with local variables, you may make assignments to a function's formal parameters or you may use them in any allowable C expression inside the function. Even though these variables perform the special task of receiving the values of the arguments that are passed to the function, you can use them like any other local variable.

Call by Value and Call by Reference

In general, you can pass arguments to subroutines in one of two ways. The first way is called *call by value*. This method copies the *value* of an argument into the formal parameter of the subroutine. Therefore, changes that you make to the parameters of the subroutine have no effect on the variables that you use to call it.

The second way that you can pass arguments to a subroutine is *call by reference*. This method copies the *address* of an argument into the parameter. Inside the subroutine, the address is used to access the actual argument used in the call. This means that changes that you make to the parameter will affect the variable that is used to call the routine.

C uses the call by value method to pass arguments. In general, using this method does not allow you to alter the variables used to call the function. Later in this chapter, you will find out how to "force" a call by reference by using pointers to allow changes to the calling variables. Consider the following function:

```
main()
{
    int t=10;
```

```
   printf("%d %d", sqr(t), t);
}

sqr(x)
int x;
{
   x = x*x;
   return(x);
}
```

This function copies the value of the argument to **sqr()**, which is 10, into the parameter **x**. When the assignment **x = x∗x** takes place, the only thing that is modified is the local variable **x**. The variable **t**, used to call **sqr()**, will still have the value 10. Hence, the output of the function will be 100 10.

Remember that the computer passes a copy of the value of the argument into that function. What occurs inside the function will have no effect on the variable used in the call.

Creating a Call by Reference

Even though C's parameter-passing convention is call by value, you can simulate a call by reference by passing a pointer to the argument. Since this process will cause the computer to pass the address of the argument to the function, you can then change the value of the argument outside the function.

You can pass pointers to functions just as you do with any other value. Of course, you must declare the parameters as pointer types. For example, consider the function **swap()**, which exchanges the value of its two integer arguments:

```
swap(x, y)
int *x, *y;
{
   int temp;

   temp = *x;   /* save the value at address x */
   *x = *y;     /* put y into x */
   *y = temp;   /* put x into y */
}
```

The function uses the ∗ operator to access the variable that its operand points to. Hence, the function will swap the contents of the variables that are used to call the function.

Remember that you must call **swap()** (or any other function that uses pointer parameters) with the *addresses of the arguments*. This program shows the correct way to call **swap()**.

```
main()
{
   int x, y;

   x = 10;
   y = 20;
   swap(&x, &y);
}
```

In this example, the program assigns the value 10 to the variable **x** and the value 20 to the variable **y**. The program then calls **swap()** with the addresses of **x** and **y**. The program uses the unary operator **&** to produce the address of the variables. Therefore, the program passes the addresses of **x** and **y** — not their values — into the function **swap()**.

At this point, you should understand why you had to put the **&** in front of the arguments of **scanf()** that were to receive values: you were actually passing their addresses so that you could modify the calling variable.

Calling Functions with Arrays

When you use an array as an argument to a function, you are passing only the address of the array and not a copy of the entire array. When you call a function with an array name, you are passing a pointer to the first element in the array into the function. (Remember that, in C, an array name without any index is a pointer to the first element in the array.) This means that the parameter declaration must be of a compatible pointer type. There are three ways to declare a parameter that will receive an array pointer. First, you may declare it as an array, as shown here:

```
main()  /* print some numbers */
{
   int t[10],i;

   for(i=0;i<10;++i) t[i]=i;
   display(t);
}

display(num)
int num[10];
{
```

```
   int i;

   for(i=0;i<10;i++) printf("%d ",num[i]);
}
```

Even though this program declares the parameter **num** to be an integer array of 10 elements, the C compiler will automatically convert **num** to an integer pointer because no parameter can receive an entire array. Therefore, only a pointer to an array will be passed, so you must include a pointer parameter to receive it.

A second way to declare an array parameter is to specify the parameter as an unsized array, as shown here:

```
display(num)
int num[];
{
  int i;

  for(i=0;i<10;i++) printf("%d ",num[i]);
}
```

This code declares **num** to be an integer array of unknown size. Since C provides no array-boundary checking, the actual size of the array is irrelevant to the parameter (but not to the program, of course). This method of declaration also defines **num** as an integer pointer.

The final way that you can declare an array parameter, and the most common form in professionally written C programs, is as a pointer, as shown here:

```
display(num)
int *num;
{
  int i;

  for(i=0;i<10;i++) printf("%d ",num[i]);
}
```

The C language allows this type of declaration because you may index any pointer by using [] as if the pointer were an array. All three methods of declaring an array parameter yield the same result: a pointer.

However, Turbo C treats an array *element* that is used as an argument just like any other simple variable. For example, you could have written the same program just shown without passing the entire array:

```
main() /* print some numbers */
{
   int t[10],i;

   for(i=0;i<10;++i) t[i]=i;
   for(i=0;i<10;i++) display(t[i]);
}

display(num)
int num;
{
   printf("%d ",num);
}
```

As you can see, the parameter to **display()** is of type **int**. It is irrelevant that the program calls **display()** by using an array element because the program uses only that value of the array.

It is important to understand that when you use an array as a function argument, the computer passes the array's address to a function. This point is an exception to C's parameter-passing convention of call by value. Thus, the code inside the function will be operating on, and potentially altering, the actual contents of the array that you have used to call the function. For example, consider the function **print_upper()** that prints its string argument in uppercase:

```
main()  /* print string as uppercase */
{
   char s[80];

   gets(s);
   print_upper(s);
}

print_upper(string)
char *string;
{
   register int t;

   for(t=0;string[t];++t)  {
     string[t]=toupper(string[t]);
     printf("%c", string[t]);
   }
}
```

After the call to **print—upper()**, the program will change the contents of array s in **main()** to uppercase. If you do not want this to happen, you could write the program like this:

```
main()  /* print string as uppercase */
{
  char s[80];

  gets(s);
  print_upper(s);
}

print_upper(string)
char *string;
{
  register int t;

  for(t=0;string[t];++t)
    printf("%c", toupper(string[t]));
}
```

In this version, the contents of array s remain unchanged because the program does not change its values.

You can find a classic example of passing arrays into functions in the standard library function **gets()**. Although **gets()** in Turbo C's standard library is much more sophisticated and complex, the function shown here will give you an idea of how it works. To avoid confusion with the standard function, this version is called **xgets()**.

```
xgets(s)  /* very simple version of the standard
              gets() library function */
char *s;
{
  char ch;
  int t;

  for(t=0; t<80; ++t) {
    ch=getchar();
    switch(ch) {
        case '\n':
          s[t]='\0'; /* terminate
                        the string */
          return;
        case '\b':
          if(t>0) t--;
```

```
            break;
        default:
            s[t]=ch;
    }
  }
  s[80]='\0';
}
```

The **xgets()** function must be called with a character array, which by definition is a character pointer. Upon entry, **xgets()** establishes a **for** loop from 0 to 80. This loop prevents you from entering larger strings at the keyboard. If you type more than 80 characters, the function will return. Because C has no built-in bounds checking, make sure that any variable that is used to call **xgets()** can accept at least 80 characters. As you type characters, the function enters the characters in the string. If you type a backspace, the function reduces the counter t by 1. When you strike a carriage return, **xgets()** places a null, which signals termination, at the end of the string. Because the function modifies the actual array used to call it, upon return the array will contain the characters typed.

The Arguments *argc* and *argv* to *main()*

Sometimes, it is useful to pass information into a program when you run it. Generally you pass information into **main()** by using *command-line arguments*. A command-line argument is the information that follows the program's name on the command line of the operating system. For example, you can start Turbo C with a program from the command line by typing

>**tcc** *program—name*

where *program—name* is the program that you wish to compile. The computer passes the name of the program into Turbo C as an argument.

You use two special built-in arguments—**argv** and **argc**—to receive command-line arguments. These are the only arguments that **main()** can have. The **argc** parameter holds the number of arguments on the command line, and is an integer. It will always be at least 1 because the name of the program qualifies as the first argument. The **argv** parameter is a pointer to an array of character pointers. Each element in this array points to a command-line argument. All command-line arguments are strings—a program must convert any numbers into the proper internal format. The following short program illustrates the use of command-line arguments and will print **Hello** followed by your name on screen if you type your name directly after the program name.

```
main(argc,argv)  /* name program */
int argc;
char *argv[];
{
  if(argc!=2) {
    printf("You forgot to type your name\n");
    exit(0);
  }
  printf("Hello %s", argv[1]);
}
```

If you titled this program **name** and your name was Tom, then you would type **name Tom** to run the program. The output from the program would be **Hello Tom**. For example, if you were logged into drive A and were running PC DOS, you would see

```
A>name Tom
Hello Tom
A>
```

after running **name**.

You must separate each command-line argument by a space or a tab. The C language does not consider commas, semicolons, and the like to be separators. For example,

```
run Spot, run
```

is made up of three strings, while

```
Herb,Rick,Fred
```

is one single string because the commas are not legal separators.

You must declare **argv** properly. The most common method is

```
char *argv[];
```

The empty brackets indicate that **argv** is an array of undetermined length. You can now access the individual arguments by indexing **argv**. For example, **argv[0]** will point to the first string, which is always the program's name; **argv[1]** will point to the first argument; and so on. (In versions of DOS before version 3.0, **argv[0]** was blank.)

A short example that uses command-line arguments is the program called **countdown**, shown here. The program counts down from a value that you specify on the command line and beeps when the program reaches 0. Notice that the program converts the first argument that contains the number into an integer by using the standard function **atoi()**. If the string **"display"** is present as the second command-line argument, the program will also display the count on screen.

```
main(argc, argv)  /* countdown */
int argc;
char *argv[];
{
   int disp, count;

   if(argc<2) {
     printf("you must enter the length of the count\n");
     printf("on the command line.  Try again.\n");
     exit(0);
   }

   if(argc==3 && !strcmp(argv[2],"display")) disp=1;
   else disp=0;

   for(count=atoi(argv[1]); count; --count)
     if(disp) printf("%d ", count);

   printf("%c", 7); /* beep the bell */
}
```

Notice that if you specify no arguments, the program will print an error message. A program that uses command-line arguments commonly issues instructions if you attempt to run it without the proper information being present.

You access an individual character in one of the command strings by adding a second index to **argv**. For example, this program will display on screen a character at a time the arguments with which it was called.

```
/* print all command line arguments */
main(argc, argv)
int argc;
char *argv[];
{
  int t, i;

  for(t=0; t<argc; ++t) {
    i = 0;
    while(argv[t][i]) {
      printf("%c", argv[t][i]);
      ++i;
    }
    printf(" ");
  }
}
```

Remember that the first index accesses the string and the second index accesses that character of the string.

Usually, you use **argc** and **argv** to get initial commands into your program. In Turbo C, you can have as many command-line arguments as the operating system will allow. DOS limits you to one 128-character line. You normally use these arguments to indicate a filename or an option. Using command-line arguments will give your program a professional appearance, and will facilitate the program's use in batch files.

Functions that Return Noninteger Values

If you do not explicitly declare the type of a function, the computer automatically declares it, by default, as **int**. The vast majority of C functions will use this default. However, when you must return a different data type, you must use a two-step process. First, you must give an explicit type specifier to the function; second, you must identify the type of the function before you make the first call to it. This process is the only way that the C compiler can generate correct code for functions that return noninteger values.

You may declare functions to return any valid C data type. The method of declaration is similar to the method that you use for variables: the type specifier precedes the function name. The type specifier tells the compiler what type of data the function will return. This information is critical if the program is going to run correctly because different data types have different sizes and internal representations.

Before you can use a function that returns a noninteger type, you must make its type known to the rest of the program. The reason for doing this is easy to understand. Unless directed to the contrary, Turbo C will assume that a function is going to return an integer value. If your program calls a function that returns a different type before that function's declaration, then the compiler will generate the wrong code for the function call. To prevent this mistake, you must place near the top of your program a special form of the declaration statement to tell the compiler what value that function is really returning. To see how this is done, examine this short example.

```
float sum();  /* identify the function */

main()
{
   float first, second;

   first=123.23;
   second=99.09;
   printf("%f",sum(first,second));
}

float sum(a,b) /* return a float */
float a,b;
{
   return a+b;
}
```

The first function-type declaration tells the compiler that **sum()** will return a floating-point data type. This step allows the compiler to generate code correctly for calls to **sum()**.

The function-type declaration statement has the general form

$$type\_specifier\ function\_name();$$

Even if the function takes arguments, you do not list any in its type declaration.

Without the type-declaration statement, a mismatch will occur between the type of data that the function returns and the type of data that the calling routine expects. This mismatch will cause bizarre and unpredictable results. If both functions are in the same file, the compiler will catch the type mismatch and not compile the program. However, if they are in different files, the compiler will not find the error. The compiler does type-checking not at link-time or run-time, but only at compile time. Therefore, you must be careful to make sure that both types are compatible.

When a character is returned from a function that you declared to be of type integer, the computer converts the character value into an integer. Because C handles the conversion from character to integer and back again cleanly, often you simply let functions returning characters default to integer, relying upon the automatic type conversion of characters into integers and back again.

Returning Pointers

Although you handle functions that return pointers in exactly the same way as any other type of function, a few important concepts need to be discussed.

Pointers to variables are *neither* integers *nor* unsigned integers. They are the memory addresses of a certain type of data. The reason for this distinction lies in the fact that, when the computer performs pointer arithmetic, it is relative to the base type; that is, if an integer pointer is incremented, it will contain a value that is two greater than its previous value. More generally, each time a pointer is incremented, the pointer will point to the next data item of its type. Since each data type may be a different length, the compiler must know what type of data the pointer is pointing to in order to make it point to the next data item.

For example, here is a function that returns a pointer into a string at the place where the computer finds a character match.

```
char *match(c, s)
char c, *s;
{
  int count;

  count=0;
  while(c!=s[count] && s[count]!='\0') count++;
  return(&s[count]);
}
```

The function **match()** will attempt to return a pointer to the place in a string where the computer finds the first match with **c**. If no match is found, the function will return a pointer to the null terminator. Here is a short program that uses **match()**:

```
char *match();  /* declare match's type */

main()
{
  char s[80], *p, ch;

  gets(s);
  ch = getche();
  p = match(ch, s);
  if(p)  /* there is a match */
    printf("%s ", p);
  else
    printf("no match found");
}
```

This program reads first a string and then a character. If the character is in the string, then it prints the string from the point of the character. Otherwise, it prints **no match found**. For example, if you entered **hi there** as the string and **t** as the character, the program will respond with **there**.

Functions of Type *void*

One of the extensions to the old UNIX standard for C is the **void** data type. One of its uses is to declare explicitly those functions that do not return values. Using **void** prevents the use of these functions in any expression, and helps to head off accidental misuse. For example, the function **print_vertical()** prints its string argument vertically down the side of the screen. Since it returns no value, it is declared as **void**.

```
void print_vertical(str)
char *str;
{
  while(*str)
    printf("%c\n", *str++);
}
```

Before you can use this function—or any other **void** function—you must declare it. If you do not, Turbo C will assume that it is returning an integer. Thus, when actually reaching the function, the compiler will declare a type mismatch. This program shows a proper example of declaring such a function.

```
void print_vertical();

main()
{
   print_vertical("hello");
}

void print_vertical(str)
char *str;
{
   while(*str)
     printf("%c\n", *str++);
}
```

In the past, functions that did not return values were simply allowed to default to type **int**. This practice is expected to continue in the less-demanding programming situations. However, where large, multiprogrammer projects are involved and where there is substantial room for error, it is a good idea to declare functions with no return values as **void**. From this point on, the examples in this book will use **void** where appropriate.

Function Prototypes

As you know, prior to using a function that returns a value other than **int**, you must define it. In Turbo C, you can take this idea one step further by also declaring the number and types of the function's arguments. This expanded definition is called a *function prototype*. Function prototypes are not part of the original UNIX C but were added by the ANSI-standard committee. They enable C to provide strong type-checking similar to that provided by such languages as Turbo Pascal. In a strongly typed language, the compiler issues errors if you call a function with arguments of types that are different from those that you defined it as having. For example, this program will cause the compiler to issue an error message because it attempts to call **func()** with two integer arguments instead of the **int** and **float** required.

```
/* This program uses function prototypes to
   enforce strong type checking in the calls
   to func().
*/

float func(int, float); /* prototype */

main()
{
  int x, y;

  x = 10;   y = 10;
  func(x, y);   /* type mismatch */
}

float func(x, y)
int x;
float y;
{
  printf("%f", y/(float)x);
}
```

Not only does the use of function prototypes help you trap bugs before they occur, but also function prototypes help to verify that your program is working correctly by not allowing you to call functions with mismatched arguments. Generally, it is a good idea to use function prototypes in larger programs or in those situations where several programmers are working on the same project.

Recursion

In C, functions may call themselves. A function is *recursive* if a statement in the body of the function calls itself. Sometimes called *circular definition*, recursion is the process of defining something in terms of itself.

Examples of recursion abound. A recursive way to define an integer number is as the digits 0, 1, 2, 3, 4, 5, 6, 7, 8, and 9, plus or minus an integer number. For example, the number 15 is the number 7 plus the number 8; 21 is 9 plus 12; 12 is 9 plus 3; and so on.

For a computer language to be recursive, a function must be able to call itself. A simple example is the function **factr()**, which computes the *factorial* of an integer. The factorial of a number N is the product of all of the whole numbers between 1 and N. For example, 3 factorial is $1 \times 2 \times 3$, or 6. Both **factr()** and its iterative equivalent are shown here:

```
factr(n)   /* recursive */
int n;
{
  int answer;

  if(n==1) return(1);
  answer=factr(n-1)*n;
  return(answer);
}


fact(n)      /* non-recursive */
int n;
{
  int t,answer;

  answer=1;
  for(t=1; t<=n; t++) answer=answer*(t);
  return(answer);
}
```

The operation of the nonrecursive version of **fact()** should be clear: it uses a loop that starts at 1 and ends at the number, and progressively multiplies each number times the increasing product.

The operation of the recursive **factr()** is more complex. If **factr()** is called with an argument of 1, the function returns 1; if it is called with any other argument, it returns the product of **factr(n−1)*n**. To evaluate this expression, **factr()** is called with **n−1** recursively. This process continues until **n** equals 1 and the calls to the function begin to return.

When you compute the factorial of 2, the first call to **factr()** will cause a second call to be made with the argument of 1. This second call will return 1, which is then multiplied by 2 (the original **n** value). The answer is then 2. You might find it interesting to insert **printf()** statements into **factr()**, which will show at what level each call is and what the intermediate answers are.

When a function calls itself, the computer allocates storage for new local variables and parameters on the stack, and executes the function code with these new variables from the start. A recursive call does not make a new copy of the function. Only the arguments are new. As each recursive call returns, the computer removes the old local variables and parameters from the stack, and resumes execution at the point of the function call inside the function. Recursive functions could be said to "telescope" out and back.

Most recursive routines do not significantly save code size or variable storage. Also, recursive versions of most routines may execute a bit more slowly than their iterative equivalents because of the added function calls; but this decrease in speed will not be noticeable in most cases. Although unlikely, many recursive calls to a function could cause a stack overrun. Because storage for function parameters and local variables is on the stack, and because each new call creates a new copy of these variables, it is possible that the stack could "walk on" some other data or program memory. However, you probably will not have to worry about this problem unless a recursive function runs wild.

The main advantage of recursive functions is that you can use them to create clearer and simpler versions of several algorithms than their iterative siblings. For example, the QuickSort sorting algorithm is quite difficult to implement in an iterative way. Also, some problems—especially AI-related ones—seem to lend themselves to recursive solutions. Finally, some people find it easier to think recursively than iteratively.

When writing a recursive function, you must have an **if** statement somewhere to force the function to return without executing the recursive call. If you do not do this, after you call the function, it will never return. This is a common error to make when you write recursive functions. Use **printf()** and **getche()** liberally during development so that you can watch what is going on and abort execution if you have made a mistake.

Implementation Issues

There are a few important issues to remember when you create C functions that affect their efficiency and usability. These issues are the subject of this section.

Parameters and General-Purpose Functions

A general-purpose function is one that can be used in a variety of situations, perhaps by many different programmers. Typically, you should not make general-purpose functions depend on global data. It is best to allow the parameters to pass to a function all of the information that it needs.

Besides making your functions general-purpose, parameters keep your code readable and less susceptible to bugs that can result from side effects.

Efficiency

Functions are the building blocks of C, and are crucial to the creation of all but the most trivial programs. Let nothing said in this section be construed to be otherwise. However, in certain specialized applications, you may need to eliminate a function and replace it with *in-line code* instead. In-line code is the equivalent of a function's statements that you use without a call to that function. You use in-line code instead of function calls only when execution time is critical.

There are two reasons why in-line code is faster than a function call. First, a "call" instruction takes time to execute. Second, if you want to pass arguments, the computer places them on the stack—a process that also takes time. For almost all applications, this slight increase in execution time is of no significance. However, if execution time is crucial, remember that each function call uses time that you would save if you placed the code in the function in line. For example, here are two versions of a program that prints the square of the numbers from 1 to 10. The in-line version will run faster than the other because the function call takes time.

```
in line

main()
{
  int x;

  for(x=1; x<11; ++x)
    printf("%d", x*x);
}
```

```
function call

main()
{
  int x;

  for(x=1; x<11; ++x)
    printf("%d", sqr(x));
}

sqr(a)
int a;
{
  return a*a;
}
```

Now that you have seen the power of Turbo C functions, you are ready to explore its I/O system.

Input and Output

CHAPTER 10

In C, you accomplish input and output through the use of library functions; C has no keywords that perform I/O operations. The ANSI standard, which Turbo C follows, defines one complete set of I/O functions. However, the UNIX standard contains two distinct systems of routines that handle I/O operations. The first, which both the ANSI standard and UNIX C define, is called the *buffered-file system* (sometimes the terms *formatted* or *high-level* are used instead). The second, which is defined under only the UNIX de facto standard, is the *unbuffered-file system* (sometimes called either *unformatted* or *UNIX-like*).

The ANSI standard does not define the unbuffered-file system. Instead, the ANSI standard expands the definition of the buffered system. The approach of the ANSI standard is justified by several arguments, including the fact that the two file systems are largely redundant. However, because both file systems are currently in widespread use, Turbo C supports both approaches. Hence, this chapter will cover both systems, but will place the greatest emphasis on the ANSI standard I/O system. The reason for this is that the use of the UNIX-like system, which the ANSI standard does not define, is expected to decline. Therefore, new code should be written by using the ANSI I/O functions.

The purpose of this chapter is to present an overview of I/O in Turbo C, and to illustrate the way that the core functions of each file system work together. The Turbo C library contains a very rich and diverse assortment of I/O routines—more routines than this chapter can cover. However, the functions presented in this chapter are sufficient for all but the most unusual circumstances. Study the Turbo C user manual to see what other functions are available.

Before beginning your exploration of Turbo C's I/O system, you will need to learn about two special compiler directives and some terminology.

Two Preprocessor
Directives

You can include various instructions to the Turbo C compiler in the source code of a program. These instructions are called *preprocessor directives* and, although not actually part of the C language, they expand the scope of the C programming environment. All preprocessor directives begin with a # sign. Although Part Three of this book will cover most of the preprocessor directives, you must understand two of them now in order to use Turbo C's file system.

The #define Directive

You use the **#define** directive to define an identifier and a string that the compiler will substitute for the identifier each time it is encountered in the source file. The identifier is called the *macro-name*, and the replacement process is called *macro-substitution*. The general form of the directive is

#define identifier string

Notice that there is no semicolon in this statement. You may include any number of spaces between the *identifier* and the *string* but, after the string begins, you can only terminate it by using a newline.

For example, to use **TRUE** for the value 1 and **FALSE** for the value 0, you would declare two macro **#define**s, as shown:

```
#define TRUE 1
#define FALSE 0
```

These two lines cause the compiler to substitute a 1 or a 0 each time that the compiler encounters **TRUE** or **FALSE** in your source file. For example, the following will print **0 1 2** on screen:

```
printf("%d %d %d",FALSE, TRUE, TRUE+1);
```

After you define a macro-name, you may use it as part of the definition of other macro-names. For example, this code defines the names **ONE**, **TWO**, and **THREE** to their respective values.

```
#define ONE      1
#define TWO      ONE+ONE
#define THREE    ONE+TWO
```

It is important to understand that the macro-substitution is simply the replacing of an identifier with its associated string. Therefore, to define a standard error message, you might write something like this:

```
#define E_MS "standard error on input\n"
    .
    .
    .
printf(E_MS);
```

This code causes the compiler to substitute the string **standard error on input \n** when it encounters the identifier **E—MS**. Thus, the compiler sees the **printf( )** statement as

```
printf("standard error on input\n");
```

No text substitutions will occur if the identifier occurs within a string. For example,

```
#define XYZ this is a test
    .
    .
    .
printf("XYZ");
```

will not print **this is a test**, but rather will print **XYZ**.

A common usage of #**define** is to define the size of elements, such as an array dimension, that might change over the evolution of a program. For example, this simple program uses the macro **MAX—SIZE** both to give dimensions to an integer array and to control the loop condition of the **for** loop that initializes the array.

```
#define MAX_SIZE 16

unsigned int  pwrs_of_two[MAX_SIZE];

/* display powers of 2 */
main()
{
    int i;

    pwrs_of_two[0] = 1; /* start the sequence */

    for(i=1; i<MAX_SIZE; i++)
      pwrs_of_two[i] = pwrs_of_two[i-1] * 2;

    printf("The first 16 powers of 2: \n");
    for(i=0; i<MAX_SIZE; i++)
      printf("%u ", pwrs_of_two[i]);
}
```

You will use #**define** to define system-related constants in your programs that use disk-file functions.

The #include *Directive*

The #**include** preproccessor directive instructs the compiler to include another source file with the one that contains the #**include** directive. You must enclose the source file to be read in double quotes or angle brackets. For example, each of these two statements

```
#include "stdio.h"
#include <stdio.h>
```

instructs the C compiler to read and compile the file that contains information about the disk-file library routines.

It is valid to have #**include** directives in included files. These #**include** directives are called *nested includes*. If you specify explicit pathnames as part of the filename identifier, then the compiler will only search those directories for the included file. However, if you enclose the filename in quotes, the compiler searches the current working directory first. If the compiler does not find the file, then it searches any directories that you specified on the command line by using the −**I** compiler option. If the compiler still has not found the file, it searches the standard directories, as defined by the implementation.

If you don't specify explicit pathnames and if you enclose the filename in angle brackets, the compiler first searches for the file in the directories that are specified in the compiler command-line −**I** option. If the compiler does not find the file, then it searches the standard directories. At no time is the current working directory searched.

The *stdio.h*
Header File

Many Turbo C library functions require that certain data types or other pieces of information be part of any program that uses them. You use the

#include directive to place this information into a separate file that is included in your program. In C, these files are called *header files*, or *headers* for short. The header file that you will need for the buffered I/O system is called **stdio.h**. The one that the UNIX-like file system uses is called **io.h**.

For example, you must place this line of code near the top of any program that uses the buffered I/O system:

```
#include "stdio.h"
```

Streams and Files

Before you begin to read about Turbo C's I/O system, it is important to understand the difference between the terms *streams* and *files*. The C I/O system supplies C programmers with a consistent interface that is independent of the actual device being accessed; that is, the C I/O system provides a level of abstraction between the programmer and the device being used. This abstraction is called a *stream* and the actual device is called a *file*. The following sections will explain the way that a stream and a file interact.

Streams

The buffered-file system is designed to work with a wide variety of devices, which include terminals, disk drives, and tape drives. Even though each device is different, the buffered-file system transforms each one into a logical device called a stream. All streams behave similarly. Because streams are largely device-independent, the same functions that can write to a disk file also can write to the console. There are two types of streams: text and binary.

Text Streams

A *text stream* is a sequence of characters that is organized into lines that are terminated by newline characters. The proposed ANSI standard states that the newline character is optional, depending upon the implementation. In a text stream, certain character translations may occur as the host environment requires. For example, the computer may convert a newline into a carriage-return-linefeed pair. Therefore, there may not be a one-to-one relationship between the characters that the computer writes (reads) and those characters in the external device. Also, because of possible translations, the number of characters written (read) may not be the same as those found in the external device.

Binary Streams

A *binary stream* is a sequence of bytes that have a one-to-one correspondence to those bytes in the external device. Thus, no character translations will occur. In addition, the number of bytes written (read) will be the same as the number of bytes found in the external device. However, the proposed ANSI standard does specify that a binary stream may have an implementation-defined number of null bytes that are appended to its end. For example, the computer might use these null bytes to pad the information so that it fills a sector on a disk.

Files

In C, a file is a logical concept that the system may apply to everything from disk files to terminals. You associate a stream with a specific file by performing an open operation. Once a file is open, you may exchange information between it and your program.

Not all files have the same capabilities. For example, a disk file can support random access while a terminal cannot. This difference illustrates an important point about the C I/O system: all streams are the same, but all files are not.

If the file can support random access (sometimes referred to as *position requests*), then opening that file also initializes the *file-position indicator* to the start of the file. As each character is read from or written to the file, the computer increments the position indicator—thus ensuring progression through the file.

You disassociate a file from a specific stream by using a close operation. On a stream that you opened for output, closing a stream causes the computer to write any contents of the associated stream to the external device. Generally referred to as *flushing the stream*, this process guarantees that the computer does not accidentally leave any information in the disk buffer. The computer will close all files automatically when your program terminates normally by **main( )** returning to the operating system or by a call to **exit( )**. The computer will not close files when a program terminates through a crash.

At the beginning of a program's execution, the computer opens three predefined text streams. They are **stdin**, **stdout**, and **stderr**. They refer to the standard I/O device that is connected to the system. For most systems, this device is the console. However, remember that most operating systems, including DOS, allow *I/O redirection*, so you may redirect routines that read or write to these files to other devices. (Redirection of I/O is the process whereby the operating system reroutes information that would normally go to one device to another device.) You should never try to open or close these files explicitly.

Each stream that is associated with a file has a file-control structure of type **FILE**. This structure is defined in the header **stdio.h**. You must not make modifications to this file-control structure. (You will learn about structures in Part Three. Briefly, a structure is simply a group of variables that is accessed under one name. Thus, a structure is similar to a RECORD in Turbo Pascal. For now, you do not need to know anything about structures in order to use the I/O routines.)

Conceptual Versus Actual

In light of the discussion just given, this section summarizes the way that the C I/O system operates. As far as you the programmer are concerned, all I/O takes place through streams, which are sequences of characters. Further, all streams are the same. The file system links a stream to a file. In the language of C programmers, a file is any external device that is capable of I/O. Because different devices have various capabilities, all files are not the same. However, the C I/O system minimizes these differences as they relate to the programmer because it converts the raw information that comes from the device into a stream (and back again). Aside from the limitation that only certain types of files support random access, programmers do not need to worry about the actual physical device, and are free to concentrate on the logical device called the stream.

If this approach seems confusing or strange, you need to see it in the context of languages like BASIC or FORTRAN, in which each device that the implementation supports has its own separate file system. In C's approach, you only need to think in terms of streams, and you only need to use one file system to accomplish all I/O operations.

Console I/O

Console I/O refers to operations that occur at the keyboard and on the screen of your computer. Generally, you perform console I/O by using a special case of the unbuffered file system. Because input and output to the console are so common, a subsystem of the buffered-file system was created that deals exclusively with console I/O. Technically, the functions in this subsystem will direct their operations to the standard input and standard output of the system. As stated, in many operating systems, including PC DOS, you can redirect the console I/O to other devices. However, for simplicity, this discussion assumes that the console will be the device used since it is the most common.

The Functions *getche()* and *putchar()*

The simplest of the console I/O functions are **getche()**, which reads a character from the keyboard, and **putchar()**, which prints a character to the screen. The **getche()** function waits until you press a key and then returns its value. The function also "echoes" the key pressed to the screen automatically. The **putchar()** function writes its character argument to the screen at the current cursor position.

This program will input characters from the keyboard and will print them in reverse case; that is, uppercase will print as lowercase, and lowercase will print as uppercase. The program halts when you type a period.

```
#include "stdio.h"

main()   /* case switcher */
{
  char ch;

  do {
    ch = getche();
    if(islower(ch)) putchar(toupper(ch));
    else putchar(tolower(ch));
  } while (ch!='.'); /* use a period to stop*/
}
```

There are two important variations of **getche()**. The first is **getchar()**, which is the original, UNIX-based character input function. The trouble with **getchar()** is that it buffers input until you enter a carriage return. The reason for this is that the original UNIX systems would line-buffer terminal input—that is, you had to hit a carriage return before anything you just typed in order to send it to the computer. The effect of line-buffering is that one or more characters will be waiting in the input queue after **getchar()** returns. This effect is quite annoying in today's interactive environments, and the use of **getchar()** cannot be recommended. Turbo C supports **getchar()** to ensure portability with UNIX-based programs. You may want to experiment with **getchar()** a little to understand its effect better.

A second and more useful variation of **getche()** is **getch()**, which operates precisely like **getche()**—except that **getch()** does not echo the typed character to the screen.

The Functions ***gets()*** *and* ***puts()***

On the next higher level of complexity and power are the functions **gets()** and **puts()**. They enable you to read and write strings of characters at the console.

The **gets()** function reads a string of characters that you enter at the keyboard, and places them at the address that its character-pointer argument points to. You may type characters at the keyboard until you enter a carriage return. The carriage return does not become part of the string; the computer places instead a null terminator at the end and **gets()** returns. In fact, it is impossible to use **gets()** to return a carriage return (however, you can use **getchar()** to do so). You can correct typing mistakes by using the backspace before pressing RETURN. Here is the general form that you use to declare **gets()**:

char *gets(char *s)

Here *s* is a character array. The **gets()** function returns a pointer to *s*. For example, this program reads a string into the array **str** and prints its length:

```
main()
{
  char str[80];

  gets(str);
  printf("length is %d",strlen(str));
}
```

The **puts()** function writes its string argument and then a newline to the screen. It is declared as

char *puts(char *s)

The **puts()** function recognizes the same backslash codes as **printf()**, such as \t for tab. A call to **puts()** requires far less overhead than the same call to **printf()** because **puts()** can only output a string of characters—it cannot output numbers or do format conversions. Therefore, **puts( )** takes up less space and runs faster than **printf( )**. For these reasons, programmers often use **puts( )** when it is important to have highly optimized code. The **puts( )** function returns a pointer to its string argument. The following statement writes **hello** on the screen:

```
puts("hello");
```

Table 10-1 summarizes the simplest functions that perform console I/O operations.

Formatted
Console I/O

In addition to the simple console I/O functions described earlier, the Turbo C standard library contains two functions that perform formatted input and output on the built-in data types: **printf( )** and **scanf( )**. The term *formatted* refers to the fact that these functions can read and write data in various

Table 10-1.   The Basic Console I/O Functions

Function	Operation
getchar( )	reads a character from the keyboard; waits for carriage return
getche( )	reads a character with echo; does not wait for carriage return
getch( )	reads a character without echo; does not wait for carriage return
putchar( )	writes a character to the screen
gets( )	reads a string from the keyboard
puts( )	writes a string to the screen

formats that are under your control. You can use **printf( )** to write data to the console; you can use **scanf( )**, the complement of **printf( )**, to read data from the keyboard. Both **printf( )** and **scanf( )** can operate on any of the built-in data types, which include characters, strings, and numbers. Although you have been using these functions since the start of this book, they will be examined in detail here.

The Function printf( )

You use this general form to declare **printf( )**:

printf("*control string*",*argument list***);**

The *control string* consists of two types of items. The first type is made up of characters that the function will print on screen. The second type contains format commands that define the way that the arguments are displayed. A format command contains first a percent sign (%) and then the format code. Table 10-2 presents the format commands. There must be exactly the same number of arguments as there are format commands, and the format commands and the arguments must match in order. For example, this **printf( )** call

```
printf("Hi %c %d %s",'c',10,"there!");
```

displays **Hi c 10 there!**.

The format commands may have modifiers that specify the field width, the number of decimal places, and a left-justification flag. An integer that is placed between the % sign and the format command acts as a *minimum field-width specifier*. This specifier causes the computer to pad the output with blanks or zeros to ensure that the output is a certain minimum length. If the string or number is greater than that minimum, **printf( )** will print it in full, even if it overruns the minimum. By default, the computer uses spaces to pad the output. If you wish to pad with zeros, place **0** before the field-width specifier. For example, **%05d** will pad a number of less than five digits with zeros so that the number's total length is five.

To specify the number of decimal places that you want to print for a floating-point number, place a decimal point after the field-width specifier and then the number of decimal places that you wish to display. For example,

Table 10-2. Format Commands of **printf( )**

Code	Format
%c	a single character
%d	decimal
%i	decimal
%e	scientific notation
%f	decimal floating point
%g	uses %e or %f —whichever is shorter
%o	octal
%s	string of characters
%u	unsigned decimal
%x	hexadecimal
%%	prints a % sign
%p	displays a pointer
%n	the associated argument will be an integer pointer into which is placed the number of characters written so far

%10.4f will display a number at least ten characters wide with four decimal places. When you apply a format like this to strings or integers, the number that follows the period specifies the maximum field length. For example, %5.7s will display a string at least five characters long and no longer than seven characters long. If the string is longer than the maximum field width, the computer will truncate the characters off the end.

By default, all output is *right-justified:* if the field width is larger than the data printed, the computer will place the data on the right edge of the field. You can force the information to be left-justified by placing a minus sign directly after the %. For example, %−10.2f will left-justify a floating-point number with two decimal places in a ten-character field.

There are two format command modifiers that allow **printf( )** to display **long** and **short** integers. You may apply these modifiers to the type modifiers **d, i, o, u,** and **x.** The l modifier tells **printf( )** that a **long** data type follows.

For example, **%ld** tells the computer that a **long int** will be displayed. The **l** modifier may also prefix the floating-point commands of **e**, **f**, and **g**, and indicates that a **double** follows. The **h** modifier instructs **printf( )** to display a **short int**. Therefore, **%hu** indicates that the data is of type **short unsigned int**.

With **printf( )**, you can output virtually any format of data you desire. Figure 10-1 presents some examples.

The Function scanf( )

The general-purpose console-input routine is **scanf( )**. It can read all of the built-in data types, and can automatically convert numbers into the proper internal format. It is almost the reverse of **printf( )**. The general form of **scanf( )** is

scanf("*control string*", *argument list*);

The *control string* consists of three classifications of characters:

- Format specifiers
- White-space characters
- Nonwhite-space characters

printf( ) statement	Output
("%−5.2f",123.234)	123.23
("%5.2f",3.234)	3.23
("%10s","hello")	hello
("%−10s","hello")	hello
("%5.7s","123456789")	1234567

Figure 10-1.   Some **printf( )** examples

You place a % sign in front of the input format specifiers, which tell **scanf( )** what type of data will be read next. Table 10-3 lists these codes. For example, **%s** reads a string, while **%d** reads an integer.

A white-space character in the control string causes **scanf( )** to skip over one or more white-space characters in the input stream. A white-space character is either a space, a tab, or a newline. In essence, one white-space character in the control string causes **scanf( )** to read, but not store, any number (including zero) of white-space characters, up to the first nonwhite-space character.

A nonwhite-space character in the control string causes **scanf( )** to read and discard a matching character. For example, the control string "%d,%d" causes **scanf( )** first to read an integer, then to read and discard a comma, and finally to read another integer. If the computer does not find the specified character, **scanf( )** will terminate.

Table 10-3.   Format Codes of **scanf( )**

Code	Meaning
%c	read a single character
%d	read a decimal integer
%i	read a decimal integer
%e	read a floating-point number
%f	read a floating-point number
%h	read a short integer
%o	read an octal number
%s	read a string
%x	read a hexadecimal number
%p	read a pointer
%n	receives an integer value equal to the number of characters read so far

All the variables used to receive values through **scanf( )** must be passed by their addresses. This means that all arguments must be pointers to the variables used as arguments. Remember that this is C's way of creating a call by reference, and it allows a function to alter the contents of an argument. For example, to read an integer into the variable **count**, you would use this **scanf( )** call:

```
scanf("%d",&count);
```

The **scanf( )** function reads strings into character arrays, and the array name without an index is the address of the first element of the array. So, to read a string into the character array **address**, you would use

```
scanf("%s",address);
```

In this case, **address** is already a pointer and does not need to be preceded by the **&** operator.

You must separate the input data items by using spaces, tabs, or newlines. The C language does not count punctuation such as commas, semicolons, and the like as separators. Thus,

```
scanf("%d%d",&r,&c);'
```

accepts an input of **10 20**, but fails with the input **10,20**. As in **printf( )**, the **scanf( )** format codes are matched in order with the variables that receive input in the argument list.

An * that is placed after the % and before the format code will read data of the specified type, but will suppress its assignment. Thus,

```
scanf("%d%*c%d",&x,&y);
```

given the input **10/20** places the value 10 into **x**, discards the division sign, and gives the value 20 to **y**.

The format commands can specify a maximum field-length modifier. This modifier is an integer number that you place between the % and the format-command code that limits the number of characters read for any field. For example, to read no more than 20 characters into **str**, you would write

```
scanf("%20s", str);
```

If the input stream is greater than 20 characters, then a subsequent call to input begins where this call leaves off. For example, if you enter

ABCDEFGHIJKLMNOPQRSTUVWXYZ

as the response to the call just given, **scanf( )** places only the first 20 characters, or up to the **T**, into **str** because of the maximum-size specifier. The function does not yet use the remaining characters, **UVWXYZ**. If you make another **scanf( )** call, such as

```
scanf("%s", str);
```

then the computer places **UVWXYZ** into **str**. Input for a field may terminate before it reaches the maximum field length if the computer encounters a white-space character. In this case, **scanf( )** moves on to the next field.

Although you use spaces, tabs, and newlines as field separators, when reading a single character, the computer reads them just like any other character. For example, with an input stream of **x y**,

```
scanf("%c%c%c",&a,&b,&c);
```

will return with the character **x** in **a**, a space in **b**, and the character **y** in **c**.

Be careful: if you have any other characters—including spaces, tabs, and newlines—in the control string, the computer will use those characters to match and discard characters from the input stream. The computer will discard any character that matches. For example, given the input stream **10t20**,

```
scanf("%st%s",&x,&y);
```

will place 10 into **x** and 20 into **y**. The computer will discard the character **t** because of the **t** in the control string. For another example,

```
scanf("%s ",name);
```

will *not* return until you type a character *after* you type a white-space character. This happens because the space after **%s** has instructed **scanf( )** to read and discard spaces, tabs, and newline characters.

You may not use **scanf( )** to display a prompting message. Therefore, you must display all prompts explicitly prior to the **scanf( )** call.

The Buffered I/O System

The buffered I/O system is comprised of several related functions. Table 10-4 presents the most common functions. These functions require you to include the header file **stdio.h** in any program in which you use them.

The File Pointer

The common thread that holds the buffered I/O system together is the *file pointer*. A file pointer is a pointer to information that defines various aspects

Table 10-4. The Most Common Buffered-File System Functions

Name	Function
fopen( )	opens a stream
fclose( )	closes a stream
putc( )	writes a character to a stream
getc( )	reads a character from a stream
fseek( )	seeks to specified byte in a stream
fprintf( )	is to a stream what **printf( )** is to the console
fscanf( )	is to a stream what **scanf( )** is to the console
feof( )	returns true if **EOF** mark is reached
ferror( )	returns true if an error has occurred
rewind( )	resets the file-position locator to the beginning of the file
remove( )	erases a file

of the file, including its name, status, and current position. In essence, the file pointer identifies a specific disk file, and is used by its associated stream to direct each of the buffered I/O functions to the place where they perform operations. A file pointer is a pointer variable of type **FILE**, which is defined in **stdio.h**.

The Function *fopen()*

The **fopen()** function serves two purposes: first, it opens a stream for use; and, second, it links a file with that stream. Most often, and for the rest of this discussion, the file is a disk file. The **fopen()** function is declared as

FILE *fopen(char *filename*, char *mode*);

Here, *mode* is a string that contains the desired open status. Table 10-5 presents the legal values for *mode* in Turbo C. The *filename* must be a string of characters that make up a valid filename for the operating system and may include a path specification.

As Table 10-5 shows, you may open a file in either text mode or binary mode. In text mode, the computer translates carriage-return-linefeed sequences to newline characters on input. On output, the reverse occurs: the computer translates newlines to carriage-return-linefeed sequences. No such translations occur on binary files.

To open a file for writing with the name **test**, you would write

```
fp = fopen("test","w");
```

where **fp** is a variable of type **FILE** *. The variable **fp** is the file pointer. Aside from assigning it a value by using **fopen()**, your code should never alter it. However, you will usually see the code written like this:

```
if ((fp = fopen("test","w"))==NULL) {
  puts("cannot open file\n");
  exit(1);
}
```

Table 10-5.   The Legal Values of *mode*

Mode	Meaning
"r"	open a text file for reading
"w"	create a text file for writing
"a"	append to a text file
"rb"	open a binary file for reading
"wb"	create a binary file for writing
"ab"	append to a binary file
"r+"	open a text file for read/write
"w+"	create a text file for read/write
"a+"	open or create a text file for read/write
"r+b"	open a binary file for read/write
"w+b"	create a binary file for read/write
"a+b"	open a binary file for read/write
"rt"	open a text file for reading
"wt"	create a text file for writing
"at"	append to a text file
"r+t"	open a text file for read/write
"w+t"	create a text file for read/write
"a+t"	open or create a text file for read/write

This method detects any error in opening a file, such as trying to open a write-protected disk or a full disk, before the computer attempts to write to it. This method uses a null, which is 0, because no file pointer will ever have that value. **NULL** is a macro that is defined in **stdio.h.**

If you use **fopen( )** to open a file for writing, then the computer will erase any preexisting file of that name and start a new file. If no file of that name exists, then one will be created. If you want to add to the end of the file, then you must use mode **a**. If you use **a** and the file does not exist, the function will return an error. Opening a file for read operations requires that the file exists. If it does not, **fopen( )** will return an error. Finally, if you open a file for read/write operations, the computer will not erase it if it exists; however, if it does not exist, the computer will create it.

The Function *putc()*

You use the **putc( )** function to write characters to a stream that you previously opened for writing through the **fopen( )** function. The function is declared as

int putc(int *ch*, **FILE** *∗fp***);**

where *fp* is the file pointer returned by **fopen( )**, and *ch* is the character to be output. The file pointer tells **putc( )** which disk file to write to. For historical reasons, *ch* is formally called an **int**, but the computer only uses the low-order byte.

If a **putc( )** operation is successful, then it will return the character written. Upon failure, it will return an **EOF**. **EOF** is a macro defined in **stdio.h** that stands for *end-of-file*.

The Function *getc()*

You use the **getc( )** function to read characters from a stream that **fopen( )** has opened in read mode. The function is declared as

int getc(FILE *∗fp***);**

fp is a file pointer of type **FILE** that is returned by **fopen( )**. For historical reasons, **getc( )** returns an integer, but the high-order byte is zero.

The **getc( )** function returns an **EOF** mark when the computer reaches the end of the file. Therefore, to read a text file to the end-of-file mark, you could use the following code:

```
ch = getc(fp);

while(ch!=EOF) {
   ch = getc(fp);
}
```

As stated earlier, the buffered-file system can also operate on binary data. When you open a file for binary input, it is possible that the computer may read an integer value that is equal to the **EOF** mark. If this happens, it would cause the routine just given to indicate an end-of-file condition, even though the computer has not reached the physical end of the file. To solve this problem, Turbo C includes the function **feof( )**, which determines where the end-of-file mark is when reading binary data. The **feof( )** function takes a file-pointer argument and returns 1 if the computer has reached the end of the file; the function returns 0 if the computer has not reached the end. Therefore, this routine reads a binary file until the computer encounters the end-of-file mark.

```
while(!feof(fp)) ch = getc(fp);
```

You may apply this same method to text files as well as binary files.

The Function fclose( )

You use the **fclose( )** function to close a stream that was opened by a call to **fopen( )**. Remember: *You must close all streams before your program terminates.* The **fclose( )** function writes to the file data that still remains in the disk buffer, and does a formal operating-system-level close on the file. Failure to close a stream invites all kinds of trouble, including lost data, destroyed files, and possible intermittent errors in your program. Using **fclose( )** also frees the file-control block associated with the stream, and makes it available for reuse. As you probably know, the operating system limits the number of open files that you may have at any one time—so you may need to close one file before you can open another.

The general form to declare **fclose( )** is

int fclose(FILE **fp***);**

where *fp* is the file pointer that is returned by the call to **fopen( )**. A return value of zero signifies a successful close operation; any other return value indicates an error. You can use the standard function **ferror( )** (which will be discussed next) to determine and report any problems. Generally, the only times that **fclose( )** will fail are either when you remove a diskette prematurely from the drive or when there is no more space on the diskette.

The Functions *ferror()* and *rewind()*

The **ferror()** function determines if a file operation has produced an error. The general form to declare **ferror()** is

int ferror(FILE *fp)

where *fp* is a valid file pointer. The **ferror()** function returns true if an error has occurred during the last file operation; it returns false if the file operation was successful. Because each file operation sets the error condition, you should call **ferror()** immediately after each file operation; if you do not, an error may be lost.

The **rewind()** function will reset the file-position locator to the beginning of the file that is specified as its argument. The general form of the declaration is

void rewind(FILE *fp)

where *fp* is a valid file pointer.

Using the Functions *fopen()*, *getc()*, *putc()*, and *fclose()*

The functions **fopen()**, **get()**, **putc()**, and **fclose()** make up the minimal set of file routines. A simple example of using **putc()**, **fopen()**, and **fclose()** is the program **ktod**, which follows. It simply reads characters from the keyboard and writes them to a disk file until you type a dollar sign. You specify the output file from the command line. For example, if you call this program **ktod**, then typing **ktod test** will allow you to enter lines of text into the file called **test**. Here is the program:

```
#include "stdio.h"

main(argc, argv)   /* ktod - key to disk */
int argc;
char *argv[];
{
   FILE *fp;
   char ch;
```

```
if(argc!=2) {
  printf("You forgot to enter the filename\n");
  exit(1);
}

if((fp=fopen(argv[1],"w")) == NULL) {
  printf("cannot open file\n");
  exit(1);
}

do {
  ch = getchar();
  putc(ch, fp);
} while (ch!='$');

fclose(fp);

}
```

The complement of **ktod** is **dtos**, which will read any ASCII file and display the contents on screen:

```
#include "stdio.h"

main(argc, argv)     /* dtos - disk to screen */
int argc;
char *argv[];
{
  FILE *fp;
  char ch;

  if(argc!=2) {
    printf("You forgot to enter the filename\n");
    exit(1);
  }

  if((fp=fopen(argv[1], "r")) == NULL) {
    printf("cannot open file\n");
    exit(1);
  }

  ch=getc(fp);    /* read one character */

  while (ch!=EOF) {
    putchar(ch);  /* print on screen */
    ch=getc(fp);
  }

  fclose(fp);
}
```

The following program will copy a file of any type.

```
#include "stdio.h"

main(argc, argv)   /* copy one file to another */
int argc;
char *argv[];
{
  FILE *in, *out;
  char ch;

  if(argc!=3) {
    printf("You forgot to enter a filename\n");
    exit(1);
  }

  if((in=fopen(argv[1], "rb")) == NULL) {
    printf("cannot open source file\n");
    exit(1);
  }
  if((out=fopen(argv[2], "wb")) == NULL) {
    printf("cannot open destination file\n");
    exit(1);
  }

  /* this line of code acutally copies the file */
  while(!feof(in)) putc(getc(in),out);

  fclose(in);
  fclose(out);
}
```

Notice that the program opens the files in binary mode and uses **feof( )** to check for the end of the file. (The program does not perform any error checking on output; however, in a real-world situation, doing so would be a good idea and you should try to add some as an exercise.)

The Functions *getw( )* and *putw( )*

In addition to **getc( )** and **putc( )**, Turbo C supports two additional buffered I/O functions: **putw( )** and **getw( )**. You use these functions to read and write integers to and from a disk file. These functions work exactly the same as **putc( )** and **getc( )**, with one exception: instead of reading or writing a single character, **putw( )** and **getw( )** read or write an integer. For example, this code fragment will write an integer to the disk file that **fp** points to:

```
putw(100, fp);
```

The Functions *fgets()* and *fputs()*

Turbo C's buffered I/O system includes two functions that can read and write strings from streams: **fgets()** and **fputs()**. The general forms of their declarations are

char *fputs(char *str, **FILE** *fp);
char *fgets(char *str, **int** *length*, **FILE** *fp);

The function **fputs()** works exactly like **puts()**, except that **fputs()** writes the string to the specified stream. The **fgets()** function reads a string from the specified stream until it reads either a newline character or length−1 characters. If **fgets()** reads a newline, it will be part of the string (unlike **gets()**). However, when **fgets()** is terminated, the resultant string will be null-terminated.

The Functions *fread()* and *fwrite()*

The buffered I/O system provides two functions—**fread()** and **fwrite()**—that allow you to read and write blocks of data. The general forms of their declarations are

int fread(void *buffer, **int** *num__bytes*, **int** *count*, **FILE** *fp)
int fwrite(void *buffer, **int** *num__bytes*, **int** *count*, **FILE** *fp)

In the case of **fread()**, *buffer* is a pointer to a memory region that will receive the data read from the file. For **fwrite()**, *buffer* is a pointer to the information that will be written to the file. For both, *num__bytes* specifies the number of bytes to be read or written. The argument *count* determines how many items (each one being *num__bytes* in length) will be read or written. Finally, *fp* is a file pointer to a previously opened stream.

As long as the file is opened for binary data, **fread()** and **fwrite()** can read and write any type of information. For example, this program writes a **float** to a disk file:

```
/* write a floating point number to a disk file */
#include "stdio.h"
```

```
main()
{
  FILE *fp;
  float f=12.23;

  if((fp=fopen("test","wb"))==NULL) {
    printf("cannot open file\n");
    return;
  }

  fwrite(&f, sizeof(float), 1, fp);

  fclose(fp);
}
```

As this program illustrates, the buffer can be, and often is, simply a variable. One of the most useful applications of **fread( )** and **fwrite( )** involves the reading and writing of arrays or, as you will see in the next chapter, structures. For example, this fragment writes the contents of the floating-point array **balance** to the file **balance** by using a single **fwrite( )** statement.

```
#include "stdio.h"

main()
{
  FILE *fp;
  float balance[100];

  if((fp=fopen("balance","w+"))==NULL) {
    printf("cannot open file\n");
    return;
  }
  .
  .
  .
  /* this saves the entire balance array in one step */
  fwrite(balance, sizeof(balance), 1, fp);
  .
  .
  .
  fclose(fp);
}
```

Later in this book, you will see several other, more complex examples of the way that you can use these functions.

Random-Access I/O and fseek()

You can perform random read and write operations under the buffered I/O system with the help of **fseek()**, which sets the file-position locator. The general form of the declaration of **fseek()** is

> int fseek(FILE *fp*, long int *num_bytes*, int *origin*);

where *fp* is a file pointer that is returned by a call to **fopen()**; *num_bytes*, which is a long integer, is the number of bytes from *origin* to reach the new position, and *origin* is one of the following macros:

Origin	Name
beginning of file	SEEK_SET
current position	SEEK_CUR
end of file	SEEK_END

Therefore, to seek *num_bytes* from the start of the file, *origin* should be **SEEK_SET**. To seek *num_bytes* from the current position, *origin* should be **SEEK_CUR**; and from the end of the file, it should be **SEEK_END**.

Remember that *num_bytes* must be a **long int** in order to support operations on files that are larger than 64K bytes.

The use of **fseek()** on text files is not recommended because the character translations will result in position errors. Therefore, its use is suggested only for binary files.

For example, to read the 234th byte in a file called **test**, you could use the following code.

```
func1()
{
  FILE *fp;

  if((fp=fopen("test", "rb")) == NULL) {
    printf("cannot open file\n");
    exit(1);
  }

  fseek(fp, 234L, 0);
```

```
      return getc(fp);    /* read one character */
                          /* at 234th position */

   }
```

Notice that this code appends the L modifier to the constant **234** in order to force the compiler to treat the constant as a **long int**. You could also use a cast to accomplish the same thing. (Remember that trying to use a regular integer will cause errors when the computer expects a long integer.)

A return value of zero means that **fseek()** succeeded. A nonzero value indicates failure.

A more interesting example is the DUMP program shown next that uses **fseek()** to let you examine the contents in both ASCII and hexadecimal of any file that you choose. You can look at the file in 128-byte "sectors," as you move about in the file in either direction. The style of the output displayed is similar to the format used by the DOS program DEBUG when given the **D** (dump memory) command. You exit the program by typing −**1** when prompted for the sector.

In the program, notice the usage of **fread()** to read the file. At the end of the file, it is likely that the program has read less than **SIZE** number of bytes so the program passes the number returned by **fread()** to **display()**. (Remember that **fread()** returns the number of items actually read.) Enter this program into your computer now and study it until you understand the way that it works.

```
/* DUMP: A simple disk look utility using fseek */
#include "stdio.h"
#include "ctype.h"

#define SIZE 128

char buf[SIZE];
void display();

main(argc, argv)
int argc;
char *argv[];
{
   FILE *fp;
   int sector, numread;
```

```
  if(argc!=2) {
    printf("usage: dump filename\n");
    exit(1);
  }

  if((fp=fopen(argv[1], "rb"))==NULL) {
    printf("cannot open file\n");
    exit(1);
  }

  do {
    printf("enter sector: ");
    scanf("%ld", &sector);
    if(fseek(fp, sector*SIZE, SEEK_SET)) {
      printf("seek error\n");
    }
    if((numread=fread(buf, 1, SIZE, fp)) != SIZE) {
      printf("EOF reached\n");
    }

    display(numread);
  } while(sector>=0);
}

/* display  the file */
void display(numread)
int numread;
{
  int i, j;

  for(i=0; i<numread/16; i++) {
    for(j=0; j<16; j++) printf("%3X", buf[i*16+j]);
    printf("   ");
    for(j=0; j<16; j++) {
      if(isprint(buf[i*16+j])) printf("%c", buf[i*16+j]);
      else printf(".");
    }
    printf("\n");
  }
}
```

The DUMP program introduces the use of a library function called **isprint( )**, which determines which characters are printing characters and which characters are not. The **isprint( )** function returns true if the character is printable, and returns false if not. The **isprint( )** function requires you to use the header file **ctype.h**, which is included at the top of the DUMP

program. This header is needed by the **isprint( )** function. An example output
with DUMP as used on itself is shown in Figure 10-2.

The Streams **stdin,** **stdout,** *and* **stderr**

Whenever a Turbo C program starts execution, the computer opens three
streams automatically. They are standard input (**stdin**), standard output
(**stdout**), and standard error (**stderr**). Normally, these streams refer to the
console, but the operating system may redirect them to some other stream
device. Because these are file pointers, the buffered I/O system may use
them to perform I/O operations on the console. For example, you could define
putchar( ) as

```
putchar(c)
char c;
{
   putc(c,stdout);
}
```

```
A:\>dump dump.c
enter sector: 0
 2F 2A 20 44 55 4D 50 3A 20 41 20 73 69 6D 70 6C    /* DUMP: A simpl
 65 20 64 69 73 6B 20 6C 6F 6F 6B 20 75 74 69 6C    e disk look util
 69 74 79 20 75 73 69 6E 67 20 66 73 65 65 6B 20    ity using fseek
 2A 2F  D  A 23 69 6E 63 6C 75 64 65 20 22 73 74    */..#include "st
 64 69 6F 2E 68 22  D  A 23 69 6E 63 6C 75 64 65    dio.h"..#include
 20 22 63 74 79 70 65 2E 68 22  D  A  D  A 23 64    "ctype.h"....#d
 65 66 69 6E 65 20 53 49 5A 45 20 31 32 38  D  A    efine SIZE 128..
  D  A 63 68 61 72 20 62 75 66 5B 53 49 5A 45 5D    ..char buf[SIZE]
enter sector: 2
 20 70 72 69 6E 74 66 28 22 75 73 61 67 65 3A 20      printf("usage:
 64 75 6D 70 20 66 69 6C 65 6E 61 6D 65 5C 6E 22    dump filename\n"
 29 3B  D  A 20 20 20 20 65 78 69 74 28 31 29 3B    );..    exit(1);
  D  A 20 20 7D  D  A  D  A 20 20 69 66 28 28 66    ..  }.... if((f
 70 3D 66 6F 70 65 6E 28 61 72 67 76 5B 31 5D 2C    p=fopen(argv[1],
 20 22 72 62 22 29 29 3D 3D 4E 55 4C 4C 29 20 7B     "rb"))==NULL) {
  D  A 20 20 20 20 70 72 69 6E 74 66 28 22 63 61    ..      printf("ca
 6E 6E 6F 74 20 6F 70 65 6E 20 66 69 6C 65 5C 6E    nnot open file\n
enter sector:
```

Figure 10-2.   Sample output from the DUMP program

In general, you use **stdin** to read from the console, **stdout** to write to the console, and **stderr** to write to the console. You may use **stdin**, **stdout**, and **stderr** as file pointers in any function that uses a variable of type **FILE** *.

Keep in mind that **stdin**, **stdout**, and **stderr** are not variables but are constants, and as such may not be altered. Also, just as the computer creates these file pointers automatically at the start of your program, it closes them automatically at the end; you should not try to close them.

The Functions *fprintf()* and *fscanf()*

In addition to the basic I/O functions discussed so far, the buffered I/O system includes **fprintf()** and **fscanf()**. These functions behave exactly the same as **printf()** and **scanf()**, except that they operate with disk files. The general forms of declarations of **fprintf()** and **fscanf()** are

> **fprintf**(*fp*, "*control string*", *argument list*);
> **fscanf**(*fp*, "*control string*", *argument list*);

where *fp* is a file pointer that is returned by a call to **fopen()**. As stated earlier, except for directing their output to the file defined by *fp*, they operate exactly like **printf()** and **scanf()**, respectively.

To illustrate how useful these functions can be, the following program maintains a simple telephone directory in a disk file. You may enter names and numbers, or you can look up a number that corresponds to the name that you are interested in.

```
/* A simple telephone directory */

#include "stdio.h"

void add_num(), lookup();

main()   /* fscanf - fprintf example */
{
 char choice;

  do {
    choice = menu();
    switch(choice) {
      case 'a': add_num();
        break;
      case 'l': lookup();
        break;
```

```
      }
  } while (choice!='q');

}

/* display menu and get request */
menu()
{
  char ch;

  do {
    printf("(A)dd, (L)ookup, or (Q)uit: ");
    ch = tolower(getche());
    printf("\n");
  } while(ch != 'q' && ch != 'a' && ch != 'l');

  return ch;
}

/* add a name and number to the directory */
void add_num()
{
  FILE *fp;
  char name[80];
  int a_code, exchg, num;

  /* open it for append */
  if((fp=fopen("phone","a")) == NULL) {
    printf("cannot open directory file\n");
    exit(1);
  }

  printf("enter name and number: ");
    fscanf(stdin, "%s%d%d%d", name, &a_code, &exchg, &num);
  fscanf(stdin, "%*c"); /* remove CR from input stream */

  /* write to file */
  printf("%d",fprintf(fp,"%s %d %d %d\n", name, a_code, exchg, num));

  fclose(fp);
}

/* find a number given a name */
void lookup()
{
  FILE *fp;
  char name[80], name2[80];
  int a_code, exchg, num;

  /* open it for read */
```

```
if((fp=fopen("phone","r")) == NULL) {
  printf("cannot open directory file\n");
  exit(1);
}

printf("name? ");
gets(name);

/* look for number */
while(!feof(fp)) {
  fscanf(fp,"%s%d%d%d", name2, &a_code, &exchg, &num);
  if(!strcmp(name, name2)) {
    printf("%s: (%d) %d-%d\n",name, a_code, exchg, num);
    break;
  }
}
fclose(fp);
}
```

Enter this program and run it at this time. After you enter a couple of names and numbers, examine the file **phone**. It should appear in the same way that it would if you had used **printf( )** to display the information on screen.

Be careful: although using **fprintf( )** and **fscanf( )** often is the easiest way to write and read assorted data to disk files, it is not always the most efficient. Because you are writing formatted ASCII data just as it would appear on the screen, instead of in binary, you use extra overhead with each call. So, if speed or file size is a concern, you should probably use **fread( )** and **fwrite( )**.

Erasing Files

The **remove( )** function erases a file that you specify. The general form of its declaration is

int **remove(char** *filename*);

If successful, **remove( )** returns zero; if unsuccessful, it returns nonzero.

Unbuffered I/O—
the UNIX-like File
Routines

Because C was originally developed under the UNIX operating system, a second disk-file I/O system was created. This second system uses functions that are separate from the functions of the buffered-file system. These second-system functions are low-level UNIX-like disk I/O functions. Table 10-6 presents these functions. All of the functions require you to include the header file **io.h** near the beginning of any program that uses them.

The disk I/O subsystem that is comprised of these functions is called the *unbuffered I/O system* because, as the programmer, you must provide and maintain *all* disk buffers—the routines will not maintain them for you. Unlike **getc()** and **putc()**, which write and read characters from or to a stream of data, **read()** and **write()** read or write one complete buffer of information with each call. (This process is similar to that of **fread()** and **fwrite()**.)

As stated at the beginning of this chapter, the proposed ANSI standard does not define the unbuffered-file system. This implies that programs that use it will have portability problems at some point in the future. Therefore, it is expected that the unbuffered-file system's use will diminish over the next few years. At the time of this writing, however, many existing C programs use the system, which is supported by virtually all existing C compilers, including Turbo C. Hence, it is included in this chapter.

Table 10-6.   The UNIX-like Unbuffered I/O Functions

Name	Function
read()	reads a buffer of data
write()	writes a buffer of data
open()	opens a disk file
close()	closes a disk file
lseek()	seeks to the specified byte in a file
unlink()	removes a file from the directory

The Functions *open()*, *creat()*, and *close()*

Unlike the high-level I/O system, the low-level system does not use file pointers of type **FILE**, but rather uses file descriptors called *handles* of type **int**. The general form of the declaration of **open()** is

int open(char **filename,* **int** *mode,* **int** *access***)**;

where *filename* is any valid filename and *mode* is one of the following macros that are defined in **io.h**.

Mode	Effect
O _RDONLY	read-only
O _WRONLY	write-only
O _RDWR	read/write

Turbo C also allows you to add some options to these basic modes; consult your manual for more information on the options.

The *access* parameter only relates to UNIX environments and is included in the declaration for compatibility. Turbo C also defines a DOS-specific version called **_open()**. The general form of its declaration is

int _open(char **filename,* **int** *mode***)**;

which bypasses the *access* parameter altogether. In the examples in this chapter, *access* will be set to zero.

A successful call to **open()** returns a positive integer. A return value of −1 means that **open()** cannot open the file.

You will usually see the call to **open()** like this:

```
if((fd=open(filename, mode, 0)) == -1) {
   printf("cannot open file\n");
   exit(1);
}
```

If the file that you specify in **open()** does not appear on the disk, the operation will fail and will not create the file.

The general form of the declaration of **close( )** is

int close(int *fd*);

If **close( )** returns −1, it was unable to close the file. This could occur if you removed the diskette from the drive, for example.

A call to **close( )** releases the file descriptor so that you can reuse it for another file. There is always some limit to the number of open files that may exist simultaneously, so you should use **close( )** to close a file when you no longer need it. More important, a close operation forces the computer to write to disk any information in the internal disk buffers of the operating system. Failure to close a file will usually lead to loss of data.

You will use **creat( )** to create a new file for write operations. The general form of the declaration of **creat( )** is

int creat(char *filename*, int *access*);

where *filename* is any valid filename. You use the *access* argument to specify access modes and to mark the file as being either binary or text.

Because the use of *access* in **creat( )** relates to the UNIX environment, Turbo C provides a special MS-DOS version called **_creat( )**, which takes a file-attribute byte for *access* instead. In DOS, each file has an associated attribute byte that specifies various bits of information. Table 10-7 shows the organization of this attribute byte. The values in Table 10-7 are additive; that is, if you wish to create a hidden file that is read only, you would use the value 3 (1 + 2) for *access*. Generally, to create a standard file, *access* will be 0.

The Functions *write( )* and *read( )*

After you open a file for writing, you may access it by using **write( )**. The general form of declaration of the **write( )** function is

int write(int *fd*, void *buf*, int *size*);

Each time the computer executes a call to **write( )**, it writes *size* characters from the buffer pointed to by *buf* to the disk file that is specified by *fd*.

Table 10-7. The Organization of the DOS-Attribute Byte

Bit	Value	Meaning
0	1	read-only file
1	2	hidden file
2	4	system file
3	8	volume label name
4	16	subdirectory name
5	32	archive
6	64	unused
7	128	unused

You may wonder why **write()** does not write the entire contents of the buffer to disk automatically. The answer is that **write()** can write a partially full buffer. The **write()** function will return the number of bytes that it wrote during a successful write operation. Upon failure, **write()** returns −1.

The function **read()** is the complement of **write()**. The general form of its declaration is

$$\textbf{int read(int } \textit{fd}, \textbf{ void } *\textit{buf}, \textbf{ int } \textit{size});$$

Here, *fd*, *buf*, and *size* are the same as for **write()**, except that **read()** will place the data read into the buffer that is pointed to by *buf*. If **read()** is successful, it returns the number of characters actually read. If it is unsuccessful, it returns 0 upon the physical end of the file; and if errors occur, it returns −1.

The program shown here illustrates some aspects of the unbuffered I/O system. The program will read lines of text from the keyboard and writes them to a disk file. After writing the lines, the program will read them back.

```
#include "io.h"

#define BUF_SIZE   128

main()   /* read and write using unbuffered I/O */
{
```

```
    char buf[BUF_SIZE];
    int fd1, fd2, t;

    if((fd1=_creat("oscar",  O_WRONLY ))==-1) { /* open for write */
      printf("cannot open file\n");
      exit(1);
    }

    input(buf, fd1);

    /* now close file and read back */
    close(fd1);

    if((fd2=open("oscar", 0, O_RDONLY))==-1) { /* open for write */
      printf("cannot open file\n");
      exit(1);
    }

    display(buf,fd2);
    close(fd2);
}

input(buf, fd1)
char *buf;
int fd1;
{
  register int t;

  do {
    for(t=0; t<BUF_SIZE; t++) buf[t]='\0';
    gets(buf); /* input chars from keyboard */
    if(write(fd1, buf, BUF_SIZE)!=BUF_SIZE) {
      printf("error on write\n");
      exit(1);
    }
  } while (strcmp(buf, "quit"));
}



display(buf, fd2)
char *buf;
int fd2;
{
  for(;;) {
    if(read(fd2, buf, BUF_SIZE)==0) return;
    printf("%s\n",buf);
  }
}
```

The Function *unlink()*

To remove a file from the directory, you use **unlink( )**. Although **unlink( )** is considered part of the UNIX-like I/O system, it will remove any file from the directory. The standard form of the call is

int unlink(char *filename*);

where *filename* is a character pointer to any valid filename. The **unlink( )** function will return an error (usually −1) if it could not erase the file. This could happen if the file was not present on the diskette, or if the diskette was write-protected.

Random-Access Files and *lseek()*

Turbo C supports random-access file I/O under the unbuffered I/O system through calls to **lseek( )**. The general form of its declaration is

long lseek(int *fd*, long *num_bytes*, int *origin*);

where *fd* is a file descriptor that is returned by **creat( )** or **open( )**. The *num_bytes* must be a **long int**, and *origin* must be one of the following macros:

Origin	Name
beginning of file	SEEK_SET
current position	SEEK_CUR
end of file	SEEK_END

Therefore, to seek *num_bytes* from the start of the file, you should make *origin* **SEEK_SET**. To seek from the current position, use **SEEK_CUR**; to seek from the end of the file, use **SEEK_END**.

The **lseek( )** function returns *num_bytes* on success. Therefore, **lseek( )** will return a **long** integer, and must be declared as such at the top of your program. Upon failure, **lseek( )** returns −**1L**.

A simple example that uses **lseek( )** is another version of the DUMP program developed earlier. This version is recoded to use the UNIX-like I/O system. The version not only shows the operation of **lseek( )** but also illustrates many of the unbuffered I/O functions.

```c
#include "io.h"
#include "ctype.h"

#define SIZE   128

char buf[SIZE];
void display();

main(argc, argv)  /* read buffers using lseek() */
int argc; char *argv[];
{
  char s[10];
  int fd, sector, numread;
  long pos;

  if(argc!=2) {
    printf("You forgot to enter the file name.");
    exit(1);
  }

  if((fd=open(argv[1], O_RDONLY, 0))==-1) { /* open for read */
    printf("cannot open file\n");
    exit(1);
  }
  do {
    printf("\n\nbuffer: ");
    gets(s);

    sector = atoi(s); /* get the sector to read */

    pos = (long) (sector*SIZE);
    if(lseek(fd, pos, SEEK_SET)!=pos)
      printf("seek error\n");

    if((numread=read(fd, buf, SIZE))!=SIZE)
      printf("EOF reached\n");
    display(numread);
  } while(sector>=0);
  close(fd);
}

void display(numread)
int numread;
{
  int i, j;
```

```
for(i=0; i<numread/16; i++) {
  for(j=0; j<16; j++) printf("%3X", buf[i*16+j]);
  printf("   ");
  for(j=0; j<16; j++) {
    if(isprint(buf[i*16+j])) printf("%c", buf[i*16+j]);
    else printf(".");
  }
  printf("\n");
}
}
```

Choosing an Approach

For new projects, using the buffered I/O system that the ANSI standard defines is recommended. Because the ANSI-standard committee has elected not to standardize the UNIX-like unbuffered I/O system, it cannot be recommended for future projects. However, existing code should remain maintainable for a number of years, and there is probably no reason to rush to rewrite at this time.

Within the buffered I/O system, you should use text mode, **getc()**, and **putc()** when you are working with character files, such as text files that a word processor creates. However, when you need to store binary data or complex data types, you should use binary files, **fread()**, and **fwrite()**.

A final word of warning: never try to mix the I/O systems inside the same program. The way that the systems approach files is different, and they could accidentally interfere with each other.

Advanced Topics

PART THREE

▲

Congratulations! Having reached this point in the book, you can call yourself a Turbo C programmer. However, you really have just scratched the surface. Part Three of this book presents many of Turbo C's advanced features, including advanced data types, user-defined data types, and advanced operators. You will also learn more about Turbo C's libraries. The book finishes with a discussion of the various compiler options, the MAKE utility program, and debugging.

▼

Advanced Data Types

C H A P T E R   1 1

Up to this point, you have been using only the five basic data types. Although these types are sufficient for many programming situations, they cannot satisfy all of the demands of the serious programmer. Towards this end, Turbo C allows you to apply various *type modifiers* to the basic types. These type modifiers fall into these categories:

- Access modifiers
- Storage modifiers
- Turbo C specific function-type modifiers
- Memory model modifiers

A type modifier precedes the base type that it modifies in the declaration statement; that is, the general form of a variable declaration is expanded to look like this:

type-modifier type-specifier variable-list;

As was stated earlier, the subject of memory models, segments, and over-rides is a complex one that is beyond the scope of this book; thus, the memory model modifiers **near**, **far**, and **huge** will not be discussed. However, this topic is fully explained in the next book in this series called *Advanced Turbo C*, by Herbert Schildt (Borland-Osborne/McGraw-Hill, available Summer, 1987). This chapter will look at the other modifiers in turn and will examine a special type of pointer: the *function pointer*.

Access Modifiers

Turbo C has two type modifiers that you use to control the ways in which variables may be accessed or modified. These modifiers are called **const** and **volatile**.

The *const* Modifier

During execution, your program may not change a variable declared with the **const** modifier, except that you may give the variable an initial value. For example,

```
const float version = 3.20;
```

creates a **float** variable called **version** that your program may not modify. However, you can use **version** in other types of expressions. A **const** variable will receive its value from an explicit initialization or through some hardware-dependent means. Applying the **const** modifier to a variable's declaration ensures that other parts of your program will not modify the variable.

Variables of type **const** have one very important use: they can protect the arguments to a function from being modified by that function. When your program passes a pointer to a function, it is possible for that function to modify the actual variable that the pointer points to. However, if you specify the pointer as **const** in the parameter declaration, the function code will not be able to modify what it points to. For example, the **code( )** function in this short program shifts each letter in a message by one. Therefore, an **A** becomes a **B**, and so forth. Using **const** in the parameter declaration ensures that the code inside the function cannot modify the object that the parameter points to.

```
void code();

main()
{
  code("this is a test");
}

void code(str)
const char *str;
{
  while(*str) printf("%c", (*str++)+1);
}
```

If, for some reason, you had written **code( )** in such a way that the argument to it would be modified, Turbo C would not compile it. For example, if you had written **code( )** like this

```
/* this is wrong */
void code(str)
const char *str;
{
  while(*str) {
    *str = *str + 1;
    printf("%c", *str++);
  }
}
```

you would see the following compiler-error message:

```
Cannot modify a const object in function code
```

The volatile Modifier

You use the modifier **volatile** to tell Turbo C that a variable's value may be changed in ways that the program does not explicitly specify. For example, a program may pass a global variable's address to the clock routine of the operating system and may use the variable to hold the real-time of the system. In this situation, the variable is altered without using any explicit assignment statements. The reason that the external alteration of a variable may be important is that Turbo C will automatically optimize certain expressions by assuming that the content of a variable is unchanged if it does not occur on the right side of an assignment statement. For example, assume that the computer's clock mechanism updates **clock** every tenth of a second. If you do not declare **clock** as **volatile**, then the following statements might not work properly:

```
int clock, timer;
   .
   .
   .
timer = clock;
/* do something */
printf("elapsed type is %d\n", clock-timer);
```

Because the program does not alter **clock** and does not declare it as **volatile**, Turbo C is free to optimize the code in such a way that the value of **clock** is not reexamined in the **printf()** statement. However, declaring **clock** as

```
volatile int clock;
```

ensures that no such optimization will take place and Turbo C will examine **clock**'s value each time that it is referenced.

Although it seems strange at first, you can use **const** and **volatile** together. For example, assume that 0×30 is the value of a port that is changed only by external conditions. Then the following declaration would be precisely what you would want to prevent any possibility of accidental side effects:

```
const volatile unsigned char *port=0x30;
```

Storage Class Specifiers

C supports four storage-class specifiers. They are

> **auto**
> **extern**
> **static**
> **register**

These specifiers tell the compiler how to store the variable that follows. The storage specifier precedes the rest of the variable declaration, which has the general form

storage-specifier type-specifier variable-list;

This section will examine each specifier in turn.

The *auto* Specifier

You use the **auto** specifier to declare local variables. However, it is rarely (if ever) used because local variables are **auto** by default.

The *extern* Specifier

All of the programs that you have been working with so far have been quite small—so small, in fact, that many fit in the 25 lines of the screen. However, in actual practice, programs tend to be much larger. Even though Turbo C is extremely fast at compiling, as the file grows, the compilation time eventually takes long enough to be annoying. When this happens, you should break your program into two or more separate files. Turbo C contains the **extern** specifier, which helps support the multiple-file approach. In this book, each of the programs developed easily fits in one file. However, in real-world programming projects, this is seldom the case. Although the subject of multiple files and separate compilation will have to wait until Chapter 16, you will take a quick look at it here because it relates to **extern**.

Because Turbo C allows you to link separately compiled modules of a large program in order to speed up compilation and to aid in the management of large projects, there must be some way of telling all of the files about the global variables that the program requires. A problem occurs if you simply declare in each file all of the global variables that your program needs. Although the compiler does not issue any error messages at compile time, you are actually trying to create two (or more) copies of each variable. The trouble starts when you attempt to link your modules together. The linker will display a warning message because it will not know which variable to use. The solution is to declare all of your global variables in one file and use **extern** declarations in the other, as shown in Figure 11-1.

In file two of Figure 11-1, the code copies the global-variable list from file one and adds the **extern** specifier to the declarations. The **extern** specifier tells the compiler that the variable types and names that follow have already been declared elsewhere. In other words, **extern** lets the compiler know what the types and names are for these global variables without actually creating storage for them again. When the linker links the two modules together, it resolves all references to the external variables. This book will look more closely at programs that use multiple files later.

When you use a global variable inside a function that is in the same file as the declaration for the global variable, you may elect to use **extern**, although you do not have to. (Frankly, you will rarely see this use of **extern**.) The following program fragment shows the use of this option:

```
int first, last;  /* global definition of first
                     and last */

main()
{
   extern int first;  /* optional use of the
                         extern declaration */
}
```

Although **extern** variable declarations can occur inside the same file as the global declaration, they are not necessary. If Turbo C finds a variable that has not been declared, the compiler will see if it matches any of the

```
          File one                    File two
     _____            _____

     int x, y;                   extern int x, y;

     char ch;                    extern char ch;

     main()                      func22()
     {                           {
         .                           x=y/10;
         .                       }
         .
     }                           func23()
                                 {
     func1()                         y=10;
     {                           }
         x=123;
     }
```

Figure 11-1. Using global variables in separately compiled modules

global variables. If it does, then the compiler will assume that it is the variable being referenced.

The *static* Variables

The **static** variables are permanent variables within either their own function or file. They differ from global variables because they are unknown outside their function or file, but they do maintain their values between calls. This characteristic can make **static** variables useful when you write generalized functions and function libraries that other programmers may use. Because **static** has different effects when you use it upon local variables than it does upon global ones, this chapter examines them separately.

The static Local Variables When you apply the **static** modifier to a local variable, it causes Turbo C to create permanent storage for the local variable in much the same way that it does for a global variable. The key difference between a **static** local variable and a global variable is that the **static** local variable is known only to the block in which it is declared. In simple terms, a **static** local variable is a local variable that retains its value between function calls.

It is important to the creation of stand-alone functions that **static** local variables are available because there are several types of routines that must preserve a value between calls. If a programming language did not allow **static** variables, then you would have to use global variables—which would open the door to possible side effects. A good example of a function that would require such a variable is a number-series generator that produces a new number based on the last one. While you could declare a global variable for this value, any program that uses the function would have to declare that global variable, making sure that it did not conflict with any other global variables already declared; this requirement would be a major drawback. Also, using a global variable would make this function difficult to place in a function library. The better solution is to declare the variable that holds the generated number as **static**, as shown in this program fragment:

```
series()
{
   static int series_num;

   series_num=series_num + 23;
   return(series_num);
}
```

In this fragment, the variable **series_num** continues to exist between function calls, instead of coming and going the way that a normal local variable would. Thus, each call to **series()** can produce a new member of the series that is based on the previous number, without declaring **series_num** globally.

You may have noticed something unusual about the function **series()** as it stands in the program fragment. The function never gives an initial value to the static variable **series_num**. This means that the initial value will be zero because Turbo C initializes **static** local variables to zero. While this initialization step is acceptable for some applications, most series generators will need a well-defined starting point. To do this requires you to initialize **series_num** prior to the first call to **series()**, which you can do easily only if

series_num is a global variable. However, avoiding the need to make **series_num** global was the entire point of making it **static** to begin with, which leads to the second use of **static**.

The static Global Variables   When you apply the **static** specifier to a global variable, **static** instructs the compiler to create a global variable that is known only to the *file* in which you declared the **static** global variable. Thus, even though the variable is global, other routines in other files may have no knowledge of it and may not alter its contents directly; it is not subject to side effects. Therefore, for the few situations where a **static** local variable cannot do the job, you can create a small file that contains only the functions that need the **static** global variable, separately compile that file, and use it without worrying about side effects.

To see how you can use a **static** global variable, the number-series generator given earlier has been recoded so that you can use a "seed" value to initialize the series through a call to a second function called **series_start()**. The entire file that contains **series()**, **series_start()**, and **series_num** is shown here:

```
/* this must all be in one file - preferably by itself */

static int series_num;

series()
{
  series_num=series_num+23;
  return(series_num);
}

/* initialize series_num */
series_start(seed)
int seed;
{
  series_num=seed;
}
```

Calling **series_start()** with a known integer value initializes the series generator. After that, calls to **series()** will generate the next element in the series.

Remember: the names of **static** local variables are known only to the function or block of code in which they are declared, and the names of **static** global variables are known only to the file in which they reside. If you place the functions **series()** and **series_start()** in a library, you can use the functions but you cannot reference the variable **series_num**. It is hidden from the rest of the code in your program. You may even declare and use another variable called **series_num** in your program (in another file) and not confuse anything. In essence, the **static** specifier allows the existence of variables that are known to the functions that need them, without confusing other functions.

The **static** variables enable you the programmer to hide portions of your program from other portions. This ability can be a tremendous advantage when you are trying to manage a large, complex program. The **static** storage specifier lets you create general functions that you can include in libraries for later use.

The register Specifier

Another important type modifier in Turbo C is called **register** and applies only to variables of type **int** and **char**. The **register** specifier requests that Turbo C keep the value of variables declared with this modifier in the register of the CPU, rather than in memory, where normal variables are stored. Operations on **register** variables can occur much faster than on variables stored in memory because Turbo C does not need memory access to determine or modify their values. (A memory access takes much longer than a register access.) This time savings makes **register** variables ideal for loop control. You can only apply the **register** specifier to local variables and to the formal parameters in a function. Hence, you cannot use **register** global variables.

Here is an example of the way to declare a **register** variable of type **int** and the way to use it to control a loop. This function computes the result of m^e for integers:

```
int_pwr(m,e)
int m;
register int e;
{
  register int temp;

  temp=1;

  for(;e;e--) temp*=m;
  return temp;
}
```

In this example, the code declares both **e** and **temp** to be **register** variables because it uses both within the loop. In general practice, you should use **register** variables where they will do the most good, which implies that you should use them in places where many references will be made to the same variable. This discrimination is important because you may not have an unlimited number of **register** variables in use at any particular time.

Both the processor type and the specific implementation of C that you are using determine the exact number of register variables allowed within any one function. For Turbo C, there may be two **register** variables active at any one time. Do not worry about declaring too many **register** variables, though, because Turbo C will automatically make **register** variables into nonregister variables when the number reaches the limit. (Turbo C does this to ensure the portability of code across a broad line of processors.)

To see the difference that register variables can make, the following program measures the execution time of two **for** loops that differ only in the type of variable that controls them. This program uses the **time( )** function that is found in Turbo C's standard library.

```
/* This program shows the difference a register
   variable can make to the speed of program
   execution.
*/

unsigned int i;   /* non-register */
unsigned int delay;

main()
{
  register unsigned int j;
  long t;

  t = time('\0');
  for(delay=0; delay<10; delay++)
    for(i=0; i<64000; i++);
  printf("time for non-register loop: %ld\n", time('\0')-t);

  t = time('\0');
  for(delay=0; delay<10; delay++)
    for(j=0; j<64000; j++) ;
  printf("time for register loop: %ld", time('\0')-t);
}
```

If you run this program, you will find that the **register**-controlled loop executes in about half the time that the nonregister-controlled loop uses.

Type Conversion
in Assignments

Type conversion refers to the situation in which variables of one type are mixed with variables of another type. When this mixing occurs in an assignment statement, the *type-conversion rule* is simple: Turbo C converts the value of the right side (the expression side) of the assignment to the type of the left side (the target variable), as illustrated by this example.

```
int x;
char ch;
float   f;

func()
{
  ch=x;     /* 1 */
  x=f;      /* 2 */
  f=ch;     /* 3 */
  f=x;      /* 4 */
}
```

In line 1, the code lops off the left high-order bits of the integer variable **x**, leaving **ch** with the lower 8 bits. If the value **x** was between 255 and 0, then **ch** and **x** would have identical values. If **x** had any other value, the value of **ch** would reflect only the lower order bits of **x**. In line 2, **x** receives the nonfractional part of **f**. Line 3 converts the value of **ch** to its equivalent floating-point format. This process also occurs in line 4, which converts the value in **x** to its equivalent floating-point format.

When you convert from integers to characters, long integers to integers, and integers to short integers, the basic rule to follow is that the appropriate amount of high-order bits will be removed. Thus, you will lose 8 bits when going from an integer to a character or short integer, and 16 bits when going from a long integer to an integer.

Table 11-1 synopsizes these assignment type conversions. You must remember one important point: The conversion of an **int** to a **float**, a **float** to a **double**, and so on, will not add any precision or accuracy. These kinds of conversions will only change the form in which the value is represented.

To use Table 11-1 to make a conversion that the table does not show directly, simply convert one type at a time until you finish. For example, to convert from a **double** to an **int**, first convert from a **double** to a **float**, and then from a **float** to an **int**.

Table 11-1.   The Outcome of Common Type Conversions, Assuming a 16-bit Word

Target type	Expression type	Possible info loss
signed char	char	If value > 127, then targets will be negative
char	short int	High-order 8 bits
char	int	High-order 8 bits
char	long int	High-order 24 bits
short int	int	None
short int	long int	High-order 16 bits
int	long int	High-order 16 bits
int	float	Fractional part and possibly more
float	double	Precision, result rounded
double	long double	None

Function-Type Modifiers

Turbo C defines three type modifiers that you may only apply to functions. These modifiers are **pascal**, **cdecl**, and **interrupt**. The proposed ANSI standard does not define these modifiers, but Turbo C does provide them in order to take the best possible advantage of the PC programming environment.

The *pascal* Type Modifier

The **pascal** type modifier tells the compiler to use a Pascal-like parameter-passing convention for the function's arguments, rather than Turbo C's normal method. This modifier allows two possibilities. First, you can write functions in Turbo C that other compilers will use. Second, you can use a Pascal compiler's library routines by declaring them at the top of your C program as being of type **pascal**.

For example, this version of the **int—pwr( )** function can be compiled for use by a Pascal compiler:

```
/* compile for Pascal compilers */
pascal int_pwr(m,e)
int m;
register int e;
{
  register int temp;

  temp=1;

  for(;e;e--) temp*=m;
  return temp;
}
```

To compile all of the functions in a file to be of type **pascal**, you could do so without utilizing **pascal** by first using the **Option** main menu selection. Next, select **Compiler** and, finally, select **Code Generation**. You can now set the calling convention to Pascal. Selecting this option tells Turbo C to treat all functions as if they were for use with a Pascal compiler. As a general rule, you should not compile using the **pascal** option unless you will be linking with actual Pascal code.

The *cdecl* Type Modifier

The **cdecl** keyword is the opposite of **pascal** because **cdecl** tells Turbo C to compile a function so that its parameters are passed in a way that is compatible with other C functions. You only use **cdecl** when you have set the compiler to compile using the Pascal calling convention and you have a few functions that you do not want compiled in the **pascal** format. The **cdecl** keyword is specific to Turbo C and is not generally portable.

The *interrupt* Type Modifier

The **interrupt** modifier tells Turbo C that the function that it modifies will be used as an interrupt handler. The modifier causes Turbo C to preserve all CPU registers each time that the program enters the function, and to exit the function with an **IRET** (return from interrupt) instruction. The development and installation of interrupt handlers is beyond the scope of this book; but if you are interested, you should study one of the excellent books on DOS or assembly language programming. (A particularly good one for DOS is *DOS: The Complete Reference* by Kris Jamsa [Osborne/McGraw-Hill, 1987].)

Pointers to Functions

A particularly confusing yet powerful feature of C is the *function pointer*. In a way, a function pointer is a new type of data. Even though a function is not a variable, it still has a physical location in memory that you can assign to a pointer. The address assigned to the pointer is the entry point of the function. You can then use this pointer in place of the function's name. The pointer also allows functions to be passed as arguments to other functions.

To understand how function pointers work, you must understand a little about the way a function is compiled and called in Turbo C. First, while compiling each function, the compiler transforms source code into object code, and establishes an entry point. When a call is made to a function while your program is running, the computer makes a machine-language "call" to this entry point. Therefore, a pointer to a function actually contains the memory address of the entry point of the function.

You obtain the address of a function by using the function's name without any parentheses or arguments. (This process is similar to the way that you obtain an array's address when you use only the array name without indices.) For example, consider this program, paying close attention to the declarations:

```
main()
{
  int strcmp(); /* declare a function */
  char s1[80], s2[80];
  void *p;

  p = strcmp;

  gets(s1);
  gets(s2);

  check(s1,s2,p);
}

check(a,b,cmp)
```

```
char *a,*b;
int (*cmp) ();
{
  printf("testing for equality\n");
  if(!(*cmp) (a,b)) printf("equal");
  else printf("not equal");
}
```

There are two reasons for the declaration of **strcmp( )** in **main( )**. First, the program must know what type of value **strcmp( )** is returning (in this case, an integer) and, second, its name must be known to the compiler as a function. In C, there is no way to declare a variable to be a function pointer directly. Instead, as shown in the program, you must declare a **void** pointer because it can receive any type of pointer. When the computer calls the function **check( )**, two character pointers and one function pointer are passed as parameters. The function **check( )** declares the arguments as character pointers and a function pointer. Notice how the function pointer is declared. You must use exactly the same method when declaring other function pointers, except that the return type of the function may be different. The parentheses around the ***cmp** are necessary to allow the compiler to interpret this statement correctly. Without the parentheses around ***cmp**, the compiler would be confused by the statement.

Once inside **check( )**, you can see how the **strcmp( )** function is called. The statement

```
(*cmp) (a,b)
```

performs the call to the function—in this case, **strcmp( )**—which **cmp** points to with the arguments **a** and **b**. Again, the parentheses around ***cmp** are necessary. This statement also represents the general form of using a function pointer to call the function that it points to.

Note that you can call **check( )** by using **strcmp** directly, as shown here:

```
check(s1,s2,strcmp);
```

This statement would eliminate the need for an additional pointer variable. However, most real-world routines that use function pointers will probably use additional pointers.

You may wonder why anyone would want to write a program in this way. Obviously, in this example, nothing is gained and significant confusion is introduced. However, sometimes it is advantageous to pass arbitrary functions into routines or to keep an array of functions.

The following example may help to illustrate a use of function pointers. When a compiler is written, it is common for the parser (that part of the compiler that evaluates arithmetic expressions) also to perform function calls to various support routines—for example, the sine, cosine, and tangent functions. Instead of having a large **switch** statement with all of these functions listed in them, you can use an array of function pointers with the proper function called. You can get the flavor of this type of usage by studying the expanded version of the example given earlier.

```
#include "ctype.h"

main()
{
   int strcmp();
   int numcmp();
   char s1[80], s2[80];

   gets(s1);
   gets(s2);

   if(tolower(*s1) <= 'z' && tolower(*s1) >= 'a')
         check(s1,s2,strcmp);
   else
         check(s1,s2,numcmp);
}

check(a,b,cmp)
char *a,*b;
int (*cmp) ();
{
   printf("testing for equality\n");
   if(!(*cmp) (a,b)) printf("equal");
   else printf("not equal");
}

numcmp(a, b)
char *a,*b;
{
   if(atoi(a)==atoi(b)) return 0;
   else return 1;
}
```

In this program, you can make **check()** check for either alphabetical equality or numeric equality, simply by calling it with a different comparison function.

User-Defined
Data Types

C H A P T E R   1 2

The C language allows you to create five different kinds of custom data types. The first type is the *structure*, which is a group of variables under one name. The structure is sometimes called a *conglomerate data type*. The second user-defined type is the *bitfield*, which is a variation of the structure and allows easy access to the bits within a word. The third type is the *union*, which enables you to define the same piece of memory as two or more different types of variables. A fourth custom data type is the *enumeration*, which is a list of symbols. You create the final type by using **typedef**, and it simply creates a new name for an existing type.

Structures

In C, a structure is a collection of variables that you reference under one name. A structure provides a convenient means of keeping related information together. A *structure definition* forms a template that you may use to create structure variables. The variables that make up the structure are called *structure elements*. (Structures in C are the equivalent of **RECORD**s in Turbo Pascal.)

Generally, all elements in the structure are logically related to each other. For example, you can normally represent the name-and-address information of a mailing list in a structure. This code fragment declares a structure template that defines the name and address fields. The keyword **struct** tells the compiler that you are defining a structure template.

```
struct addr {
   char name[30];
   char street[40];
   char city[20];
   char state[3];
   unsigned long int zip;
};
```

Notice that a semicolon terminates the definition. The reason for the semicolon is that a structure definition is a statement. In addition, the structure tag **addr** identifies this particular data structure, and is its type specifier.

At this point in the code, *no variable has actually been declared*. The code has only defined the form of the data. To declare an actual variable with this structure, you would write

```
struct addr addr_info;
```

This line will declare a structure variable of type **addr** called **addr—info**. When you define a structure, you are essentially defining a complex variable type that is made up of the structure elements. Only when you declare a variable of that type will one actually exist.

Turbo C automatically allocates sufficient memory to accommodate all of the variables that make up a structure variable. Figure 12-1 shows the way that **addr—info** would appear in memory, assuming one-byte characters and two-byte integers.

You may also declare one or more variables when you define a structure. For example:

```
struct addr {
  char name[30];
  char street[40];
  char city[20];
  char state[3];
  unsigned long int zip;
} addr_info, binfo, cinfo;
```

This code defines a structure type called **addr**, and declares variables **addr—info**, **binfo**, and **cinfo** of the same type.

If you only need one structure variable, you do not need to include the structure name.

```
struct  {
  char name[30];
  char street[40];
  char city[20];
  char state[3];
  unsigned long int zip;
} addr_info;
```

declares one variable named **addr—info**, as defined by the structure that precedes it.

Name	30 bytes	
Street	40 bytes	
City	20 bytes	addr—info
State	3 bytes	
ZIP	4 bytes	

Figure 12-1.   The **addr—info** structure as it appears in memory

The general form of a structure definition is

```
struct struct-type-name {
    type variable_name;
    type variable_name;
    type variable_name;
       .
       .
       .
} structure_variables;
```

where you may omit either the structure type name *struct-type-name* or the *structure_variables*, but not both.

Referencing Structure Elements

You reference individual structure elements by using the . operator, which is sometimes called the *dot operator*. For example, the following code will assign the Zip code **12345** to the **zip** field of the structure variable **addr_info** that was declared earlier.

```
addr_info.zip = 12345;
```

The structure-variable name, which is followed by a period, and the structure element name will reference that individual structure element. You access structure elements by using this format. The general form is

structure_name.element_name

Therefore, to print the Zip code to the screen, you could write

```
printf("%d", addr_info.zip);
```

which prints the Zip code in the **zip** variable of the structure variable **addr_info**.

In the same fashion, you can use the character array **addr_info.name** to call **gets( )**, as shown here.

```
gets(addr_info.name);
```

This call to **gets( )** will pass a character pointer to the start of the element **name**.

To access the individual elements of **addr—info.name**, you could index **name**. For example, you could print the contents of **addr—info.name** one character at a time by using this code:

```
register int t;

for(t=0; addr_info.name[t]; ++t) putchar(addr_info.name[t]);
```

Arrays of Structures

Perhaps the most common use of structures is in *arrays of structures*. To declare an array of structures, you must first define a structure, and then declare an array variable of that type. For example, to declare an 100-element array of structures **addr** that had been defined earlier, you would write

```
struct addr addr_info[100];
```

This code creates 100 sets of variables that are organized as defined in the structure **addr**.

To access a specific structure, you index the structure name. For example, to print the Zip code of structure 3, you would write

```
printf("%d", addr_info[2].zip);
```

Like all array variables, arrays of structures begin their indexing at zero.

A Mailing-List Example

To help illustrate the way to use structures and arrays of structures, this section develops a simple mailing-list program that uses an array of structures to hold the address information. The functions in this program interact with structures and their elements.

In this example, the information that will be stored includes

> name
> street
> city, state, zip

To define the basic data structure **addr** that will hold this information, you would write

```
struct addr {
  char name[30];
  char street[40];
  char city[20];
  char state[3];
  unsigned long int zip;
} addr_info[SIZE];
```

The Zip code field is an unsigned long integer because the computer cannot represent Zip codes greater than 64,000—such as 94564—in a two-byte integer. In this example, the program uses an integer to hold the Zip code to illustrate a numeric structure element. However, the more common practice is to use a character string that accommodates postal codes with letters as well as numbers, like those used by Canada and other countries. The array **addr_info** contains **SIZE** structures of type **addr**, where you may define **SIZE** to suit the specific need.

The first function that you need for the program is **main( )**, which is shown here:

```
main()
{
  char choice;

  init_list();

  for(;;) {
    choice = menu();
    switch(choice) {
      case 'e': enter();
        break;
      case 'd': display();
        break;
      case 's': save();
        break;
```

```
      case 'l': load();
        break;
      case 'q': exit(1);
    }
  }
}
```

First, **init_list()** prepares the structure array for use by putting a null character into the first byte of the **name** field. The program assumes that a structure variable is not in use if the **name** field is empty. You could write **init_list()** as

```
/* initialize the addr_info array */
void init_list()
{
  register int t;

  for(t=0; t<SIZE; t++) *addr_info[t].name='\0';
  /* a zero length name signifies empty */
}
```

The **menu_select()** function will display the option messages and return the user's selection:

```
/* get a menu selection */
menu()
{
  char s[80];

  do {
    printf("(E)nter\n");
    printf("(D)isplay\n");
    printf("(L)oad\n");
    printf("(S)ave\n");
    printf("(Q)uit\n\n");
    printf("choose one: ");
    gets(s);
  } while(!strrchr("edlsq", tolower(*s)));
  return tolower(*s);
}
```

The **enter()** function prompts the user for input, and places the information entered into the next free structure. If the array is full, then **enter()** prints the message **list full** on the screen. Here is **enter()**:

```
/* put names into addr_info */
void enter()
{
  register int i;

  for(i=0; i<SIZE;i++)
    if(!*addr_info[i].name) break;

  if(i==SIZE) {
    printf("addr_info full\n");
    return;
  }
  printf("name: ");
  gets(addr_info[i].name);

  printf("street: ");
  gets(addr_info[i].street);

  printf("city: ");
  gets(addr_info[i].city);

  printf("state: ");
  gets(addr_info[i].state);

  printf("zip: ");
  gets(addr_info[i].zip);
}
```

The program uses the routines **save( )** and **load( )**, shown here, to save and load the mailing-list database. Each routine contains little code because of the power of **fread( )** and **fwrite( )**.

```
/* save the list */
void save()
{
  FILE  *fp;
  register int i;

  if((fp=fopen("maillist","wb"))==NULL) {
    printf("cannot open file\n");
    return;
  }

  for(i=0;i<SIZE;i++)
    if(*addr_info[i].name)
      if(fwrite(&addr_info[i],sizeof(struct addr),1,fp)!=1)
        printf("file write error\n");
  fclose(fp);
}
```

```
/* load the file */
void load()
{
  FILE  *fp;
  register int i;

  if((fp=fopen("maillist","rb"))==NULL) {
    printf("cannot open file\n");
    return;
  }

  init_list();
  for(i=0; i<SIZE; i++)
      if(fread(&addr_info[i],sizeof(struct addr),1,fp)!=1) {
        if(feof(fp)) {
          fclose(fp);
          return;
        }
        printf("file read error\n");
      }
}
```

Both **save()** and **load()** confirm a successful file operation by checking the return value of **fread()** or **fwrite()**. In addition, **load()** must explicitly check for an end-of-file mark by using **feof()** because **fread()** returns the same value if the computer reaches the end-of-file mark or if an error has occurred.

The final function that the program needs is **display()**, which prints the entire mailing list on screen.

```
/* display the addr_info */
void display()
{
  register int t;

  for(t=0; t<SIZE; t++) {
    if(*addr_info[t].name) {
      printf("%s\n", addr_info[t].name);
      printf("%s\n", addr_info[t].street);
      printf("%s\n", addr_info[t].city);
      printf("%s\n", addr_info[t].state);
      printf("%s\n\n", addr_info[t].zip);
    }
  }
}
```

Here is the complete listing for the mailing-list program.

```c
/* A simple mailing list that uses an array
   of structures. */

#include "stdio.h"
#include "ctype.h"

#define SIZE 100

struct addr {
  char name[40];
  char street[40];
  char city[30];
  char state[3];
  char zip[10];
} addr_info[SIZE];

void enter(), init_list(), display(), save(), load();

main()
{
  char choice;

  init_list();

  for(;;) {
    choice = menu();
    switch(choice) {
      case 'e': enter();
        break;
      case 'd': display();
        break;
      case 's': save();
        break;
      case 'l': load();
        break;
      case 'q': exit(1);
    }
  }
}

/* initialize the addr_info array */
void init_list()
{
  register int t;

  for(t=0; t<SIZE; t++) *addr_info[t].name='\0';
  /* a zero length name signifies empty */
}

/* get a menu selection */
menu()
{
  char s[80];
```

```
  do {
    printf("(E)nter\n");
    printf("(D)isplay\n");
    printf("(L)oad\n");
    printf("(S)ave\n");
    printf("(Q)uit\n\n");
    printf("choose one: ");
    gets(s);
  } while(!strrchr("edlsq", tolower(*s)));
  return tolower(*s);
}


/* put names into addr_info */
void enter()
{
  register int i;

  for(i=0; i<SIZE;i++)
    if(!*addr_info[i].name) break;

  if(i==SIZE) {
    printf("addr_info full\n");
    return;
  }
  printf("name: ");
  gets(addr_info[i].name);

  printf("street: ");
  gets(addr_info[i].street);

  printf("city: ");
  gets(addr_info[i].city);

  printf("state: ");
  gets(addr_info[i].state);

  printf("zip: ");
  gets(addr_info[i].zip);
}

/* display the addr_info */
void display()
{
  register int t;

  for(t=0; t<SIZE; t++) {
    if(*addr_info[t].name) {
      printf("%s\n", addr_info[t].name);
      printf("%s\n", addr_info[t].street);
      printf("%s\n", addr_info[t].city);
      printf("%s\n", addr_info[t].state);
      printf("%s\n\n", addr_info[t].zip);
```

```
      }
    }
  }

/* save the list */
void save()
{
  FILE  *fp;
  register int i;

  if((fp=fopen("maillist","wb"))==NULL) {
    printf("cannot open file\n");
    return;
  }

  for(i=0;i<SIZE;i++)
    if(*addr_info[i].name)
      if(fwrite(&addr_info[i],sizeof(struct addr),1,fp)!=1)
        printf("file write error\n");
  fclose(fp);
}


/* load the file */
void load()
{
  FILE  *fp;
  register int i;

  if((fp=fopen("maillist","rb"))==NULL) {
    printf("cannot open file\n");
    return;
  }

  init_list();
  for(i=0; i<SIZE; i++)
    if(fread(&addr_info[i],sizeof(struct addr),1,fp)!=1) {
      if(feof(fp)) {
        fclose(fp);
        return;
      }
      printf("file read error\n");
    }
}
```

If you have any doubts about your understanding of structures, enter this program into your computer and study its execution by making changes and watching their effect. Further, try to add functions that search the list, remove an address from the list, and send the list to the printer.

Passing Structures to Functions

So far, the examples in the book have assumed all structures and arrays of structures to be either global or defined within the function that uses them. This section will give special consideration to passing structures and their elements to functions.

Passing Structure Elements to Functions

When you pass an element of a structure variable to a function, you are actually passing the value of that element. Thus, you are passing a simple variable—unless that element is complex, such as an array of characters. For example, consider this structure:

```
struct fred {
  char x;
  int y;
  float z;
  char s[10];
} mike;
```

Here is the way that you can pass each element to a function.

```
func(mike.x);   /* passes character value of x */

func2(mike.y); /* passes integer value of y */

func3(mike.z); /* passes float value of z */

func4(mike.s); /* passes address of string s */

func(mike.s[2]); /* passes character value of s[2] */
```

However, to pass the address of an individual structure element so that you achieve call-by-value parameter passing, you would place the **&** operator before the variable name. For example, to pass the addresses of the elements in the structure variable **mike**, you would write

```
func(&mike.x);  /* passes address of character x */

func2(&mike.y); /* passes address of integer y */

func3(&mike.z); /* passes address of float z*/

func4(mike.s);  /* passes address of string s */

func(&mike.s[2]); /* passes address of character s[2] */
```

Notice that the **&** operator precedes the structure variable name, and not the individual element name. In addition, note that the string element s already signifies an address so that the use of **&** is not required in that line of code.

Passing Entire Structures to Functions

When you use a structure as an argument to a function, Turbo C passes the entire structure by using the standard call-by-value method. This method means that any changes that you make to the structure's contents inside the function to which the structure is passed do not affect the structure that you use as an argument.

The most important consideration to keep in mind when you use a structure as a parameter is that the type of the argument must match the type of the parameter. For example, this program declares both the argument **arg** and the parameter **parm** to be of the same type of structure:

```
main()
{
  struct {
    int a,b;
    char ch;
  } arg;

  arg.a=1000;

  f1(arg);
}
```

```
arg(parm)
struct {
  int x,y;
  char ch;
} parm;

{
  printf("%d",parm.x);
}
```

As you can see, this program will print **1000** on the screen. Although it is not uncommon to see parallel structure declarations of this type, a more common approach—and one that requires less work from you—is to define a structure globally, and then to use its name to declare structure variables and parameters as needed. Using this method, the program just shown changes as follows:

```
/* define a structure type */
struct struct_type {
  int a,b;
  char ch;
} ;

main()
{
  struct struct_type arg;  /* declare arg */

  arg.a=1000;

  f1(arg);
}

arg(parm)
struct struct_type parm;
{
  printf("%d",parm.a);
}
```

Not only does this version save programming effort, but more important, it helps to ensure that the arguments and the parameters do in fact match.

Pointers to Structures

C allows pointers to structures in the same way that it allows pointers to any other type of variable. However, there are some special aspects of structure pointers that you must be aware of.

Declaring a Structure Pointer

You declare structure pointers by placing the * in front of a structure variable's name. For example, if you assume the structure **addr** defined earlier, the following declares **addr __pointer** to be a pointer to data of that type:

```
struct addr *addr_pointer;
```

Using Structure Pointers

There are two primary uses for structure pointers. The first use is to achieve a call-by-reference call to a function. The second use is to create linked lists and other dynamic data structures by using Turbo C's allocation system. This chapter will only be concerned with the first use; the second use is covered in detail in *Advanced Turbo C*, this book's sequel.

There is one major drawback to passing all but the simplest structures to functions: it is the overhead needed to push (and pop) all structure elements onto the stack. In simple structures with few elements, this overhead is not important, but if a structure uses several elements, or if some of the elements are arrays, then run-time performance may degenerate to unacceptable levels. The solution to this problem is to pass only a pointer.

When you pass a pointer to a structure to a function, the computer pushes (and pops) only the address of the structure on the stack. This means that Turbo C can execute a very fast function call. Also, because the function will be referencing the actual structure and not a copy, the function can modify the contents of the elements of the structure used in the call.

To find the address of a structure variable, you place the **&** operator before the structure variable's name. For example, given the following fragment

```
struct bal {
  float balance;
  char name[80];
} person;

struct bal *p;  /* declare a structure pointer */
```

then

```
p=&person;
```

places the address of **person** into the pointer **p**. To reference the **balance** element, you would write

```
(*p).balance
```

The parentheses are necessary around the pointer because the dot operator has a higher priority than the * operator.

Actually, there are two methods that you may use to reference an element in a structure variable, given a pointer to that variable. The first method uses *explicit pointer references*, and is considered archaic by today's standards. However, because some older, existing C code may use this approach, it is important that you are familiar with it. Also, it lays important groundwork that enables you to understand the second, more common method. This second method of accessing elements of structures by using pointers utilizes the —> operator, which is essentially a shorthand for the first method.

To see how you can use a structure pointer, examine this simple program that prints the hours, minutes, and seconds on the screen by using a software-delay timer.

```
/* display a software timer */
struct tm {
  int hours;
  int minutes;
  int seconds;
```

```
} ;
main()
{
  struct tm time;

  time.hours=0;
  time.minutes=0;
  time.seconds=0;

  for(;;) {
    update(&time);
    display(&time);
  }
}

update(t) /* version 1 - explicit pointer references */
struct tm *t;
{
  (*t).seconds++;
  if((*t).seconds==60) {
    (*t).seconds=0;
    (*t).minutes++;
  }
  if((*t).minutes==60) {
    (*t).minutes=0;
    (*t).hours++;
  }
  if((*t).hours==24) (*t).hours=0;
  delay();
}

display(t)
struct tm *t;
{
  printf("%d:",(*t).hours);
  printf("%d:",(*t).minutes);
  printf("%d\n",(*t).seconds);
}
delay()
{
  long int t;
  for(t=1;t<128000;++t) ;
}
```

You can adjust the timing of this program by varying the loop count in **delay()**.

As you can see, the program defines a global structure called **tm**, but declares no variable. Inside **main()**, the structure **time** is declared and initialized to 00:00:00; thus, **time** is known directly only to **main()**.

The program passes the address of **time** to two functions: **update()**, which changes the time, and **display()**, which prints the time. In both functions, the argument is declared to be of structure type **tm** so that the compiler will know how to reference the structure elements.

The program accomplishes the actual referencing of each structure element through the use of a pointer. For example, to set the hours back to zero when the program reaches 24:00:00, you would write

```
if((*t).hours==24) (*t).hours=0;
```

This line of code tells the compiler to take the address of **t**—which is **time** in **main()**—and assign zero to its element called **hours**. (Remember that the parentheses are necessary around *t because the dot operator has a higher priority than the * operator.)

As stated earlier, you will seldom, if ever, see references made to a structure's elements through the explicit use of the * operator. Because this type of operation is so common, C defines a special operator to perform this task. This operator is the —> operator, which most C programmers call the *arrow operator*. You form the arrow operator by using the minus sign followed by a greater-than sign. You use the arrow operator in place of the dot operator when accessing a structure element, given a pointer to the structure variable. For example,

```
(*t).hours
```

is the same as

```
t->hours
```

Therefore, you could rewrite **update()** as

```
update(t) /* version 2 with the arrow operator */
struct tm *t;
{
  t->seconds++;

  if(t->seconds==60) {
    t->seconds=0;
    t->minutes++;
  }
```

```
if(t->minutes==60) {
  t->minutes=0;
  t->hours++;
}

if(t->hours==24) t->hours=0;

delay();

}
```

Remember that you use the dot operator to access structure elements when operating on the structure itself. When you have a pointer to a structure, then you should use the arrow operator. Also, remember that you have to pass the address of the structure to a function by using the **&** operator.

Arrays and Structures Within Structures

A structure element may be either simple or complex. A simple element is one of the built-in data types, such as integer or character. You have already seen one complex element: the character array used in **addr_info**. Other complex data types are single arrays and multidimensional arrays of the other data types and structures.

The computer treats a structure element that is an array as you might expect from the earlier examples. For example, consider this structure:

```
struct x {
  int a[10][10]; /* 10 x 10 array of ints */
  float b;
} y;
```

To reference integer **3,7** in **a** of structure **y**, you would write

```
y.a[3][7]
```

When a structure is an element of another structure, it is called a *nested structure*. For example, the structure variable element **address** is nested inside **emp** in this example.

```
struct emp {
  struct addr address;
  float wage;
} worker;
```

Here, **addr** is the structure that was defined previously. The example defines the structure **emp** as having two elements. The first element is the structure of type **addr** that will contain an employee's address. The second element is **wage**, which holds the employee's wage. The following code fragment will assign the Zip code 98765 to the **zip** field of **address** of **worker**.

```
worker.address.zip = 98765;
```

As you can see, this fragment references the elements of each structure from left to right from the outermost to the innermost.

Bitfields

Unlike most other computer languages, C has a built-in method to access a single bit within a byte. This method can be useful for a number of reasons: first, if storage is limited, you can store several *Boolean* (true or false) variables in one byte; second, certain device interfaces transmit information that is encoded into bits within one byte; and third, certain encryption routines need to access the bits within a byte. Although you can perform all of these operations with the bitwise operators, a *bitfield* can add more structure and efficiency to your code. The bitfield might also make a program more portable.

The method that C uses to access bits is based on the structure. A bitfield is just a special type of structure that defines the length in bits that each element will be. The general form of a bitfield definition is

> **struct** *struct-type-name* {
>   *type name 1 : length;*
>   *type name 2 : length;*
>   .
>   .
>   .
>   *type name 3 : length;*
> }

You must declare a bitfield as either **int, unsigned,** or **signed**. You should declare bitfields of length 1 as **unsigned** because a single bit cannot have a sign.

For example, consider this structure definition:

```
struct device {
   unsigned active : 1;
   unsigned ready : 1;
   unsigned xmt_error : 1;
} dev_code;
```

This structure defines three variables of one bit each. To see how you can use a bitfield, imagine that your system has tape backup and that you want to use the structure variable **dev—code** to decode information from the port of a tape drive. The following code fragment will write a byte of information to the tape, and check for errors by using **dev—code** given earlier.

```
wr_tape(c)
char c;
{
   while(!dev_code.ready) rd(&dev_code); /* wait */

   wr_to_tape(c); /* write out byte */

   while(dev_code.active) rd(&dev_code); /* wait till
           info is written */

   if(dev_code.xmt_error) printf("write error");
}
```

Here, **rd( )** returns the status of the tape drive and **wr—to—tape( )** writes the data. Figure 12-2 shows what the bitfield variable **dev—code** looks like in memory.

As you can see from the example, the code accesses each bitfield by using the dot operator. However, if the code references the structure through a pointer, you must use the —> operator.

You do not have to name each bitfield. This freedom makes it easy to reach the bit that you want, and allows you to pass up unused ones. For example, if the tape drive also returned an end-of-tape flag in bit 5, you could alter the structure **device** to accommodate this end-of-tape flag by using

```
struct device {
   unsigned active : 1;
   unsigned ready : 1;
```

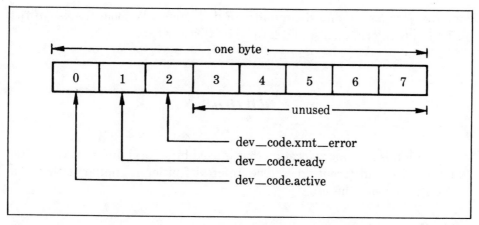

Figure 12-2. The bitfield variable **dev—code** in memory

```
    unsigned xmt_error : 1;
    unsigned : 2;
    unsigned EOT : 1;
} dev_code;
```

Bitfield variables have certain restrictions. First, you cannot take the address of a bitfield variable. Second, you cannot array bitfield variables. Third, you cannot overlap integer boundaries. Finally, you cannot know, from machine to machine, whether the fields will run from right to left or from left to right; this limitation implies that any code that uses bitfields may have some machine dependencies.

It is valid to mix normal structure elements with bitfield elements, as shown here:

```
struct emp {
  struct addr address;
  float pay;
  unsigned lay_off:1;   /* lay off or active */
  unsigned hourly:1:    /* hourly pay or wage */
  unsigned deductions:3: /* IRS deductions */
};
```

This structure defines an employee record that uses only one byte to hold three pieces of information: the employee's status, whether or not the employee is salaried, and the number of deductions. Without the use of the bitfield, this information would have used three bytes.

unions

In C, a **union** is a memory location that is used by several different variables, which can be of different types. The **union** definition is similar to that of a structure, as shown here:

```
union u_type {
   int i;
   char ch;
} ;
```

As with a structure declaration, this definition does not declare any variables. You may declare a variable either by placing its name at the end of the definition, or by using a separate declaration statement. To declare a **union** variable **cnvt** of type **u_type** using the definition just given, you would write

```
union u_type cnvt;
```

In **cnvt**, both integer **i** and character **ch** share the same memory location. (However, **i** occupies two bytes and **ch** uses only one.) Figure 12-3 shows the way that **i** and **ch** share the same address.

When you declare a **union**, Turbo C will automatically create a variable large enough to hold the largest variable type in the **union**.

To access a **union** element, you use the same syntax that you would use for structures: the dot operator and the arrow operator. If you are accessing the **union** element directly, use the dot operator. If you are accessing the **union** variable through a pointer, use the arrow operator. For example, to assign the integer 10 to element **i** of **cnvt**, you would write

```
cnvt.i=10;
```

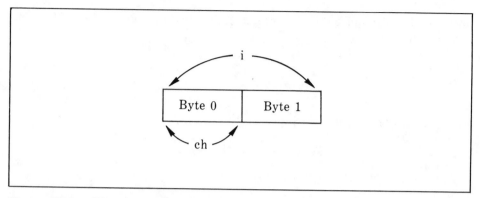

Figure 12-3. How **i** and **ch** utilize the **union cnvt**

In the following example, the code passes a pointer to **cnvt** to a function:

```
func1(un)

union u_type *un;

{
   un->i=10; /* assign 10 to cnvt using
               a pointer */
}
```

Using a **union** can aid in the production of machine-independent, or portable, code. Because the compiler keeps track of the sizes of the variables that
make up the **union**, using a **union** does not produce machine dependencies.
You need not worry about the size of an integer, a character, a floating-point
variable, or whatever.

In C, **union**s are used frequently when type conversions are necessary.
For example, the standard library function **putw( )** will write the binary
representation of an integer to a disk file. Although there are many ways to
code this function, the one shown here uses a **union**. First, this code creates a

union that is comprised of one integer and a two-byte character array:

```
union pw {
  int i;
  char ch[2];
};
```

Now, you can create **putw( )** by using the **union**, as shown here:

```
putw(word,fp)   /* putw with union */
union pw word;
FILE *fp;
{
  putc(word->ch[0]); /* write first half */
  putc(word->ch[1]); /* write second half */
}
```

Although called with an integer, **putw( )** can still use the standard function **putc( )** to write an integer to a disk file.

An interesting program that combines **union**s with bitfields displays the ASCII code in binary that is generated when you press a key at the keyboard. The **union** allows **getche( )** to assign the value of the pressed key to a character variable, while the program uses the bitfield to display the individual bits. Study this program to make sure that you fully understand its operation.

```
/* display the ASCII code in binary for characters */

/* a bitfield that will be decoded */
struct byte {
  int a : 1;
  int b : 1;
  int c : 1;
  int d : 1;
  int e : 1;
  int f : 1;
  int g : 1;
  int h : 1;
};

union bits {
  char ch;
  struct byte bit;
} ascii ;

void decode();

main()
{
  do {
    ascii.ch = getche();
```

```
      printf(": ");
      decode(ascii.bit);
   } while(ascii.ch!='q');
}

/* display the bit pattern for each character */
void decode(b)
union bits b;
{
  if(b.bit.h) printf("1 ");
    else printf("0 ");
  if(b.bit.g) printf("1 ");
    else printf("0 ");
  if(b.bit.f) printf("1 ");
    else printf("0 ");
  if(b.bit.e) printf("1 ");
    else printf("0 ");
  if(b.bit.d) printf("1 ");
    else printf("0 ");
  if(b.bit.c) printf("1 ");
    else printf("0 ");
  if(b.bit.b) printf("1 ");
    else printf("0 ");
  if(b.bit.a) printf("1 ");
    else printf("0 ");
  printf("\n");
}
```

Figure 12-4 shows a sample run of the program.

```
A:\>ascii
a: 0 1 1 0 0 0 0 1
b: 0 1 1 0 0 0 1 0
c: 0 1 1 0 0 0 1 1
d: 0 1 1 0 0 1 0 0
e: 0 1 1 0 0 1 0 1
f: 0 1 1 0 0 1 1 0
g: 0 1 1 0 0 1 1 1
h: 0 1 1 0 1 0 0 0
i: 0 1 1 0 1 0 0 1
j: 0 1 1 0 1 0 1 0
k: 0 1 1 0 1 0 1 1
l: 0 1 1 0 1 1 0 0
m: 0 1 1 0 1 1 0 1
n: 0 1 1 0 1 1 1 0
o: 0 1 1 0 1 1 1 1
p: 0 1 1 1 0 0 0 0
=: 0 0 1 1 1 1 0 1
-: 0 0 1 0 1 1 0 1
0: 0 0 1 1 0 0 0 0
9: 0 0 1 1 1 0 0 1
8: 0 0 1 1 1 0 0 0
q: 0 1 1 1 0 0 0 1

A:\>
```

Figure 12-4.   A sample run of the ASCII program

Enumerations

An *enumeration* is a set of named integer constants, and specifies all of the legal values that a variable of that type may have. Enumerations are not uncommon in everyday life. For example, an enumeration of the coins used in the United States is

penny, nickel, dime, quarter, half-dollar, dollar

You define enumerations in almost the same way that you define structures, with the keyword **enum** signaling the start of an enumeration type. The general form is shown here:

enum *enum-type-name { enumeration list } variable list;*

Here, both the enumeration type name *enum-type-name* and the *variable list* are optional. As with structures, you use the enumeration type name to declare variables of its type. The following fragment defines an enumeration called **coin** that declares **money** to be of that type.

```
enum coin { penny, nickel, dime, quarter,
        half_dollar, dollar};

enum coin money;
```

Given this definition and declaration, the following statements are valid:

```
money=dime;

if(money==quarter) printf("is a quarter\n");
```

The key point about an enumeration is that each symbol stands for an integer value. As such, you may use the symbols in any integer expression. Unless initialized otherwise, the value of the first enumeration symbol is zero, the value of the second symbol is 1, and so forth. Therefore,

```
printf("%d %d",penny, dime);
```

displays **0 2** on screen.

You can specify the value of one or more of the symbols by using an initializer. To do so, place an equal sign and an integer value after the symbol. Whenever you use an initializer, the computer assigns values greater than the previous initialization value to symbols that appear after the initializer. For example, the following assigns the value of 100 to **quarter**:

```
enum coin { penny, nickel, dime, quarter=100,
        half_dollar, dollar};
```

The values of these symbols are as follows:

penny	0
nickel	1
dime	2
quarter	100
half_dollar	101
dollar	102

One common, but erroneous, assumption about enumerations is that the symbols can be input and output directly. However, this is not the case. For example, the following code fragment will not perform as desired:

```
/* this will not work */

money = dollar;

printf("%s",money);
```

Remember that the symbol **dollar** is simply a name for an integer; it is not a string. For the same reason, you cannot use this code to achieve the desired results:

```
/* this code is wrong */

gets(s);

strcpy(money,s);
```

Thus, this code does not cause the computer to convert a string that contains the name of a symbol automatically to that symbol.

Actually, creating code to input and output enumeration symbols is quite tedious (unless you are willing to settle for their integer values). For example, you need to use this code to display, in words, the kind of coins that **money** contains:

```
switch(money) {
  case penny: printf("penny");
        break;
  case nickel: printf("nickel");
        break;
  case dime: printf("dime");
        break;
  case quarter: printf("quarter");
        break;
  case half_dollar: printf("half_dollar");
        break;
  case dollar: printf("dollar");
}
```

Sometimes, to translate an enumeration value into its corresponding string, you can declare an array of strings and use the enumeration value as an index. For example, this code fragment will also output the proper string:

```
char name[][20]={
  "penny",
  "nickel",
  "dime",
  "quarter",
  "half_dollar",
  "dollar"
};
   .
   .
   .
printf("%s",name[money]);
```

This fragment will only work if you do not use symbol initializations because you must index the string array starting at zero. For example, this program prints the names of the coins:

```
enum coin { penny, nickel, dime, quarter,
            half_dollar, dollar};

enum coin money;

char name[][20]={
  "penny",
  "nickel",
  "dime",
  "quarter",
```

```
  "half_dollar",
  "dollar"
};

main()
{
  enum coin money;

  for(money=penny; money<=dollar; money++)
    printf("%s ",name[money]);
}
```

Given the fact that you must convert enumeration values manually to their human-readable string values for console I/O, you can find the greatest use of enumeration values in routines that do not make such conversions. For example, it is common to see an enumeration used to define a compiler's symbol table. Another use of enumerations is to help prove the validity of a program by providing a compile-time redundancy check.

Using *sizeof* to Ensure Portability

So far, you have seen that you can use structures, **unions**, and enumerations to create variables of varying sizes, and that the actual size of these variables may change from machine to machine. You can use the **sizeof** unary operator to compute the size of any variable or type, and to help eliminate machine-dependent code from your programs.

For example, Turbo C has the following sizes for data types:

Type	Size (bytes)
char	1
int	2
long int	4
float	4
double	8

Therefore, this code will print the numbers 1, 2, and 8 on the screen:

```
char ch;
int i;
double f;

printf("%d",sizeof(ch));

printf("%d",sizeof(i));

printf("%d",sizeof(f));
```

The **sizeof** operator is a compile-time operator: the computer knows all of the information necessary to compute the size of any variable at compile time. For example, consider this code:

```
union x {
   char ch;
   int i;
   float f;
} tom;
```

The **sizeof(tom)** will be 4. At run-time, it does not matter what the **union tom** is *actually* holding; all that matters is the size of the largest variable it can hold because the **union** must be as large as its largest element.

The Keyword
typedef

Turbo C allows you to define new data type names explicitly by using the **typedef** keyword. You are not actually *creating* a new data class, but rather are defining a new name for an existing type. This process can help make machine-dependent programs more portable; you only need to change the **typedef** statements. The process also can aid in documenting your code by allowing descriptive names for the standard data types. The general form of the **typedef** statement is

typedef type name;

where *type* is any allowable data type and *name* is the new name for this type. The name that you define is in addition to, and not a replacement for, the existing type name.

For example, you could create a new name for **float** by using

```
typedef float balance;
```

This statement tells the compiler to recognize **balance** as another name for **float**. Next, you could create a **float** variable by using **balance**:

```
balance over_due;
```

Here, **over—due** is a floating-point variable of type **balance**, which is another word for **float**.

You can use **typedef** to create names for more complex types, too, as shown here:

```
typedef struct client {
  float due;
  int over_due;
  char name[40];
};

client clist[NUM_CLIENTS]; /* define array of
         structures of type client */
```

Using **typedef** can help make your code easier to read and easier to port to a new machine. However, remember that you are *not* creating any new data types.

Now that you have seen the power of Turbo C's custom data types, you are ready to move on to Turbo C's advanced operators, which can give your programs true "turbo power"!

Advanced Operators

C H A P T E R   1 3

In Part Two you learned about the more common Turbo C operators. Unlike most languages, Turbo C contains several special operators that greatly increase its power and flexibility—especially for system-level programming. You will study these operators in this chapter.

Bitwise Operators

Unlike most other languages, C supports a complete arsenal of bitwise operators. Since C was designed to replace assembly language in most programming tasks, it had to have the ability to support all (or at least many) operations that can be done in assembler. *Bitwise operations* refer to the testing, setting, or shifting of the actual bits in a byte or word, both of which correspond to Turbo C's **char** and **int** data types. You may not use bitwise operations on type **float**, **double**, **long double**, **void**, or other more complex types. Table 13-1 lists the operators.

The bitwise AND, OR, and one's complement (NOT) are governed by the same truth table that governs their logical equivalents, except that they work on a bit-by-bit level. Given that **p** and **q** are Boolean variables, the exclusive OR, ^, has the truth table shown here.

p	q	$p \wedge q$
0	0	0
1	0	1
1	1	0
0	1	1

As the table indicates, the outcome of an XOR is true only if exactly one of the operands is true; it is false if any other condition exists.

Bitwise operations most often find application in device drivers—such as modem programs, disk-file routines, and printer routines—because you can use the bitwise operations to mask off certain bits, such as parity. (You use the parity bit to confirm that the rest of the bits in the byte are unchanged. It is usually the high-order bit in each byte.)

In terms of its most common usage, you can think of the bitwise AND as a way to turn bits off; that is, any bit that is 0 in either operand will cause the outcome of the operation to be 0. For example, the following function first reads a character from the modem port by using the library function **bioscom( )**, and then resets the parity bit to zero. You can use the **bioscom( )** function to access the asynchronous serial ports on an IBM PC or compatible. (You can find a complete description in *The Turbo C Reference Guide*.)

```
char get_char_from_modem()
{
  char ch;

  ch = bioscom(2, 0, 0); /* get a character from
                            COM1 */
  return(ch & 127);
}
```

Table 13-1. The Bitwise Operators

Operator	Action
&	AND
¦	OR
^	exclusive OR (XOR)
~	one's complement (NOT)
>>	shift right
<<	shift left

Parity is indicated by the eighth bit, which is set to zero by ANDing it with a byte that has bits 1 through 7 set to 1 and bit 8 set to 0. The expression **ch & 127** means to AND together the bits in **ch** with the bits that make up the number 127. The result is that the eighth bit of **ch** will be set to 0. In the following example, assume that **ch** had received the character **A** and had the parity bit set:

```
Parity bit
      1 1 0 0 0 0 0 1   ch that contains an A with parity set
      0 1 1 1 1 1 1 1   127 in binary
&     _____  Do bitwise AND
      0 1 0 0 0 0 0 1   A without parity
```

You can use the bitwise OR as the reverse of AND, to turn bits on. Any bit that is set to 1 in either operand will cause the corresponding bit in the variable to be set to 1. For example, here is **128 ¦ 3.**

```
      1 0 0 0 0 0 0 0   128 in binary
      0 0 0 0 0 0 1 1   3 in binary
¦     _____  Bitwise OR
      1 0 0 0 0 0 1 1   Result
```

An exclusive OR, which is usually abbreviated as XOR, will set a bit on if

and only if the bits that you are comparing are different. For example, **127** ^
120 is

```
   0  1  1  1  1  1  1  1   127 in binary
   0  1  1  1  1  0  0  0   120 in binary
^  ─────────────────────   Bitwise XOR
   0  0  0  0  0  1  1  1   Result
```

Generally, bitwise ANDs, ORs, and XORs apply their operations directly
to each bit in the variable individually. For this reason, bitwise operations
are usually not used in conditional statements in the way that the relational
and logical operators are. For example, if **X** equals 7, then **X && 8** evaluates
to true (1), whereas **X & 8** evaluates to false (0).

Remember: *relational and logical operators always produce a result that
is either 0 or 1, whereas the similar bitwise operations may produce any arbitrary value in accordance with the specific operation.* In other words, the logical and relational operators will always evaluate to 0 or 1, while bitwise
operations may have values other than 0 or 1.

The AND operator is also useful when you want to check to see if a bit is
on or off. For example, this statement checks to see if bit 4 in **status** is set:

```
if(status & 8) printf("bit 4 is on");
```

The reason that the statement uses 8 is that, in binary, 8 is represented as
0000 1000. Thus, the number 8, when translated into binary, has only the
fourth bit on. Hence, the **if** statement can only succeed when bit 4 of **status** is
also on. An interesting use of this procedure is the **disp—binary( )** function
shown here. It displays, in binary format, the bit pattern of its argument.
You will use **disp—binary( )** later in this chapter to watch the effects of
other bitwise operations.

```
/* display the bits within a byte */
void disp_binary(i)
int i;
{
  register int t;

  for(t=128; t>0; t = t/2)
    if(i & t) printf("1 ");
    else printf("0 ");
  printf("\n");
}
```

The **disp—binary( )** function works by successively testing each bit in the byte, by using the bitwise AND, to determine if the bit is on or off. If it is on, the function displays **1**; if it is off, the function displays **0**.

The shift operators, $>>$ and $<<$, move all bits in a variable to the right or the left as specified. The general form of the shift-right statement is

$$variable >> number\ of\ bit\ positions$$

and the general form of the shift-left statement is

$$variable << number\ of\ bit\ positions$$

As the statements shift bits off one end, the computer brings zeros in the other end. Remember that a shift is *not* a rotate: the bits shifted off one end *do not* come back around to the other. The bits shifted off are lost, and zeros are brought in to replace them.

Bitwise-shift operations can be useful when you decode external-device input such as D/A converters, and when you read status information. You can also use the bitwise-shift operators to perform quick multiplication and division of integers. As shown in Figure 13-1, a shift left will effectively multiply a number by 2 and a shift right will divide it by 2. The figure assumes that zeros are shifted in.

The following program graphically shows the effect of the shift operators.

```
/* Example of bitshifting. */

void disp_binary();

main()
{
  int i=1, t;

  for(t=0; t<8; t++) {
    disp_binary(i);
    i = i << 1;
  }

  printf("\n");

  for(t=0; t<8; t++) {
    i = i >> 1;
    disp_binary(i);
  }
}
```

```
/* display the bits within a byte */
void disp_binary(i)
int i;
{
  register int t;

  for(t=128; t>0; t=t/2)
    if(i & t) printf("1 ");
    else printf("0 ");
  printf("\n");
}
```

It produces the following output:

```
0 0 0 0 0 0 0 1
0 0 0 0 0 0 1 0
0 0 0 0 0 1 0 0
0 0 0 0 1 0 0 0
0 0 0 1 0 0 0 0
0 0 1 0 0 0 0 0
0 1 0 0 0 0 0 0
1 0 0 0 0 0 0 0

1 0 0 0 0 0 0 0
0 1 0 0 0 0 0 0
0 0 1 0 0 0 0 0
0 0 0 1 0 0 0 0
0 0 0 0 1 0 0 0
0 0 0 0 0 1 0 0
0 0 0 0 0 0 1 0
0 0 0 0 0 0 0 1
```

	x as Each Statement Executes								Value of x
char x;									
x=7;	0	0	0	0	0	1	1	1	7
x << 1;	0	0	0	0	1	1	1	0	14
x << 3;	0	1	1	1	0	0	0	0	112
x << 2;	1	1	0	0	0	0	0	0	192
x >> 1;	0	1	1	0	0	0	0	0	96
x >> 2;	0	0	0	1	1	0	0	0	24

Note: Each left shift multiplies by 2. After x<<2, information has been lost because a bit was shifted off each end. Each right shift divides by 2. Subsequent divisions will not bring back any lost bits.

Figure 13-1. Multiplication and division with shift operators

Although C does not contain a rotate operator, you can easily create a function to perform this task. A rotate operation is similar to a left-shift operation except that a rotate operation shifts the bits that are shifted off the left end onto the right end. For example, 1010 rotated once is 0101. One way to perform a rotate requires using a **union** of two different types of data. The first type is a two-element array of the type of data that you wish to rotate. The second type is larger than the data that you will be rotating. Using this **union**

```
union rotate {
   char ch[2];
   unsigned int i;
} rot;
```

the following function performs a byte rotation:

```
/* rotate a byte */
rotate_it(rot)
union rotate *rot;
{
   rot->ch[1] = 0;  /* clear the high-order byte */

   rot->i = rot->i << 1;  /* shift once to the left */

   /* see if a bit has been shifted out of ch[0] */
   if(rot->ch[1]) rot->i = rot->i ¦ 1;  /* OR it back in */
}
```

The function first clears the high-order byte of the integer **i** so that if a bit is shifted in, the function can detect it. By applying the left-shift operator to the entire integer, the function will not lose a bit that leaves the byte **ch[0]**, but will move the bit into **ch[1]**. If a bit is shifted out, it is ORed into the lower-order bit of **ch[0]**. A program that uses this function is shown here.

```
/* How to do a rotation */

union rotate {
   char ch[2];
   unsigned int i;
} rot;

void disp_binary();

main()
{
   register int t;

   rot.ch[0] = 101;
```

```
    for(t=0; t<7; t++) {
      disp_binary(rot.i);
      rotate_it(&rot);
    }
}

/* rotate a byte */
rotate_it(rot)
union rotate *rot;
{
  rot->ch[1] = 0;  /* clear the high-order byte */

  rot->i = rot-> i << 1;  /* shift once to the left */

  /* see if a bit has been shifted out of ch[0] */
  if(rot->ch[1]) rot->i = rot->i ¦ 1;  /* OR it back in */
}

/* display the bits within a byte */
void disp_binary(i)
int i;
{
  register int t;

  for(t=128; t>0; t=t/2)
    if(i & t) printf("1 ");
    else printf("0 ");
  printf("\n");
}
```

This program produces this output by rotating the original byte six times.

```
0 1 1 0 0 1 0 1
1 1 0 0 1 0 1 0
1 0 0 1 0 1 0 1
0 0 1 0 1 0 1 1
0 1 0 1 0 1 1 0
1 0 1 0 1 1 0 0
0 1 0 1 1 0 0 1
```

The one's complement operator, ~, will reverse the state of each bit in the specified variable: all 1's are set to 0 and all 0's are set to 1. An interesting use for the one's complement operator allows you to see the extended character set that is hiding inside your computer. You may not realize that you can directly generate only a small amount of the character set at the keyboard.

However, the following program uses the one's complement operator to reverse the bits in the characters that you type. These reversed-bit patterns correspond to much of the extended character set. For example, when you type **d**, the cents sign is displayed. You will be surprised how many different characters are available. Here is the program:

```
/* A window into the PC's extended character set */
main()
{
  char ch;

  do {
    ch = getch();
    printf("%c", ~ch);
  }while(ch!='q');
}
```

Cipher routines often use the bitwise operators. To make a disk file appear unreadable, you could perform some bitwise manipulations on it. One of the simplest methods would be to complement each byte by using the one's complement to reverse each bit in the byte as is shown here:

Original byte	0	0	1	0	1	1	0	0	
After first complement	1	1	0	1	0	0	1	1	Same
After second complement	0	0	1	0	1	1	0	0	

Notice that a sequence of two complements will always produce the original number. Hence, the first complement would represent the coded version of that byte. The second complement would decode this version to its original value.

You could use the **encode( )** function shown here to encode a character. To decode a coded character, you would simply use **encode( )** a second time.

```
char encode(ch)  /* a simple cipher function */
char ch;
{
  return(~ch); /* complement it */
}
```

The ? Operator

You can use the ? operator to replace **if/else** statements of the general form

> **if**(*condition*)
> > *expression*
> **else**
> > *expression*

The key restriction of the ? operator is that the target of both the **if** and the **else** must be a single expression—not another C statement.

The **?** is called a *ternary operator* because it requires three operands and takes the general form

$$Exp1 \; ? \; Exp2 : Exp3$$

where *Exp1*, *Exp2*, and *Exp3* are expressions. Notice the use and placement of the colon.

You can determine the value of a ? expression like this. Imagine that you are evaluating *Exp1*. If it is true, then you evaluate *Exp2* and it becomes the value of the entire ? expression. If *Exp1* is false, then you evaluate *Exp3* and its value becomes the value of the expression. For example, consider

```
x = 10;

y = x>9 ? 100 : 200;
```

This example will assign the value 100 to **y**. If **x** is less than 9, **y** will receive the value 200. If you used the **if/else** statement, the same code would be

```
x = 10;

if(x>9) y=100;
else y=200;
```

However, the use of the ? operator to replace **if/else** statements is not restricted to only assignments. To see how you can expand its use, it is important to remember that all functions (except those declared as **void**) may return a value. Hence, it is permissible to use one or more function calls in a C expression. After encountering the function's name, the computer executes the function so that it can determine the function's return value. Therefore, you can execute one or more function calls that use the ? operator by placing them in the expressions that form the operands.

Here is an example:

```
main()
{
  int t;

  printf(": ");
  scanf("%d",&t);

  /* print proper message */
  t ? f1(t)+f2() : printf("zero entered");

}

f1(n)
int n;
{
  printf("%d ",n);
}

f2()
{
  printf("entered");
}
```

In this simple example, if you enter a zero, then the **printf( )** function will be called and the message **zero entered** will appear. If you enter any other number, then the program will execute both **f1( )** and **f2( )**. It is important to note that the value of the ? expression is discarded in this example. It is not necessary to assign the value to anything.

A word of warning: Turbo C may rearrange the order of evaluation of an expression in an attempt to optimize the object code. This rearranging could cause functions that form the operands of the ? operator to execute in a sequence other than you intended.

Using this scheme, you can again rewrite the magic number program developed in Chapter 6 as shown here.

```
main()  /* magic number program - final version*/
{
  int magic = 123;  /* magic number */
  int guess;

  scanf("%d",&guess);
  if (guess == magic) {
     printf("** Right ** ");
```

```
        printf("%d is the magic number",magic);
  }
  else
        guess > magic ? printf("High") : printf("Low");
  }
```

Here, the ? operator causes the computer to display the proper message based on the outcome of the test **guess>magic**.

C Shorthand

C has a special shorthand that simplifies the coding of a certain type of assignment statement. For example, you can rewrite

```
x = x+10;
```

in C shorthand as

```
x += 10;
```

The operator pair += tells the compiler to assign to **x** the value of **x** plus 10.

This shorthand will work for all of the binary operators in C. (Remember, a binary operator is one that requires two operands.) The general form of the shorthand is

$$var\ op = expression;$$

Here is another example:

```
x = x-100;
```

is the same as

```
x -= 100;
```

You will see shorthand notation used widely in professionally written C programs and you should become familiar with it.

The Comma Operator

You use the comma operator to string together several expressions. The compiler always evaluates the left side of the comma operator as **void**. Thus, the expression on the right side will become the value of the total comma-separated expression. For example,

```
x = (y=3, y+1);
```

first assigns the value 3 to **y** and then assigns the value of 4 to **x**. The parentheses are necessary because the comma operator has a lower precedence than the assignment operator.

Essentially, the comma's effect is to cause a sequence of operations to be performed. When you use it on the right side of an assignment statement, the value assigned is the value of the last expression of the comma-separated list. For example, after the computer executes

```
y = 10;

x = (y=y-5, 25/y);
```

x will have the value 5 because the original value of **y**, 10, is reduced by 5, and then the value of **x** is divided into 25, which yields 5 as the result.

In some ways, you can think of the comma operator as having the same meaning as the word *and* has in English, as in the phrase "do this and this and this."

Parentheses and Square Brackets

The C language considers parentheses and square brackets to be operators. Parentheses do the expected job of increasing the precedence of the operations that are inside the parentheses. Square brackets perform array-indexing and have been discussed earlier in this book. It is interesting to note that most other computer languages do not consider parentheses and the array-indexing symbols to be operators.

Table 13-2. The Precedence of C Operators

```
       Highest  ()  []  —  .
                !  ~  ++  ——  —  (type) * & sizeof
                *  /  %
                +  —
                <<  >>
                <  <=  >  >=
                ==  !=
                &
                ^
                |
                &&
                ||
                ?
                =  +=  —=  *=  /=
       Lowest   ,
```

Precedence Summary

Table 13-2 lists the precedence of all C operators. Please note that all operators, except the unary operators and ?, associate from left to right. The unary operators, which are *, &, —, and ?, associate from right to left.

The Turbo C
Preprocessor and
Compiler Options

C H A P T E R   1 4

It is possible to include various instructions to the compiler in the source code for a C program. These instructions are called *preprocessor directives* and, although not actually part of the Turbo C language, they expand the scope of the C programming environment. In addition to studying the preprocessor directives, this chapter also examines Turbo C's built-in macros. The chapter concludes by looking at some of Turbo C's more important compiler options.

The Turbo C Preprocessor

As defined by the proposed ANSI standard, the C preprocessor contains the following directives.

#if
#ifdef
#ifndef
#else
#elif
#include
#define
#undef
#line
#error
#pragma

As is apparent, all preprocessor directives begin with a # sign.

The #define Directive

You use **#define** to define an identifier and a string that the compiler will substitute for the identifier each time it is encountered in the source file. The proposed ANSI standard refers to the identifier as a *macro-name*, and to the replacement process as *macro-substitution*. The general form of the directive is

#define *identifier string*

Notice that this statement contains no semicolon. There may be any number of spaces between the *identifier* and the *string* but, once the *string* begins, only a newline can terminate it.

For example, if you wish to use the word **TRUE** for the value 1 and the word **FALSE** for the value 0, then you would declare two macro **#define**s as

```
#define TRUE 1
#define FALSE 0
```

This causes the compiler to substitute a 1 or a 0 each time that it encounters the name TRUE or FALSE in your source file. For example, the following will print **0 1 2** on screen:

```
printf("%d %d %d",FALSE, TRUE, TRUE+1);
```

After you define a macro-name, you may use it as part of the definition of other macro-names. For example, this code defines the names **ONE**, **TWO**, and **THREE** to their respective values:

```
#define ONE     1
#define TWO     ONE+ONE
#define THREE   ONE+TWO
```

It is important to understand that the macro-substitution is simply the process of replacing an identifier with its associated string. Therefore, if you wish to define a standard error message, you might write something like this:

```
#define E_MS "standard error on input\n"
.
.
printf(E_MS);
```

Turbo C will actually substitute the string **standard error on input\n** when it encounters the identifier **E_MS**. To the compiler, the **printf( )** statement will actually appear to be

```
printf("standard error on input\n");
```

No text substitutions will occur if the identifier occurs within a quoted string. For example,

```
#define XYZ this is a test
.
.
printf("XYZ");
```

will not print **this is a test**, but rather will print **XYZ**.

If the string is longer than one line, you may continue the string on the next line by placing a backslash at the end of the line, as shown in this example:

```
#define LONG_STRING "this is a very long \
string that is used as an example"
```

C programmers commonly use capital letters for defined identifiers. This convention helps anyone who reads the program know at a glance that a macro-substitution will take place. Also, it is best to put all **#define** directives at the start of the file or, perhaps, in a separate header file, rather than sprinkling them throughout the program.

The most common usage of macro-substitutions is to define names for "magic numbers" that occur in a program. For example, you may have a program that defines an array and has several routines to access that array. Instead of "hard-coding" the array's size with a constant, it is better to define a size and use that name whenever you need the size of the array. This method only requires a change in one place and a recompilation to alter the size of the array if you need to change it. Here is an example of this use of macro-substitutions:

```
#define MAX_SIZE 100

float balance[MAX_SIZE];
```

The **#define** directive has another powerful feature: the macro-name can have arguments. Each time that the compiler encounters the macro-name, the actual arguments found in the program replace the arguments associated with the macro-name. Study this example:

```
#define MIN(a,b)  (a<b) ? a : b

main()
{
  int x,y;

  x=10;
  y=20;
  printf("the minimum is: %d",MIN(x,y);
}
```

When compiling this program, the compiler will substitute the expression defined by **MIN(a,b)**, except that **x** and **y** will be used as the operands. Thus, after the compiler makes the substitution, the **printf( )** statement will look like this:

```
printf("the minimum is: %d",(x<y) ? x : y);
```

The use of macro-substitutions in the place of actual functions has one major benefit: it increases the speed of the code because no overhead for a function call is incurred. However, you pay for this increased speed with an increase in the size of the program because of the duplicated code.

The #error Directive

The **#error** directive forces Turbo C to stop compilation when the compiler encounters it. It is used primarily for debugging. The general form of the directive is

> **#error** *error-message*

The *error-message* does not appear between double quotes. When the compiler encounters this directive, it displays the following information and terminates compilation.

> **Fatal:** *filename linenum Error directive: error-message*

The #include Directive

The **#include** preproccessor directive instructs the compiler to include another source file with the one that has the **#include** directive in it. You must enclose the source file to be read between either double quotes or angle brackets. For example,

```
#include "stdio.h"
#include <stdio.h>
```

both instruct the C compiler to read and compile the header for the disk-file library routines.

It is valid for "include files" to have **#include** directives in them. These files are referred to as *nested includes*. The number of levels of nesting that you can use depends on the implementation that you are using.

If you specify explicit pathnames as part of the filename identifier, then the compiler will search for the included file in only those directories. If you do not specify pathnames and if you enclose the filename in quotes, the compiler first searches the current working directory. If the file is not found, then the compiler searches any directories specified on the command line. Finally, if the file has still not been found, the compiler searches the standard directories, as defined by the implementation.

If you do not specify explicit pathnames and if you enclose the filename in angle brackets, the compiler first searches for the file in the directories that are specified in the compiler command line. If the file is not found, then the compiler searches the standard directories. At no time does the compiler search the current working directory.

Conditional Compilation Directives

Several directives allow you to compile portions of your program's source code selectively. This process is called *conditional compilation* and is used widely by commercial software houses that provide and maintain many customized versions of one program.

The #if, #else, #elif, and #endif Directives

The general idea behind the #if is that if the constant expression that follows the #if is true, then the compiler will compile the code between it and an **#endif**; if the expression is false, the compiler will skip over it. You use #endif to mark the end of an #if block.

The general form of **#if** is

> **#if** *constant-expression*
> *statement sequence*
> **#endif**

If the *constant-expression* is true, Turbo C will compile the block of code; if the *constant-expression* is false, the compiler will skip over it. For example, this program

```
/* simple #if example */

#define MAX 100
main()
{
#if MAX>99
  printf("compiled for array greater than 99\n");
#endif
}
```

will display the message on screen because, as defined, **MAX** is greater than 99. This example illustrates an important point: the expression that follows the **#if** is *evaluated at compile-time*. Therefore, the expression must contain only identifiers that have been previously defined and constants—it may not use any variables. In addition, it may not use the **sizeof** operator.

The **#else** works in much the same way as the **else** that forms part of the C language: **#else** establishes an alternative if the **#if** fails. You can expand the previous example as shown here:

```
/* simple #if/#else example */

#define MAX 10
main()
{
#if MAX>99
  printf("compiled for array greater than 99\n");
#else
  printf("compiled for small array\n");
#endif
}
```

This version defines **MAX** to be less than 99. Thus, the compiler does not compile the **#if** position of the code, but does compile the **#else** alternative.

Therefore, the program displays the message **compiled for small array**.

Notice that this version uses the #**else** to mark both the end of the #**if** block and the beginning of the #**else** block. This structure is necessary because there can only be one #**endif** associated with any #**if**.

The #**elif** stands for "else if" and is used to establish an if/else/if ladder for multiple-compilation options. A constant expression follows the #**elif**. If the expression is true, then the compiler compiles that block of code and tests no other #**elif** expressions. If the expression is false, the compiler checks the next expression in the series. The general form is

> #**if** *expression*
>   *statement sequence*
> #**elif** *expression 1*
>   *statement sequence*
> #**elif** *expression 2*
>   *statement sequence*
> #**elif** *expression 3*
>   *statement sequence*
> #**elif** *expression 4*
>
> .
>
> .
>
> .
>
> #**elif** *expression N*
>   *statement sequence*
> #**endif**

For example, this fragment uses the value of **ACTIVE—COUNTRY** to define the currency sign:

```
#define US 0
#define ENGLAND 1
#define FRANCE 2

#define ACTIVE_COUNTRY US

#if ACTIVE_COUNTRY==US
  char currency[]="dollar";
#elif ACTIVE_COUNTRY==ENGLAND
  char currency[]="pound";
#else
  char currency[]="franc";
#endif
```

You may nest **#if**s and **#elif**s to any level up to some implementation-specific limit, with the **#endif**, **#else**, or **#elif** associating with the nearest **#if** or **#elif**. For example, the following is perfectly valid:

```
#if MAX>100
   #if SERIAL_VERSION
      int port=198;
   #elif
      int port=200;
   #endif
#else
   char out_buffer[100];
#endif
```

The #*ifdef* and #*ifndef* Directives

Another method of conditional compilation uses the directives **#ifdef** and **#ifndef**, which mean "if defined" and "if not defined," respectively.

The general form of **#ifdef** is

> **#ifdef** *macro-name*
> *statement sequence*
> **#endif**

If you previously defined the *macro-name* in a **#define** statement, the compiler will compile the *statement sequence* between the **#ifdef** and **#endif**. The general form of **#ifndef** is

> **#ifndef** *macro-name*
> *statement sequence*
> **#endif**

If the *macro-name* is currently undefined by a **#define** statement, then the block of code is compiled. Both the **#ifdef** and **#ifndef** may use an **#else** statement but not the **#elif**. For example,

```
#define TED 10

main()
```

```
{
#ifdef TED
  printf("Hi Ted\n");
#else
  printf("Hi anyone\n");
#endif
#ifndef RALPH
  printf("RALPH not defined\n");
#endif
}
```

will print **Hi Ted** and **RALPH not defined**. However, if you did not define **TED**, then the code would display **Hi anyone**, followed by **RALPH not defined**.

You may nest **#ifdefs** and **#ifndefs** to any level in the same way that you nest **#ifs**.

The #undef Directive

You use **#undef** to remove a previously defined definition of the macro-name that follows the directive. The general form of **#undef** is

#undef *macro-name*

For example, this code

```
#define LEN 100
#define WIDTH 100

char array[LEN][WIDTH];

#undef LEN
#undef WIDTH
/* at this point both LEN and WIDTH are undefined */
```

defines both **LEN** and **WIDTH** until the **#undef** statements are encountered.

The principle use of **#undef** is to allow macro-names to be localized to only those sections of code that need them.

The #line Directive

You can use the #line directive to change the contents of _ _LINE_ _ and _ _FILE_ _, which are predefined identifiers in Turbo C. The basic form of the command is

#line *number* ["*filename*"]

where *number* is any positive integer and the optional *filename* is any valid file identifier. The *number* is the number of the current source line and the filename is the name of the source file. You primarily use #line for debugging purposes and special applications.

For example, the following specifies that the line count will begin with 100.

```
#line 100    /* reset the line counter */
main()       /* line 100 */
{            /* line 101 */
  printf("%d\n",__LINE__);  /* line 102 */
}
```

The **printf( )** statement displays **102** because it identifies the third line in the program after the #line 100 statement.

The #pragma Directive

The #pragma directive is an implementation-defined directive that allows you to give various instructions, defined by the compiler's creator, to the compiler. The general form of the #pragma directive is

#pragma *name*

where *name* is the name of the #pragma statement you want. Turbo C defines two #**pragma** statements: **warn** and **inline**.

The **warn** directive causes Turbo C to override warning message options. The general form of **warn** is

#**pragma warn** *setting*

where *setting* is one of the various warning error options, as defined in *The Turbo C Reference Guide*. For most applications you will not need to use this form of #**pragma**.

The second #**pragma** statement is **inline**. It has the general form

#**pragma inline**

and tells Turbo C that the program contains in-line assembly code. (In-line assembly code is covered in detail in the sequel to this book, *Advanced Turbo C*, by Herbert Schildt [Borland-Osborne/McGraw-Hill, 1987].)

Predefined Macro-Names

The proposed ANSI standard specifies five built-in predefined macro-names. They are

```
_ _LINE_ _
_ _FILE_ _
_ _DATE_ _
_ _TIME_ _
_ _STDC_ _
```

In addition to these, Turbo C also defines these built-in macros:

```
_ _CDECL_ _
_ _COMPACT_ _
_ _HUGE_ _
_ _LARGE_ _
_ _MEDIUM_ _
_ _MSDOS_ _
_ _PASCAL_ _
_ _SMALL_ _
_ _TINY_ _
_ _TURBOC_ _
```

The #**line** discussion presented earlier in this chapter discussed both the _ _LINE_ _ and _ _FILE_ _ macros.

The _ _DATE_ _ macro contains a string of the form *month/day/year*, which is the date of the translation of the source file into object code.

The _ _TIME_ _ macro contains as a string the time of the translation of the source code into object code. The form of the string is *hour:minute:second*.

The macro _ _STDC_ _ contains the decimal constant 1. This means that the implementation is an ANSI-standard-conforming implementation. If the constant is any other number, then the implementation must vary from the standard.

The _ _CDECL_ _ macro is defined if you use the standard C calling convention—that is, if the Pascal option is not in use. If the Pascal option is in use, then the macro is undefined.

The compiler defines only one of these macros, based upon the memory model that you use during compilation: _ _TINY_ _, _ _SMALL_ _, _ _COMPACT_ _, _ _MEDIUM_ _, _ _LARGE_ _, and _ _ HUGE_ _.

The _ _MSDOS_ _ macro is defined with the value 1 under all situations when you use the MS-DOS version of Turbo C.

The _ _PASCAL_ _ macro is defined only if you use the Pascal calling conventions to compile a program. If you do not use those conventions, _ _PASCAL_ _ is undefined.

Finally, _ _TURBOC_ _ contains the version number of Turbo C.

For the most part, you use these built-in macros in fairly complex programming environments when you develop or maintain several different versions of a program—perhaps running them on different computers. If you are a beginning Turbo C programmer, you should be aware that these macros are available, but you will probably not need to use one for some time.

Compiler and Linker Options

As you use Turbo C, you probably realize that you can control many options that affect the way that Turbo C compiles and links programs. Until now, you have used Turbo C's default settings without worry because they can accommodate a wide variety of programming projects. While it is beyond the scope of this book to cover all of the options available in Turbo C, the most important options will be examined here. This chapter will discuss these options from the point of view of the integrated environment. Except for those options and settings that deal exclusively with the integrated environment, all options that are available in the integrated environment are also available for use by the command-line version.

These are the options available in the **Options** menu:

- **Compiler**
- **Linker**
- **Environment**
- **Args**
- **Retrieve options**
- **Store options**

Compiler Options

After selecting **Compiler**, you will see these compiler options:

- **Model**
- **Defines**
- **Code generation**
- **Optimization**
- **Source**
- **Errors**
- **Names**

Model

The **Model** option allows you to select which memory model to use to compile your program. The default is **small** and is adequate for most applications.

Defines

The **Defines** option allows you to define temporary preprocessor symbols that your program will automatically use. This feature is most useful when you are debugging your program.

Code generation

Selecting **Code generation** presents a large number of switches that you can set. These are the available options:

- **Calling convention**
- **Instruction set**
- **Floating point**
- **Default char type**
- **Alignment**
- **Generate underbars**
- **Merge duplicate strings**
- **Standard stack frame**
- **Test stack overflow**
- **Line numbers**

You can choose between the C calling conventions and the Pascal calling conventions. A calling convention is simply the method by which a programming language calls functions and passes arguments. Generally, you should use the C calling convention.

If you know that the object code of your program will be used on a 80186/80286 processor, then you can select the **Instruction set** option to allow for this. This option will cause your program to execute a little faster, but your program will not be able to run on 8088/8086-based computers. The default is 8088/8086 instructions.

You can choose the way that Turbo C implements floating-point operations. The default—and most common—method is to use 8087/80287-emulation routines. The 8087 chip is the math co-processor for the 8086 family of CPUs, while the 80287 chip is the math co-processor for the 80286 CPU. When one of these co-processors is in the system, it allows extremely rapid floating-point operations. However, if you do not have a math co-processor, or if your program will be used in a variety of computers, you must emulate the 8087's operation in software, a process that is much slower. If you do have the co-processor, then you can select the 8087/80287 option, which uses the co-processor. Finally, you can "deselect" floating-point operations altogether when your program does not use them.

The default **char type** option determines whether the type **char** is signed or unsigned by default. By default, **char** is signed in Turbo C.

The **Alignment** option determines whether data is aligned on byte or word boundaries. On the 8086 and 80286 processors, memory accesses are quicker if data is word-aligned. However, there is no difference on the 8088. The default is word-alignment.

The **Generate underbars** option, which is on by default, determines whether or not Turbo C will add an underscore to the start of each identifier in the link file. For the most part, do not turn this option off unless you are an experienced programmer and unless you understand the inner workings of Turbo C.

A common compiler optimization that Turbo C performs is the elimination of duplicate string constants. Thus, Turbo C merges all duplicate strings into one string. You can stop this merging by toggling the **Merge duplicate strings** option.

You can use the **Standard stack frame** option to force Turbo C to generate standard calling and returning code for each function call. Doing this helps the debugging process. You will not generally have to worry about or use this option.

You can force Turbo C to check for stack overflows by turning on the **Test stack overflow** option. Doing this will cause your program to run slower, but this may be necessary in order to find certain bugs.

Finally, you can force Turbo C to enter the number of each line of the source file into the object file. Having line numbers is useful when you use a debugging program.

Optimization

Under the **Optimization** option are these four toggles:

- **Optimize for size/speed**
- **Use register variables on/off**
- **Register optimization off/on**
- **Jump optimization off/on**

Turbo C is very efficient. But for somewhat complicated reasons, some optimizations that make the object code smaller also make it slower. Other optimizations make the object code faster but larger. Therefore, Turbo C lets you decide which consideration—speed or size—is the most important by providing the **Optimize for** option. The default is size.

When toggled off, the **Use register variables** option suppresses the use of register variables. Unless you are interfacing to non-Turbo C code, leave this option turned on.

The **Register optimization** option, which is off by default, allows Turbo C to perform additional optimizations if you turn it on. However, leave this option off, until you understand the inner workings of Turbo C.

By toggling **Jump optimization** on, you allow Turbo C to rearrange the code within loops and switch statements. This setting can cause higher performance. However, if you are using a debugger on your object code, then turn this option off.

Source

The **Source** option lets you set the number of significant characters in an identifier, determine whether comments may be nested, and force Turbo C to accept only the ANSI keywords. Generally, you should leave these options in their default settings. However, let's look at a use for nested comments.

In its standard form, C (including Turbo C) does not allow one comment to be inside another. For example, in standard C, this code will cause a compile-time error:

```
/* In standard ANSI C this will not compile. */

/*
  if(x<10) printf("all OK"); /* signal status */
  else printf("failure in port 102");
*/
```

Here, the programmer is attempting to "comment out" a section of code, but failed to notice that a nested comment was created. By selecting the **Nested comments** option, you can tell Turbo C to allow situations like the example just given. This ability can be useful when you wish to remove a section of code temporarily. (The standard and portable way to do this is to use an **#ifdef** preprocessor command.)

Errors

The **Errors** option lets you determine how Turbo C reports errors during the compilation process. You may set the way that Turbo C reports many fatal and warning errors until the compilation process stops. You can toggle whether or not Turbo C displays warning errors. Furthermore, you can select precisely what type of warning errors will be displayed.

As you know, Turbo C is very forgiving and tries to understand your source code, no matter how unusual it may seem. However, if Turbo C suspects that what you have written is incorrect, it will display a warning error. A warning error does not stop compilation—it simply informs you of Turbo C's concerns over a certain construct. You must decide whether or not Turbo C is correct in its concern.

Many warning errors are generated by portability issues. An error may occur because the code that you are working on is intrinsically nonportable. In this case, you may tire of seeing the warning messages and choose to turn them off temporarily.

Keep in mind that as a beginning C programmer, you should keep all warnings active and then correct any statement that causes a warning. As you become more experienced, you will be able to better decide which warnings are important and which can be ignored.

Names

The **Names** option lets you change the names that Turbo C uses for the various memory segments used by your program. You will only need to change these names in unusual situations. Do not change them unless you truly know what you are doing.

Linker Options

If you select the **Linker** options, you will see the following choices:

- **Map file**
- **Initialize segments**
- **Default libraries**
- **Warn duplicate symbols**
- **Stack warning**
- **Case-sensitive link**

Until you become an advanced Turbo C programmer, you will probably not want to change any of these. However, let's quickly look at what you can use them for.

Map file

By default, Turbo C's linker does not create a *map file* of your compiled program. A map file shows the relative positions of the variables and functions that make up your program, and where they reside in memory. With the

Map file option, you may create a map file for debugging certain programs in complex situations. You can create a map file three ways. The first shows only the segments. The second shows the public, or global, symbols. The third creates a detailed, or complete, map.

Initialize segments

By default, the **Initialize segments** option is off. You can turn it on in highly specialized situations to force the linker to initialize segments.

Default libraries

The **Default libraries** option applies only when you are linking modules that other C compilers compiled. By default, this option is off. If you turn it on, the linker will search those libraries that are defined in those separately compiled modules before it searches Turbo C's libraries.

Warn duplicate symbols

By default, **Warn duplicate symbols** is on. Thus, if you have multiple-defined global identifiers, the linker will warn you of this fact. By turning the option off, you will not see this message and the linker will choose which symbol to use.

Stack warning

If you are using Turbo C to create routines that you will link with external assembly language programs, you might receive the link-time message **No stack specified**. You can eliminate this message by turning the **Stack warning** option off. However, this is another situation that you are unlikely to encounter.

Case-sensitive link

The **Case-sensitive link** option is on by default because C is case-sensitive. However, if you are trying to link Turbo C modules with FORTRAN modules, for example, you may need to turn this option off. Generally, though, you will not want to change the default.

The Turbo C
Integrated Environment Options

By selecting the **Environment** option from the **Options** menu, you can change the way Turbo C's integrated environment works. Here are the choices that you will see:

- **Include directories**
- **Output directory**
- **Library directory**
- **Turbo C directory**
- **Auto save edit**
- **Backup source files**
- **Zoomed windows**

The first four options let you define the paths to the indicated directories.

You can cause Turbo C to save the program in the editor automatically after each change by turning the **Auto save edit** option on. By default, this option is off.

When you save a file, Turbo C automatically renames the previous version of that file from a .C extension to a .BAK extension. This process ensures that you always have the previous version as a backup. You can prevent Turbo C from using the process by toggling the **Backup source files** option. The only reason that you would want to turn this option off is if disk space is very limited.

Finally, you can have Turbo C use zoomed windows by default by turning the **Zoomed windows** option on.

Args

As you know, when you run a program in the interactive environment, you do not type the program name as you would do from the DOS system prompt. Hence, you cannot specify command-line arguments directly when running a program in the integrated environment. However, Turbo C handles this problem by allowing you to specify command-line arguments through the **Args** option.

When you select **Args**, Turbo C prompts you to enter the command-line parameters that your program requires. Enter the desired parameters—but not the program name. Then, each time that you run the program, Turbo C will use the command-line parameters that you specified.

Saving and Loading Options

After you have customized Turbo C by changing various options, you have two choices: you can use the options during your current session only, or you can save them. The two entries **Retrieve options** and **Store options** in the **Options** menu allow you to save and load the options.

The TCCONFIG.TC File

When executing the integrated environment, Turbo C first looks for a file called TCCONFIG.TC, which holds the configuration information for the system. You can change the contents of this file by using the **Store** option. With this option, the changes that you make to Turbo C will still be in memory the next time you execute it.

Turbo C looks for the TCCONFIG.TC file first in the current working directory. If Turbo C does not find the file, it then looks in the TURBO directory, should it exist. If you are going to modify TCCONFIG.TC, you should keep a copy of the unmodified file handy in case you need to go back to the default settings later.

Using Other Configuration Files

When you save the changes that you have made to Turbo C, you do not have to save them in the TCCONFIG.TC file. You may specify any file that you desire. When beginning to execute the integrated environment, Turbo C will use the default settings. To load the options you want, simply select the **Options** menu and use the **Retrieve options** option. Then, specify the name of the file that contains the settings you want. The advantage to this approach is that Turbo C's default settings are always available if you should need them, but you still can easily customize Turbo C to your liking.

Some Common Turbo C Library Functions

CHAPTER 15

This chapter discusses a number of the more common or more important Turbo C library functions that have not been fully discussed in an earlier chapter. If you have looked through the library section in *The Turbo C Reference Guide,* you are aware that the number of library functions is quite large and that it is beyond the scope of this book to cover each function. However, those discussed here are the ones that you will need for most programming tasks.

You can group the library functions into the following categories:

- I/O functions
- String and character functions
- Mathematical functions

- Operating-system-related functions
- Dynamic allocation
- Miscellaneous functions

Chapter 10 thoroughly covered the I/O functions and this chapter will not expand their discussion here. This chapter will look at each of the other categories in turn. Keep in mind that some of the functions discussed have been presented in passing earlier. This chapter includes them for a more formal treatment.

Each function description begins with the appropriate header files and then presents the function's prototype. The prototype provides you with a way of knowing what type of argument the function takes and what type of value it returns. The chapter lists the functions alphabetically within their category.

Remember: this chapter only scratches the surface. You should study *The Turbo C Reference Guide* to see what other functions are available.

String and Character Functions

The Turbo C standard library has a rich and varied set of string- and character-handling functions. In C, a string is a null-terminated array of characters. You can find the declarations for the string functions in the header file **string.h**. The character functions use **ctype.h** as their header file.

Because C has no bounds checking on array operations, it is your responsibility as programmer to prevent an array overflow. As the proposed ANSI standard puts it, if an array has overflowed, "the behavior is undefined," which is a simple way of saying that your program is about to crash!

In C, a *printable character* is one that the computer can display on a terminal. Printable characters are usually those between a space (0x20) and a tilde (0xfE). *Control characters* have values between (0) and (0x1F), as well as DEL (0x7F).

You declare the character functions to take an integer argument. However, the function can only use the low-order byte. Generally, you are free to use a character argument because the compiler will automatically elevate it to **int** at the time of the call.

#include "ctype.h"
int isalnum(int ch)

The **isalnum( )** function returns nonzero if its argument is either a letter of the alphabet or a digit. If the character is not alphanumeric, then the function returns 0.

Example

This program checks each character read from **stdin** and reports all alphanumeric ones:

```
#include "ctype.h"
#include "stdio.h"
main()
{
  char ch;

  for(;;) {
    ch = getchar();
    if(ch==' ') break;
    if(isalnum(ch)) printf("%c is alphanumeric\n", ch);
  }
}
```

#include "ctype.h"
int isalpha(int ch)

The **isalpha( )** function returns nonzero if *ch* is a letter of the alphabet; the function returns 0 if *ch* is not a letter.

Example

This program checks each character read from **stdin** and reports all those that are letters of the alphabet:

```
#include "ctype.h"
#include "stdio.h"
main()
{
  char ch;

  for(;;) {
    ch = getchar();
    if(ch==' ') break;
    if(isalpha(ch)) printf("%c is a letter\n", ch);
  }
}
```

#include "ctype.h"
int iscntrl(int ch)

The **iscntrl( )** function returns nonzero if *ch* is between 0 and 0x1F or if *ch* is equal to 0x7F (DEL); the function returns 0 if *ch* is neither of these.

Example

This program checks each character read from **stdin** and reports all those that are control characters.

```
#include "ctype.h"
#include "stdio.h"
main()
{
  char ch;

  for(;;) {
    ch = getchar();
    if(ch==' ') break;
    if(iscntrl(ch)) printf("%c is a control character\n", ch);
  }
}
```

#include "ctype.h"
int isdigit(int ch)

If *ch* is a digit, 0 through 9, the **isdigit( )** function returns nonzero. The function returns 0 if *ch* is not a digit.

Example

This program checks each character read from **stdin** and reports all those that are digits:

```
#include "ctype.h"
#include "stdio.h"
main()
{
  char ch;

  for(;;) {
    ch = getchar();
    if(ch==' ') break;
    if(isdigit(ch)) printf("%c is a digit\n", ch);
  }
}
```

#include "ctype.h"
int isgraph(int ch)

If *ch* is any printable character other than a space, the **isgraph( )** function returns nonzero; if not, the function returns 0. Printable characters are in the range from 0x21 through 0x7E.

Example

This program checks each character read from **stdin** and reports all those that are printable characters.

```
#include "ctype.h"
#include "stdio.h"
main()
{
  char ch;

  for(;;) {
    ch = getchar();
    if(ch==' ') break;
    if(isgraph(ch)) printf("%c is a printing character\n",ch);
  }
}
```

#include "ctype.h"
int islower(int ch)

If *ch* is a lowercase letter (a to z), the **islower( )** function returns nonzero; if not, the function returns 0.

Example

This program checks each character read from **stdin** and reports all those that are lowercase letters:

```
#include "ctype.h"
#include "stdio.h"
main()
{
  char ch;

  for(;;) {
    ch = getchar();
    if(ch==' ') break;
    if(islower(ch)) printf("%c is lowercase\n", ch);
  }
}
```

#include "ctype.h"
int isprint(int ch)

The **isprint( )** function returns nonzero if *ch* is a printable character, which could also be a space; the function returns 0 if *ch* is nonprintable. Printable characters are often in the range 0x20 through 0x7E.

Example

This program checks each character read from **stdin** and reports all those that are printable.

```
#include "ctype.h"
#include "stdio.h"
main()
{
  char ch;

  for(;;) {
    ch = getchar();
    if(ch==' ') break;
    if(isprint(ch)) printf("%c is printable\n", ch);
  }
}
```

#include "ctype.h"
int ispunct(int ch)

The **ispunct( )** function returns nonzero if *ch* is a punctuation character, except a space; the function returns 0 if *ch* is another type of character. The term *punctuation*, as defined by this function, includes all printing characters that are neither alphanumeric nor a space.

Example

This program checks each character read from **stdin** and reports all those that are punctuation:

```
#include "ctype.h"
#include "stdio.h"
main()
{
  char ch;

  for(;;) {
    ch = getchar();
    if(ch==' ') break;
    if(ispunct(ch)) punctf("%c is punctuation\n", ch);
  }
}
```

#include "ctype.h"
int isspace(int ch)

The **isspace( )** function returns nonzero if *ch* is either a space, tab, or newline character; the function returns 0 if *ch* is none of these characters.

Example

This program checks each character read from **stdin** and reports all those that are white-space characters:

```
#include "ctype.h"
#include "stdio.h"
main()
{
  char ch;

  for(;;) {
    ch = getchar();
    if(ch==' ') break;
    if(isspace(ch)) spacef("%c is white-space\n", ch);
  }
}
```

#include "ctype.h"
int isupper(int ch)

The **isupper( )** function returns nonzero if *ch* is an uppercase letter (A to Z); the function returns 0 if *ch* is any other character.

Example

This program checks each character read from **stdin** and reports all those that are uppercase letters:

```
#include "ctype.h"
#include "stdio.h"
main()
{
  char ch;

  for(;;) {
    ch = getchar();
    if(ch==' ') break;
    if(isupper(ch)) printf("%c is uppercase\n", ch);
  }
}
```

#include "ctype.h"
int isxdigit(int ch)

The **isxdigit( )** function returns nonzero if *ch* is a hexadecimal digit; the function returns 0 if *ch* is not. A hexadecimal digit will be in one of these ranges: A to F, a to f, or 0 to 9.

Example

This program checks each character read from **stdin** and reports all those that are hexadecimal digits.

```
#include "ctype.h"
#include "stdio.h"
main()
{
  char ch;

  for(;;) {
    ch = getchar();
    if(ch==' ') break;
    if(isxdigit(ch)) xdigitf("%c is hexadecimal \n", ch);
  }
}
```

#include "string.h"
char *strcat(char *str1, char *str2)

The **strcat( )** function concatenates a copy of *str2* to *str1*, and terminates *str1* with a null. The first character of *str2* overwrites the null terminator that originally ended *str1*. The operation does not affect the string *str2*.

The **strcat( )** function returns *str1*.

Remember that no bounds checking takes place, so you as the programmer are responsible for ensuring that *str1* is large enough to hold both its original contents and the contents of *str2*.

Example

This program appends the first string read from **stdin** to the second. For example, if the user enters **hello** and **there**, the program will print **therehello**.

```
#include "string.h"
main()
{
  char s1[80], s2[80];

  gets(s1);
  gets(s2);
  strcat(s2, s1);
  printf(s2);
}
```

#include "string.h"
char *strchr(char *str, int ch)

The **strchr()** function returns a pointer to the first occurrence of the low-order byte of *ch* in the string that *str* points to. If the function does not find a match, it returns a null pointer.

Example .

This program prints the string **is a test** with a space preceding the string:

```
#include "string.h"
main()
{
  char *p;

  p = strchr("this is a test", (int) ' ');
  printf(p);
}
```

#include "string.h"
int strcmp(char *str1, char *str2)

The **strcmp()** function lexicographically compares two null-terminated strings and returns an integer based on the outcome, as shown here:

Value	Meaning
Less than 0	*str1* is less than *str2*
0	*str1* is equal to *str2*
Greater than 0	*str1* is greater than *str2*

Example

You can use the following function as a password-verification routine. It will return 0 upon failure, and 1 upon success.

```
password()
{
  char s[80], *strcmp();

  printf("enter password: ");
  gets(s);

  if(strcmp(s,"pass")) {
    printf("invalid password\n");
    return 0;
  }
  return 1;
}
```

#include "string.h"
char *strcpy(char *str1, char *str2)

You can use the **strcpy()** function to copy the contents of *str2* into *str1*. The string *str2* must be a pointer to a null-terminated string. The **strcpy()** function returns a pointer to *str1*.

If *str1* and *str2* overlap, the behavior of **strcpy()** is undefined.

Example

The following code fragment will copy "**hello**" into string **str**:

```
char str[80];
strcpy(str, "hello");
```

#include "string.h"
unsigned int strlen(char *str)

The **strlen()** function returns the length of the null-terminated string that *str* points to. The function does not count the null.

Example

The following code fragment will print the number 5 on screen:

```
strcpy(s, "hello");
printf("%d", strlen(s));
```

#include "stdio.h"
*char *strstr(char *str1, char *str2)*

The **strstr( )** function returns a pointer to the first occurrence in the string that *str1* points to of the string that *str2* points to (except *str2*'s null terminator). The function returns a null pointer if it does not find a match.

Example

This program displays the message **is is a test**.

```
#include "string.h"
main()
{
  char *p;

  p = strstr("this is a test","is");
  printf(p);
}
```

#include "string.h"
*char *strtok(char *str1, char *str2)*

The **strtok( )** function returns a pointer to the next token in the string that *str1* points to. The characters making up the string pointed to by *str2* are the delimiters that determine the token. The function returns a null pointer when there is no token to return.

The first time that **strtok( )** is called, the call actually uses *str1*. Subsequent calls use a null pointer for the first argument. In this way, the function can reduce the entire string to its tokens.

It is important to understand that the **strtok( )** function modifies the string that *str1* points to. Each time that the function finds a token, it places a null where it found the delimiter. In this way, **strtok( )** can continue to advance through the string.

You can use a different set of delimiters for each call to **strtok( )**.

Example

This program reduces the string "**The summer soldier, the sunshine patriot**" to tokens, with spaces and commas being the delimiters. The output will be

The¦summer¦soldier¦the¦sunshine¦patriot

```
#include "string.h"
main()
{
  char *p;

  p = strtok("The summer soldier, the sunshine patriot"," ");
  printf(p);
  do {
    p = strtok('\0', ", ");
    if(p) printf("¦%s", p);
  } while(p);
}
```

#include "ctype.h"
int tolower(int ch)

The **tolower( )** function returns the lowercase equivalent of *ch* if *ch* is a letter; the function returns *ch* unchanged if *ch* is not a letter.

Example

This fragment displays **q**:

```
putchar(tolower('Q'));
```

#include "ctype.h"
int toupper(int ch)

The **toupper( )** function returns the uppercase equivalent of *ch* if *ch* is a letter; the function returns *ch* unchanged if *ch* is not a letter.

Example

This fragment displays **A**:

```
putchar(toupper('a'));
```

The Mathematics
Functions

Turbo C contains several mathematics functions that take **double** arguments and return **double** values. These functions fall into the following categories:

- Trigonometric functions
- Hyperbolic functions
- Exponential and logarithmic functions
- Miscellaneous

All of the mathematics functions require you to include the header **math.h** in any program that uses them. In addition to declaring the mathematics functions, this header defines three macros called **EDOM, ERANGE,** and **HUGE—VAL**. If an argument to a mathematics function is not in the domain for which it is defined, then the function returns 0 and sets the global **errno** equal to **EDOM**. If a routine produces a result that is too large to be represented by a **double**, an overflow occurs. This causes the routine to return **HUGE—VAL** and sets **errno** to **ERANGE**, which indicates a range error. If an underflow happens, the routine returns 0 and sets **errno** to **ERANGE**.

#include "math.h"
double acos(double arg)

The **acos( )** function returns the arc cosine of *arg*. The argument to **acos( )** must be in the range of −1 through 1; if not, a domain error will occur.

Example

This program prints the arc cosines, in increments of one-tenth, of the values −1 through 1:

```
#include "math.h"

main()
{
  double val = -1.0;

  do {
    printf("arc cosine of %f is %f\n", val, acos(val));
    val += 0.1;
  } while(val<=1.0);
}
```

#include "math.h"
double asin(double arg)

The **asin( )** function returns the arc sine of *arg*. The argument to **asin( )** must be in the range −1 through 1; if not, a domain error will occur.

Example

This program prints the arc sines, in increments of one-tenth, of the values −1 through 1:

```
#include "math.h"

main()
{
  double val=-1.0;

  do {
    printf("arc sine of %f is %f\n", val, asin(val));
    val += 0.1;
  } while(val<=1.0);
}
```

#include "math.h"
double atan(double arg)

The **atan( )** function returns the arc tangent of *arg*.

Example

This program prints the arc tangents, in increments of one-tenth, of the values −1 through 1:

```
#include "math.h"

main()
{
  double val=-1.0;

  do {
    printf("arc tangent of %f is %f\n", val, atan(val));
    val += 0.1;
  } while(val<=1.0);
}
```

#include "math.h"
double atan2(double y, double x)

The **atan2()** function returns the arc tangent of y/x. The function uses the signs of its arguments to compute the quadrant of the return value.

Example

This program prints the arc tangents, in increments of one-tenth, of y, of the values −1 through 1:

```
#include "math.h"

main()
{
  double y=-1.0;

  do {
    printf("atan2 of %f is %f\n", val, atan2(y, 1.0));
    y += 0.1;
  } while(y<=1.0);
}
```

#include "math.h"
double ceil(double num)

The **ceil()** function returns the smallest integer, which is represented as a **double** that is not less than *num*. For example, given 1.02, **ceil()** would return 2.0. Given −1.02, **ceil()** would return −1.

Example

This fragment prints **10** on screen:

```
printf("%f", ceil(9.9));
```

#include "math.h"
double cos(double arg)

The **cos()** function returns the cosine of *arg*. The value of *arg* must be in radians.

Example

This program prints the cosines, in increments of one-tenth, of the values −1 through 1:

```
#include "math.h"

main()
{
```

```
double val=-1.0;

do {
  printf("cosine of %f is %f\n", val, cos(val));
  val += 0.1;
} while(val<=1.0);
}
```

#include "math.h"
double cosh(double arg)

The **cosh( )** function returns the hyperbolic cosine of *arg*. The value of *arg* must be in radians.

Example

This program prints the hyperbolic cosines, in increments of one-tenth, of the values -1 through 1:

```
#include "math.h"

main()
{
  double val=-1.0;

  do {
    printf("hyperbolic cosine of %f is %f\n", val, cosh(val));
    val += 0.1;
  } while(val<=1.0);
}
```

#include "math.h"
double exp(double arg)

The **exp( )** function returns the natural logarithm e raised to the *arg* power.

Example

This fragment displays the value of e (rounded to 2.718282):

```
printf("value of e to the first: %f", exp(1.0));
```

#include "math.h"
double fabs(double num)

The **fabs( )** function returns the absolute value of *num*.

Example

This program prints **1.0 1.0** on screen:

```
#include "math.h"
main()
{
  printf("%1.1f %1.1f", fabs(1.0), fabs(-1.0));
}
```

#include "math.h"
double floor(double num)

The **floor( )** function returns the largest integer, which is represented as a **double**, that is not greater than *num*. For example, given 1.02, **floor( )** would return 1.0. Given −1.02, **floor( )** would return −2.0.

Example

This fragment prints **10** on screen:

```
printf("%f", floor(10.9));
```

#include "math.h"
double log(double num)

The **log( )** function returns the natural logarithm for *num*. A domain error occurs if *num* is negative, while a range error occurs if the argument is 0.

Example

This program prints the natural logarithms for the numbers 1 through 10:

```
#include "math.h"

main()
{
  double val=1.0;

  do {
    printf("%f %f\n", val, log(val));
    val++;
  } while (val<11.0);
}
```

#include "math.h"
double log10(double num)

The **log10( )** function returns the base 10 logarithm for *num*. A domain error occurs if *num* is negative, while a range error occurs if the argument is 0.

Example

This program prints the base 10 logarithms for the numbers 1 through 10:

```
#include "math.h"

main()
{
```

```
    double val=1.0;

    do {
      printf("%f %f\n", val, log10(val));
      val++;
    } while (val<11.0);
}
```

#include "math.h"
double pow(double base, double exp)

The **pow( )** function returns *base* raised to the *exp* power (*base^exp*). A domain error occurs if *base* is 0 and if *exp* is less than or equal to 0. A domain error may also occur if *base* is negative and *exp* is not an integer. An overflow produces a range error.

Example

This program prints the first 10 powers of 10:

```
#include "math.h"

main()
{
  double x=10.0, y=0.0;

  do {
    printf("%f",pow(x, y));
    y++;
  } while(y<11);
}
```

#include "math.h"
double sin(double arg)

The **sin( )** function returns the sine of *arg*. The value of *arg* must be in radians.

Example

This program prints the sines, in increments of one-tenth, of the values −1 through 1.

```
#include "math.h"

main()
{
  double val=-1.0;

  do {
    printf("sine of %f is %f\n", val, sin(val));
    val += 0.1;
  } while(val<=1.0);
}
```

#include "math.h"
double sinh(double arg)

The **sinh( )** function returns the hyperbolic sine of *arg*. The value of *arg* must be in radians.

Example

This program prints the hyperbolic sines, in increments of one-tenth, of the values −1 through 1.

```
#include "math.h"

main()
{
  double val=-1.0;

  do {
    printf("hyperbolic sine of %f is %f\n", val, sinh(val));
    val += 0.1;
  } while(val<=1.0);
}
```

#include "math.h"
double sqrt(double num)

The **sqrt( )** function returns the square root of *num*. If you call **sqrt( )** with a negative argument, a domain error will occur.

Example

This fragment prints 4 on screen:

```
printf("%f", sqrt(16.0));
```

#include "math.h"
double tan(double arg)

The **tan( )** function returns the tangent of *arg*. The value of *arg* must be in radians.

Example

This program prints the tangent, in increments of one-tenth, of the values -1 through 1:

```
#include "math.h"

main()
{
  double val=-1.0;

  do {
    printf("tangent of %f is %f\n", val, tan(val));
    val += 0.1;
  } while(val<=1.0);
}
```

#include "math.h"
double tanh(double arg)

The **tanh( )** function returns the hyperbolic tangent of *arg*. The value of *arg* must be in radians.

Example

This program prints the hyperbolic tangent, in increments of one-tenth, of the values −1 through 1:

```
#include "math.h"

main()
{
  double val=-1.0;

  do {
    printf("Hyperbolic tangent of %f is %f\n", val, tanh(val));
    val += 0.1;.
  } while(val<=1.0);
}
```

Operating-System-Related
Functions

This section covers those functions that in one way or another are more operating-system-sensitive than others. Of the functions found in Turbo C's library, these functions include the time and date functions, and those functions that allow direct operating-system interfacing.

The time and date functions require the header **time.h**. It defines two types. The type **time_t** can represent the system time and date as a long integer, which is called the *calendar time*. The structure type **tm** holds the date and time broken down into its elements. Here is the definition of the **tm** structure:

```
struct tm {
  int tm_sec;  /* seconds, 0-59 */
  int tm_min;  /* minutes, 0-59 */
  int tm_hour; /* hours, 0-23 */
  int tm_mday; /* day of the month, 1-31 */
  int tm_mon;  /* months since Jan, 0-11 */
  int tm_year; /* years from 1900 */
  int tm_wday; /* days since Sunday, 0-6 */
  int tm_yday; /* days since Jan 1, 0-365 */
  int tm_isdst /* Daylight Savings Time indicator */
}
```

The value of **tm—isdst** will be positive if daylight-savings time is in effect, 0 if it is not in effect, and negative if there is no information available. When represented in this way, the value of **tm—isdst** is referred to as the *broken-down time.*

The PC-DOS interfacing functions that Turbo C defines require the header **dos.h,** which defines a union **REGS** that corresponds to the registers of the 8088/86 CPU and is used by some of the system-interfacing functions. REGS is defined as the union of two structures in order to allow either a word or a byte to access each register. Here is **dos.h:**

```
/* dos.h

   Defines structs, unions, macros, and functions for dealing
   with MSDOS and the Intel iAPX86 microprocessor family.

   Copyright (c) Borland International Inc. 1987
   All Rights Reserved.
*/

struct WORDREGS
       {
       unsigned int    ax, bx, cx, dx, si, di, cflag;
       };

struct BYTEREGS
       {
       unsigned char   al, ah, bl, bh, cl, ch, dl, dh;
       };
```

```
union    REGS    {
         struct  WORDREGS x;
         struct  BYTEREGS h;
         };
```

#include "time.h"
char *asctime(struct tm *ptr)

The **asctime( )** function returns a pointer to a string. This string converts the information stored in the structure that *ptr* points to into the following form:

day month date hours:minutes:seconds year **\n \0**

Here is an example:

Wed Jun 19 12:05:34 1999

The compiler generally obtains the structure pointer passed to **asctime( )** from either **localtime( )** or **gmtime( )**.

The buffer that **asctime( )** uses to hold the formatted output string is a statically allocated character array. Turbo C overwrites this buffer each time that the function is called. If you wish to save the contents of the string, you must copy it elsewhere.

Example

This program displays the local time defined by the system:

```
#include "time.h"
#include "stddef.h"
```

```
main()
{
  struct tm *ptr;
  time_t lt;

  lt = time(NULL);
  ptr = localtime(&lt);
  printf(asctime(ptr));
}
```

#include "dos.h" int bdos(int fnum, unsigned dx, unsigned al)

The **bdos()** function is not part of the proposed ANSI standard. You use the **bdos()** function to access the PC-DOS system call that *fnum* specifies. The function first places the value *dx* into the **DX** register and the value *al* into the **AL** register, and then executes an **INT 21H** instruction.

The **bdos()** function returns the value of the **AX** register which PC-DOS uses to return information. You can only use the **bdos()** function to access those system calls that either take no arguments or that require only **DX**, **AL**, or both for their arguments.

Example

This program reads characters directly from the keyboard, bypassing all of C's I/O functions, until the user types a carriage return:

```
/* do raw keyboard reads */
#include "dos.h"

main()
{
  char ch;

  while((ch=bdos(1,0,0))!=\n) ;
}
```

#include "time.h"
char *ctime(long time)

The **ctime( )** function returns a pointer to a string of the form

day month date hours:minutes:seconds year \n \0

given a pointer to the calendar time. You generally can obtain the calendar time through a call to **time( )**. The **ctime( )** function is equivalent to

```
asctime(localtime(time))
```

The buffer that **ctime( )** uses to hold the formatted output string is a statically allocated character array. Turbo C overwrites the buffer each time that the function is called. If you wish to save the contents of the string, you must copy it elsewhere.

Example

This program displays the local time defined by the system:

```
#include "time.h"
#include "stddef.h"

main()
{
   time_t lt;

   lt = time(NULL);
   printf(ctime(lt));
}
```

#include "time.h"
double difftime(time _t time2, time _t time1)

The **difftime( )** function returns the difference, in seconds, between *time1* and *time2*. Thus, the function returns the result of *time2* minus *time1*.

Example

This program times the number of seconds that the empty **for** loop needs to go from 0 to 500000.

```
#include "time.h"
#include "stddef.h"

main()
{
  time_t start,end;
  long unsigned int t;

  start = time(NULL);
  for(t=0; t<500000; t++) ;
  end = time(NULL);
  printf("loop required %f seconds\n", difftime(end, start));
}
```

#include "time.h"
struct tm *gmtime(time—t time)

The **gmtime( )** returns a pointer, in the form of a **tm** structure, to the broken-down form of *time*. The time is represented in Greenwich mean time. Generally, you can obtain the *time* value through a call to **time( )**.

The structure that **gmtime( )** uses to hold the broken-down time is statically allocated, and is overwritten each time that the function is called. If you wish to save the contents of the structure, you must copy it elsewhere.

Example

This program prints both the local time and the Greenwich mean time of the system:

```
#include "time.h"
#include "stddef.h"

/* print local and GM time */
main()
{
```

```
struct tm *local, *gm;
time_t t;

t = time(NULL);
local = localtime(&t);
printf("Local time and date: %s", asctime(local));
gm = gmtime(&t);
printf("Greenwich mean time and date: %s",gmtime(gm));
}
```

#include "dos.h"
int int86(int int__num, union REGS
*in__regs, union REGS *out__regs)

The **int86( )** function is not part of the proposed ANSI standard. You use the **int86( )** function to execute a software interrupt that *int num* specifies. The function first copies the contents of the union *in__regs* into the register of the processor, and then executes the proper interrupt.

Upon return, the union *out__regs* will contain the values of the registers that the CPU has upon return from the interrupt.

The union **REGS** is defined in the header **dos.h**.

Example

The **int86( )** function is often used to call ROM routines in the IBM PC. For example, this function executes an **INT 10H** function code 0 that causes the video mode to be set to that specified by the argument **mode**:

```
#include "dos.h"

set_mode(mode)
char mode;
{
  union REGS in, out;

  in.h.al = mode;
  in.h.ah = 0;  /* set mode function number */

  int86(0x10, &in, &out);
}
```

#include "dos.h"
int intdos(union REGS *in_regs,
union REGS *out_regs)

The **intdos( )** function is not part of the proposed ANSI standard. You use the **intdos( )** function to access the PC-DOS system call specified by the contents of the union pointed to by *in_regs*. The function executes an **INT 21H** instruction, and places the outcome of the operation in the union that *out_regs* points to. The **intdos( )** function returns the value of the **AX** register, which PC-DOS uses to return information.

You use the **intdos( )** function to access those system calls that either require arguments in registers other than **DX**, **AL**, or both, or that return information in a register other than **AX**.

The union **REGS** defines the registers of the 8088/86 family of processors, and is found in the **dos.h** header.

Example

This program reads the time directly from the system clock, bypassing all of C's time functions:

```
#include "dos.h"

main()
{
  union REGS in, out;

  in.h.ah = 0x2c;  /* get time function number */
  intdos(&in, &out);
  printf("time is %.2d:%.2d:%.2d",out.h.ch, out.h.cl, out.h.dh);
}
```

#include "time.h"
struct tm *localtime(time_t *time)

The **localtime( )** function returns a pointer, in the form of a **tm** structure, to the broken-down form of *time*. The *time* value is represented in *localtime*.

Generally, you can obtain the *time* value through a call to **time()**.

The structure that **localtime()** uses to hold the broken-down time is statically allocated and is overwritten each time that the function is called. If you wish to save the contents of the structure, you must copy it elsewhere.

Example

This program prints both the local time and the Greenwich mean time of the system:

```
/* print local and Greenwich mean time */
main()
{
  struct tm *local, *local;
  time_t t;

  t = time(NULL);
  local = localtime(&t);
  printf("Local time and date: %s", asctime(local));
  local = gmtime(&t);
  printf("Greenwich mean time and date: %s", asctime(local));
}
```

#include "time.h"
time_t time(time_t time)

The **time()** function returns the current calendar time of the system. If the system has no time, then the function returns −1.

You can call the **time()** function either with a null pointer or with a pointer to a variable of type **time_t**. If you use the latter, then the function will also assign the calendar time to the argument.

Example

This program displays the local time that the system defines:

```
#include "time.h"
#include "stddef.h"

main()
{
  struct tm *ptr;
  time_t lt;

  lt = time(NULL);
  ptr = localtime(&lt);
  printf(asctime(ptr));
}
```

Dynamic Allocation

A Turbo C program uses one of two primary ways to store information in the main memory of the computer. The first way uses global and local variables—including arrays and structures. In the case of global variables and **static** local variables, the storage is fixed throughout the run-time of your program. For dynamic local variables, Turbo C allocates storage from the stack space of the computer. Although Turbo C efficiently implements these variables, they require the programmer to know, in advance, the amount of storage needed for every situation. The second way that Turbo C can store information is through the use of Turbo C's dynamic-allocation system. In this way, Turbo C allocates storage for information from the free memory area as needed. The free memory region lies between your program with its permanent storage area, and the stack.

The proposed ANSI standard specifies that the header information necessary to the dynamic-allocation system will be in **stdlib.h**. However, Turbo C also places the allocation-header information into **alloc.h**. This book will use the proposed ANSI standard's approach because it is portable.

#include "stdlib.h"
void *calloc(unsigned num, unsigned size)

The **calloc()** function returns a pointer to the allocated memory. The amount of memory allocated is equal to *num*size*. Thus, **calloc()** allocates sufficient memory for an array of *num* objects of size *size*.

The **calloc()** function returns a pointer to the first byte of the allocated region. If there is not enough memory to satisfy the request, the function returns a null pointer. It is always important to verify that the return value is not a null pointer before you attempt to use it.

Example

This function returns a pointer to a dynamically allocated array of 100 **float**s:

```
#include "stdlib.h"

float *get_mem()
{
  float *p;

  p = (float *) calloc(100, sizeof(float));
  if(!p) {
    printf("allocation failure - aborting");
    exit(1);
  }
  return p;
}
```

#include "stdlib.h" /* malloc.h
in some systems */void free(void *ptr)

The **free()** function returns the memory that *ptr* points to back to the heap. This process makes the memory available for future allocation.

It is imperative that you only call **free()** with a pointer that was previously allocated by using one of the dynamic-allocation system's functions, such as **malloc()** or **calloc()**. Using an invalid pointer in the call most likely will destroy the memory-management mechanism and cause a system crash.

Example

This program first allocates room for the user-entered strings, and then frees it:

```
#include "stdlib.h"

main()
{
  char *str[100];
  int i;

  for(i=0; i<100; i++) {
    if((str[i] = (char *)malloc(128))==NULL) {
      printf("allocation error - aborting");
      exit(1);
    }
    gets(str[i]);
  }

  /* now free the memory */
  for(i=0; i<100; i++) free(str[i]);
}
```

#include "stdlib.h"
void *malloc(unsigned size)

The **malloc()** function returns a pointer to the first byte of a region of memory of size *size* that you have allocated from the heap. If there is insufficient memory in the heap to satisfy the request, **malloc()** returns a null pointer. It is always important to verify that the return value is not a null pointer before you attempt to use it. Attempting to use a null pointer will usually result in a system crash.

Example

This function allocates sufficient memory to hold structures of type **addr**:

```
#include "stdlib.h"

struct addr {
  char name[40];
  char street[40];
  char city[40];
  char state[3];
  char zip[10];
};
  .
  .
  .
struct addr *get_struct()
{
  struct addr *p;

  if((p=(struct addr *)malloc(sizeof(addr)))==NULL) {
    printf("allocation error - aborting");
    exit(1);
  }
  return p;
}
```

#include "stdlib.h"
*void *realloc(void *ptr, unsigned size)*

The **realloc()** function changes the size of the allocated memory that *ptr* points to to that specified by *size*. The value of *size* may be greater or less than the original. The function may return a pointer to the memory block because it may be necessary for **realloc()** to move the block in order to increase its size. If this occurs, the function copies the contents of the old block into the new block and no information is lost.

If there is insufficient free memory in the heap to allocate *size* bytes, then the function returns a null pointer and frees (loses) the original block. This process indicates the importance of verifying the success of a call to **realloc()**.

Example

This program first allocates 17 characters, copies the string "**this is 16 chars**" into them, and then uses **realloc()** to increase the size to 18 in order to place a period at the end of the string:

```
#include "stdlib.h"

main()
{
  char *p;

  p = (char *) malloc(17);
  if(!p) {
    printf("allocation error - aborting");
    exit(1);
  }

  strcpy(p,"this is 16 chars");

  p = realloc(p,18);
  if(!p) {
    printf("allocation error - aborting");
    exit(1);
  }

  strcat(p, ".");

  printf(p);

  free(p);
}
```

Miscellaneous Functions

The functions presented in this section are all of the standard functions that do not easily fit in any other category.

#include "stdlib.h"
void abort()

The **abort()** function causes immediate termination of a program. The function does not flush any files, and returns the value 3 to the calling process, which is usually the operating system.

The primary use of **abort()** is to prevent a runaway program from closing active files.

Example

This program will terminate if the user enters **A**.

```
#include "stdlib.h"

main()
{
  for(;;)
    if(getchar()=='A') abort();
}
```

#include "stdlib.h"
int abs(int num)

The **abs( )** function returns the absolute value of the integer *num*.

Example

This function converts the user-entered numbers into their absolute values:

```
#include "stdlib.h"

get_abs()
{
  char num[80];

  gets(num)
  return abs(atoi(num));
}
```

#include "stdlib.h"
double atof(char *str)

The **atof( )** function converts the string that *str* points to into a **double** value. The string must contain a valid floating-point number. If it does not, the function returns 0.

The number may be terminated by any character that cannot be part of a valid floating-point number. This character may be a white-space character, punctuation (other than periods), or a character other than **E** or **e**. Thus, if you call **atof()** with **100.00HELLO**, the function will return the value 100.00.

Example

This program reads two floating-point numbers and displays their sum:

```
#include "stdlib.h"

main()
{
  char num1[80], num2[80];

  printf("enter first: ");
  gets(num1);
  printf("enter second: ");
  gets(num2);
  printf("the sum is: %f",atoi(num1)+atoi(num2));
}
```

#include "stdlib.h"
int atoi(char *str)

The **atoi()** function converts the string that *str* points to into an **int** value. The string must contain a valid integer number. If it does not, the function returns 0.

The number may be terminated by any character that cannot be part of an integer number. This character may be a white-space character, punctuation, or a character other than **E** or **e**. Thus, if you call **atoi()** with **123.23**, the function will return the integer value 123 and ignore the 0.23 portion.

Example

This program reads two integer numbers and displays their sum:

```
#include "stdlib.h"

main()
{
   char num1[80], num2[80];

   printf("enter first: ");
   gets(num1);
   printf("enter second: ");
   gets(num2);
   printf("the sum is: %d",atoi(num1)+atoi(num2));
}
```

#include "stdlib.h"
int atol(char *str)

The **atol( )** function converts the string that *str* points to into a **long int** value. The string must contain a valid long-integer number. If it does not, the function returns 0.

The number may be terminated by any character that cannot be part of an integer number. This character can be a white-space character, punctuation, or a character other than **E** or **e**. Thus, if you call **atol( )** with **123.23**, the function will return the integer value 123 and will ignore the 0.23 portion.

Example

This program reads two long-integer numbers and displays their sum:

```
#include "stdlib.h"

main()
{
   char num1[80], num2[80];

   printf("enter first: ");
   gets(num1);
   printf("enter second: ");
   gets(num2);
   printf("the sum is: %ld",atol(num1)+atol(num2));
}
```

#include "stdlib.h"
void *bsearch(void *key, void *base,
unsigned num, unsigned size,
int (*compare)())

The **bsearch( )** function performs a binary search on the sorted array that *base* points to, and returns a pointer to the first member that matches the key that *key* points to. Here, *num* specifies the number of elements in the array and *size* describes the size (in bytes) of each element.

The **bsearch( )** function uses the function that *compare* points to to compare an element of the array with the key. The form of the *compare* function must be

*func_name(arg1, arg2)***void** *arg1, *arg2

The function must return the following values:

- A value less than 0 if *arg1* is less than *arg2*
- 0 if *arg1* is equal to *arg2*
- A value greater than 0 if *arg1* is greater than *arg2*

The array must be sorted in ascending order with the lowest address containing the lowest element.

If the array does not contain the key, then **bsearch( )** returns a null pointer.

Example

Assuming buffered keyboard I/O, this program reads characters entered at the keyboard and determines whether they belong to the alphabet:

```
#include "stdlib.h"
#include "ctype.h"
```

```
char *alpha="abcdefghijklmnopqrstuvwxyz";

main()
{
  char ch;
  char *p;
  int comp();

  do {
    printf("enter a character: ");
    scanf("%c%*c",&ch);
    ch = tolower(ch);
    p = (char *) bsearch(&ch,alpha, 26, 1, comp);
    if(p) printf("is in alphabet\n");
    else printf("is not in alphabet\n");
  } while(p);
}

/* compare two characters */
comp(ch, s)
char *ch, *s;
{
  return *ch-*s;
}
```

#include "stdlib.h"
void exit(int status)

The **exit()** function causes immediate, normal termination of a program. The function passes the value of *status* to the calling process, usually the operating system, if the environment supports it. By convention, if the value of *status* is 0, normal program termination is assumed. You may use a nonzero value to indicate an error.

Example

This function performs menu selection for a mailing-list program. If the user selects **Q**, this function terminates the program.

```
menu()
{
  char choice;

  do {
    printf("Enter names (E)\n");
    printf("Delete name (D)\n");
    printf("Print (P)\n");
    printf("Quit (Q)\n");
  } while(!strchr("EDPQ",toupper(ch));
  if(ch=='Q') exit(0);
  return ch;
}
```

#include "stdlib.h"
char *itoa(int num, char *str, int radix)

The proposed ANSI standard does not currently define the **itoa( )** function.

The **itoa( )** function converts the integer *num* into its string equivalent, and places the result in the string that *str* points to. The base of the output string is determined by *radix*, which may be in the range of 2 through 36.

The **itoa( )** function returns a pointer to *str*. Generally, *str* has no error-return value. Be sure to call **itoa( )** with a string of sufficient length to hold the converted result.

The main use of **itoa( )** is to transform integers into strings so that you can send them to a device not directly supported by the normal C I/O system — that is, a nonstream device. You may accomplish the same process by using **sprintf( )**. The reason that this discussion includes **itoa( )** is that its use is quite prevalent throughout older existing code.

Example

This program displays the value of 1423 in hexadecimal, which is 58F:

```
#include "stdlib.h"

main()
{
  char p[20];
```

```
   itoa(1423, p, 16);

   printf(p);
}
```

#include "stdlib.h"
long labs(long num)

The **labs( )** function returns the absolute value of the **long int** *num*.

Example

This function converts the user-entered numbers into their absolute values:

```
#include "stdlib.h"

long int get_labs()
{
  char num[80];

  gets(num)

  return labs(atol(num));
}
```

#include "setjmp.h"
void longjmp(envbuf, val)
jmp—buf envbuf;
int val

The **longjmp( )** function causes program execution to resume at the point of the last call to **setjmp( )**. These two functions are Turbo C's way of providing for a jump between functions. Notice that **longjmp( )** requires the header **setjmp.h**.

The **longjmp( )** function operates by resetting the stack as described in *envbuf*, which must have been set by a prior call to **setjmp( )**. This process causes program execution to resume at the statement after the **setjmp( )** invocation. Thus, you can "trick" the computer into thinking that it never left the function **setjmp( )**. (Here is a graphic explanation. The **longjmp( )** function "warps" across time and memory space to a previous point in your program, without having to perform the normal function-return process.)

The buffer *envbuf* is of type **jmp—buf**, which is defined in the header **setjmp.h**. You must have set the buffer through a call to **setjmp( )** prior to calling **longjmp( )**.

The value of *val* becomes the return value of **setjmp( )** and may be interrogated to determine where the long jump originated from. The only value that **longjmp( )** does not allow is 0.

It is important to understand that you must call the **longjmp( )** function before the **setjmp( )** function returns. If you do not, the result is technically undefined. (Actually, a crash will almost certainly occur.)

By far, the most common use of **longjmp( )** is to return from a deeply nested set of routines when a catastrophic error occurs.

Example

This program prints **1 2 3**.

```
#include "setjmp.h"

jmp_buf ebuf;

main()

{
  char first=1;
  int i;

  printf("1 ");
  i = setjmp(ebuf);
  if(first) {
    first = !first;
    f2();
    printf("this will not be printed");
  }
  printf("%d", i);
}
```

```
f2()
{
  printf("2 ");
  longjmp(ebuf,3);
}
```

#include "stdlib.h"
void qsort(void *base, unsigned num,
unsigned size, int (*compare)())

The **qsort( )** function sorts the array that *base* points to by using a *quicksort*, which was developed by C.A.R. Hoare. The quicksort is generally considered the best general-purpose sorting algorithm. Upon termination, the function will sort the array. Here, *num* specifies the number of elements in the array, and *size* describes the size in bytes of each element.

The **qsort( )** function uses the function that *compare* points to to compare an element of the array with the key. The form of the *compare* function must be

$$func\_name(arg1, arg2) \textbf{ void } *arg1, *arg2;$$

The function must return the following values:

- A value less than 0 if *arg1* is less than *arg2*
- 0 if *arg1* is equal to *arg2*
- A value greater than 0 if *arg1* is greater than *arg2*

The array is sorted into ascending order with the lowest address containing the lowest element.

Example

This program sorts a list of integers and displays the result:

```
#include "stdlib.h"  /* "search.h" in some systems */

int num[10]= {
  1,3,6,5,8,7,9,6,2,0
};

main()
{
  int i, comp();

  printf("original array: ");
  for(i=0; i<10; i++) printf("%d ", num[i]);

  qsort(num, 10, sizeof(int), comp);

  printf("sorted array: ");
  for(i=0; i<10; i++) printf("%d ", num[i]);
}

/* compare the integers */
comp(i, j)
int *i,*j;
{
  return *i-*j;
}
```

#include "stdlib.h"
int rand()

The **rand()** function generates a sequence of pseudorandom numbers. Each time that you call **rand()**, it returns an integer between 0 and **RAND_MAX**.

Example

This program displays ten pseudorandom numbers:

```
#include "stdlib.h"

main()
{
  int i;

  for(i=0; i<10; i++)
    printf("%d ",rand());
}
```

#include "setjmp.h"
int setjmp(jmp—buf envbuf)
jmp—buf envbuf

The **setjmp()** function saves the contents of the system stack in the buffer *envbuf* for later use by **longjmp()**.

The **setjmp()** function returns 0 upon invocation. However, **longjmp()** passes an argument to **setjmp()** during execution, and this value, which is always nonzero, will appear to be the value of **setjmp()** after a call to **longjmp()**.

See the discussion of **longjmp()**, given earlier, for additional information.

Example

This program prints **1 2 3**:

```
#include "setjmp.h"

jmp_buf ebuf;

main()
{
  char first=1;
  int i;
```

```
  printf("1 ");
  i = setjmp(ebuf);
  if(first) {
    first = !first;
    f2();
    printf("this will not be printed");
  }
  printf("%d",i);
}

f2()
{
 printf("2 ");
 longjmp(ebuf, 3);
}
```

#include "stdlib.h"
void srand(unsigned seed)

You use the **srand()** function to set a starting point for the sequence that **rand()** generates. (The **rand()** function returns pseudorandom numbers.)

Generally you use **srand()** to allow multiple program runs that use different sequences of pseudorandom numbers.

Example

This program uses the system time to initialize the **rand()** function randomly by using **srand()**:

```
#include "stdio.h"
#include "stdlib.h"
#include "time.h"

/* Seed rand()with the system time
   and display the first 100 numbers.
*/
main()
{
  int i,stime;
  long  ltime;

  /* get the current calendar time */
```

```
    ltime = time(NULL);
    stime = (unsigned int) ltime/2;
    srand(stime);
    for(i=0; i<10; i++) printf("%d ", rand());
}
```

Miscellaneous Topics

C H A P T E R   1 6

This final chapter covers a number of important topics, which include a brief description of compiling multiple-file programs, compiling from the command line, and Turbo C's standalone **Make** facility. The chapter concludes with a look at the most common C programming errors.

Compiling Multiple-File Programs

As mentioned earlier in this book, most real-world C programs are too large to fit easily into one file. The primary reason for this problem has to do with efficiency considerations. First, extremely large files are difficult to edit.

Second, making a small change in the program requires that you recompile the entire program. Although compiling in Turbo C is very fast, at some point no matter how fast the compiler, the time it takes to compile will become unbearable.

The solution to these problems is to break the program into smaller pieces, compile them, and then link them together. This process is known as *separate compilation and linking*, and forms the backbone of most development efforts.

The methods of creating, compiling, and linking multiple-file programs differ between the integrated-environment version and the command-line version of Turbo C. This section will focus on the integrated environment. The next section will illustrate the command-line approach.

Projects and the *Project* Option

In the Turbo C integrated environment, multiple-file programs are called *projects*. Each project is associated with a *project file*, which determines what files are part of the project. The main menu option **Project** lets you specify a project file. All project files must end with a .PRJ extension.

After you have defined a project file inside the **Project** menu, place in it the names of the files that form the project. For example, if the project file is called **MYPROJ.PRJ** and your project contains the two files **TEST1.C** and **TEST2.C**, you would edit **MYPROJ.PRJ**, and enter the two files **TEST1.C** and **TEST2.C**. Thus **MYPROJ.OBJ** will look like this:

```
TEST1.C
TEST2.C
```

For the sake of discussion, assume that you have not compiled **TEST1.C** or **TEST2.C**. There are two ways to compile and link these files together. First, you can select **Run** from the main menu. When there is a .PRJ file specified in the **Project** option, Turbo C uses this file as its guide during compilation of your program. The compiler reads the contents of the .PRJ file and compiles each file that needs to be compiled to a .OBJ file. Next, Turbo C links those files together and executes the program.

The second way that you can compile a project is to use the built-in **Make** facility. By pressing F9, or by selecting the **Make** option under the main menu option **Compile**, you cause Turbo C to compile and link all files that are specified in the project file. The only difference between the **Make** option and the **Run** option is that **Make** does not execute the program. In fact, you can think of the **Run** option as first performing a **Make** and then executing the .EXE file.

Whenever you **Make** a program, the compiler will actually compile only those files that need to be compiled. Turbo C determines which files these are by checking the time and date associated with each source file and its .OBJ file. If the .C file is newer than the .OBJ file, then Turbo C knows that the .C file has been changed and then recompiles it. If the .C file is older than the .OBJ file, then Turbo C simply uses the .OBJ file. In this situation, the *target* .OBJ file is said to depend upon the .C file. The same sort of dependency is true of the .EXE file: As long as the .EXE file is newer than all of the .OBJ files in the project, then Turbo C does not recompile anything. If the .EXE file is older, Turbo C recompiles any necessary files and relinks the project.

Trying It Yourself

To see how this process works, first select the **Project** option from the main menu and select **Project name**. Turbo C will then prompt you for the name of the project. For this example, use **MYPROJ.PRJ**. Next, using the **File** option, load the file **TEST1.C**. (This file should be new. If not, use a different name.) Enter and save the following code:

```
/* file TEST1.C */

main()
{
  printf("This is file 1.\n");

  count(); /* this is in TEST2.C */
}
```

Next, edit **TEST2.C**. Enter and save this code:

```
/* file TEST2.C */

count()
{
  int i;

  for(i=0; i<10 i++)
    printf("%d ", i);
}
```

Now, you can compile and run the program by selecting the **Run** option. Do so at this time. As you can see, Turbo C compiles both files and links them together automatically. If you select **Run** again, Turbo C merely checks the dates on the files, sees that nothing needs to be recompiled, and runs the program.

Specifying Additional Dependencies

Just as the standard library functions have header files, so may your program. In fact, customized header files are common in C programs that use multiple files because you can use them to declare **extern** variables as well as any #**define**s that your program needs. Since a change to a header file means that you must recompile any file that depends upon that header, it is important to specify this relationship.

To specify a dependency like this, you place the name of the file (or files) inside parentheses on the same line as the dependent file. For example, assume that **MYPROG.H** is a header file that is necessary to **TEST2.C** of the example just given. In this case, **MYPROJ.PRJ** will look like this.

```
TEST1
TEST2 (MYPROG.H)
```

To see how this process might actually work, make **MYPROJ.PRJ** look like the one just shown. Next, modify **TEST1.C** and **TEST2.C** as shown here. (Remember to keep them as separate files.)

```
/* file TEST1.C */
int max;

main()
{
  printf("This is file 1.\n");

  max = 100;
  count(); /* this is in TEST2.C */
}



/* file TEST2.C */

#include "myprog.h"  /* read in the header file */
```

```
count()
{
  int i;

  for(i=0; i<max i++)
    printf("%d ", i);
}
```

Finally, create the header file **MYPROG.H**, as shown here.

```
/* header file MYPROG.H */

extern int max;
```

As you can see, the keyword **extern** is used to prevent Turbo C from creating two separate copies of **max**. The header file simply specifies that *somewhere* your code declares a variable named **max** as an integer.

Now, select the **Run** option. Assuming that you entered everything correctly, the program runs fine. Now, edit the header file, change nothing, but save it back to disk. This process will cause the date of the header file to be newer than its dependent file **TEST2.C**. Now when you select **Run**, Turbo C automatically recompiles **TEST2.C** and relinks the program.

Without a doubt, the project capabilities of Turbo C are among its most important aspects because they let you manage multiple-source-file programs with little difficulty.

The Command-Line Version of Turbo C

If you are new to C, there is no doubt that you will find that using Turbo C's integrated environment provides the easiest way to develop programs. However, if you have been programming for some time and have been using your own editor, you might prefer to use the command-line version of Turbo C. For long-time C programmers, the command-line version represents the traditional method of compilation and linking. In addition, the command-line version of the compiler can do a few things that the integrated-environment version cannot. For example, if you wish to generate an assembly language listing of the code that Turbo C generated, or if you want to use in-line assembly code, you must use the command-line version. The name of the command-line compiler is **TCC.EXE**.

Compiling by Using the Command-Line Compiler

Assume that you have a program called X.C. To compile this program by using the command-line version of Turbo C, your command line with the C> prompt will look like this:

```
C>TCC X.C
```

If there are no errors in the program, this command causes Turbo C to compile and link X.C with the proper library files. This is the simplest form of the command line.

The general form of the command line is

TCC [*option1 option2...optionN*] *fname1 fname2... fnameN*

where *option* refers to either a compiler option or a linker option, and where *fname* is either a C source file, a .OBJ file, or a library file.

All compiler-linker options begin with a dash, or minus sign. Generally, placing a dash after an option turns that option off. Table 16-1 shows the options that are available in the command-line version of Turbo C. Keep in mind that the options are case-sensitive.

For example, to compile X.C with the stack checked for overflow, the command line will look like this:

```
C>TCC -N X.C
```

What's in a Filename?

The Turbo C command-line version does not require the .C extension. For example, both of these command lines function in the same way:

```
C>TCC X.C

C>TCC x
```

Table 16-1. Turbo C's Command-Line Options

Option	Meaning
−A	Recognize ANSI keywords only
−a	Use word alignment for data
−a−	Use byte alignment for data
−B	In-line assembly code in source file
−C	Accept nested comments
−c	Compile to .OBJ only
−Dname	Define a macro-name
−Dname=string	Define and give a value to a macro-name
−d	Merge duplicate strings
−efname	Specify project name
−f	Use floating-point emulation
−f−	No floating-point emulation
−f87	Use 8087
−G	Optimize code for speed
−gN	Stop after *N* warning errors
−Ipath	Specify path to include directory
−iN	Specify identifier length
−jN	Stop after *N* fatal errors
−K	**char** unsigned
−K−	**char** signed
−k	Use standard stack frame
−Lpath	Specify library directory
−M	Create map file
−mc	Use compact-memory model
−mh	Use huge-memory model
−ml	Use large-memory model
−mm	Use medium-memory model
−ms	Use small-memory model
−mt	Use tiny-memory model
−N	Check for stack overflows
−npath	Specify output directory
−O	Optimize for size
−p	Use Pascal calling conventions
−p−	Use C calling conventions
−r	Use register variables
−S	Generate assembly code output
−Uname	Undefine a macro-name
−w	Display warning errors (see *Turbo C Reference Guide*)
−w−	Do not display warning errors
−y	Embed line numbers into object code
−Z	Register optimization on
−z	Specify segment names (see *Turbo C Reference Guide*)
−1	Generate 80186/80286 instructions
−1−	Do not generate 80186/80286 instructions

You can compile a file with an extension other than .C by specifying its extension. For example, to compile **X.TMP**, the command line will look like this.

```
C>TCC X.TMP
```

You may specify additional object files to link in with the source file that you are compiling by specifying them after the source file. All of these files must have been previously compiled and have a .OBJ extension. For example, if your program consists of the files **P1**, **P2**, and **P3**, and if you have already compiled **P2** and **P3** to .OBJ files, then the following command line will first compile **P1.C**, and then link it with **P2.OBJ** and **P3.OBJ**:

```
C>TCC P1 P2.OBJ P3.OBJ
```

If you have additional libraries other than those that Turbo C supplies, you can specify them by using the .LIB extension.

The example just given assumed **P2.OBJ** and **P3.OBJ** existed. The way to produce these files from their .C source files is to compile each by using the −c compiler option. This option causes the compiler to create .OBJ files but no link process takes place.

The executable output file that the linker produces generally has the name of the source file being compiled with a .EXE extension. However, you can specify a different name by using the −e compiler option. The name that follows −e is the name of the file that the compiler will use as the executable file. There can be no spaces between the −e and the filename. For example, this command line causes the compiler to compile the file **TEST.C** and to create an executable file called **RUN.EXE**.

```
C>TCC -eRUN test
```

A Brief Overview
of the Standalone Make

Turbo C comes with a standalone version of **Make** that you can use with the command-line version of Turbo C. **Make** is a sophisticated program; this section only introduces you to it. If you intend to use the command-line compiler, then you should carefully study Appendix D of *The Turbo C Reference Guide*, which fully describes **Make**.

Make is a utility program that, when you are using the command-line version of Turbo C, automates the recompilation process for large programs that are comprised of several files. Its operation is similar in nature to the **Project/Make** facilities of the Turbo C integrated environment except that it is more flexible. In the course of program development, you will make many small changes to some of the files before you recompile and test the program. The trouble is that it is easy to forget which file needs to be recompiled. This situation leads to either a recompilation of all files — a waste of time — or accidentally not recompiling a file that should be, which potentially adds several hours of frustrating debugging. The **Make** program solves this problem by automatically recompiling only those files that you have altered.

Make is driven by a *make file*, which contains a list of *target files, dependent files*, and commands. A target file requires its dependent file or files to produce it. For example, **T.C** would be the dependent file of **T.OBJ** because Turbo C requires **T.C** to make **T.OBJ**. Like its cousin in the integrated environment, **Make** works by comparing the date and time between a dependent file and its target file. If the target file has a date that is older than that of its dependent file, or if it does not exist, then Turbo C executes the specified command sequence. The general form of the make file is

> *target-file1 : dependent-file list*
> *command-sequence*
> *target-file2 : dependent-file list*
> *command-sequence*
> *target-file3 : dependent-file list*
> *command-sequence*
> :
> :
> *target-fileN : dependent-file list*
> *command-sequence*

The target filename must start in the leftmost column, and must be followed by a colon and a list of dependent files. At least one space or tab must precede the command sequence that is associated with each target. Comments are preceded by #, and may follow the dependent-file list and the command sequence. If comments appear on a line of their own, they must start in the leftmost column. You must separate each target file specification from the next by using at least one blank line.

To see how **Make** works, try the following example, which uses a simple program. The program is divided into four, files called **test.h, test.C, test2.c,** and **test3.c**, as shown in Figure 16-1.

```
test.h    │ extern int count;                          │

          │ int count=0;                               │
          │                                            │
          │ main()                                     │
          │ {                                          │
test.c    │   printf("count=%d\n",count);              │
          │   test2();                                 │
          │   printf("count=%d\n",count);              │
          │   test3();                                 │
          │   printf("count=%d\n",count);              │
          │ }                                          │

          │ #include "test.h"                          │
          │                                            │
test2.c   │ test2()                                    │
          │ {                                          │
          │    count=30;                               │
          │ }                                          │

          │ #include "test.h"                          │
          │                                            │
test3.c   │ test3()                                    │
          │ {                                          │
          │    count=-100;                             │
          │ }                                          │
```

Figure 16-1.   A simple four-file program

A make file that you can use to recompile the program when you make changes looks like this:

```
# recreate if header file has changed
test.exe: test.h
        tcc -c test
        tcc -c test2
```

```
        tcc test test2.obj test3.obj

test.obj: test.c # test.c changed
        tcc test test2.obj test3.obj

test2.obj: test2.c # test2.c changed
        tcc -etest test2 test.obj test3.obj

test3.obj: test3.c # test3.c changed
        tcc -etest test3 test.obj test2.obj
```

If the name of this file is **MAKEFILE,** then your command line would look like this:

```
C>MAKE
```

This command causes the compiler to compile the necessary modules and create an executable program. If you specify no other filename, **Make** executes whatever is in the file called **MAKEFILE,** if it exists. To specify a different make file, use the −**f** compiler option, which tells **Make** to use the file that follows as its make file. For example, this command line tells **Make** to use the **MYMAKE** make file:

```
C>MAKE -fMYMAKE
```

Order is important in the make file because **Make** moves through the list in only the forward direction. For example, imagine that you changed the make file to look like this:

```
# this makefile is incorrect
test.obj: test.c # test.c changed
        tcc test test2.obj test3.obj

test2.obj: test2.c # test2.c changed
        tcc -etest test2 test.obj test3.obj

test3.obj: test3.c # test3.c changed
        tcc -etest test3 test.obj test2.obj

# recreate if header file has changed
test.exe: test.h
        tcc -c test
        tcc -c test2
        tcc test test2.obj test3.obj
```

This file will no longer work correctly when you change the file **test.h** and any other source file because changing a source file causes Turbo C to create a new **test.exe**. Therefore, the date of the make file will no longer be older than the date of **test.h**.

Make allows Turbo C to define macros in the make file. These macronames are simply placeholders for the information that will actually be determined either by a command-line specification or by the macro's definition in the make file. Turbo C defines macros according to this general form:

$$macro\text{-}name = definition$$

If there will be any white space in the macro *definition*, you must enclose the *definition* in double quotes.

After you have defined a macro, you use it in the make file like this:

$$\$(macro\text{-}name)$$

Each time that Turbo C encounters this, it substitutes the definition link to the macro.

Some Common
Programming Errors

As good as any computer language is, you can still make programming errors. To paraphrase Thomas Edison, programming is 10% inspiration and 90% debugging! All good programmers are good debuggers. Certain types of bugs can occur easily while you use C, and these bugs are the topic of this section.

Order-of-Process Errors

The increment and decrement operators are used in most programs in C, and the order in which the operation takes place is affected by whether these operators precede or follow the variable. Consider the following:

```
y = 10;          y = 10;

x = y++;         x = ++y;
```

These two sets of statements are not the same. The first one assigns the value of 10 to **x** and then increments **y**. The second one increments **y** to 11 and then assigns the value 11 to **x**. Therefore, in the first set, **x** contains 10; in the second set, **x** contains 11. The rule is that increment and decrement operations will occur before other operations if they precede the operand; they occur later if they follow the operand.

An order-of-process error usually occurs through changes to an existing statement. For example, you may enter the statement

```
x = *p++;
```

which assigns to **x** the value that **p** points to and then increments the pointer **p**. However, imagine that later you decide that **x** really needs the square of the value that **p** points to times the value pointed to by **p**. To do this, you try the statement

```
x = *p++ * (*p);
```

However, this statement cannot work because the statement given earlier has already incremented **p**. The solution is to write

```
x = *p * (*p++);
```

Errors like this can be very hard to find. There may be clues such as loops that do not run correctly or routines that produce results that are off by one. If you have any doubt about a statement, recode it in another way that you are sure about.

Pointer Problems

A common error in C programs is the misuse of pointers. Pointer problems fall into two general categories: those problems that arise from misunderstanding of indirection and the pointer operators, and those that develop out of the accidental use of invalid pointers. The solution to the first problem is to understand the C language; the solution to the second problem is always to verify the validity of a pointer before you use it.

Here is a typical error that beginning C programmers make. (Don't try this code unless you are willing to reformat your hard disk!!!)

```
#include "stdlib.h"

main()  /* this program is WRONG */
{
  char *p;

  *p = malloc(100); /* this line is wrong */

  gets(p);
  printf(p);

}
```

This program will crash the computer by overwriting the vector-interrupt table that helps to drive the operating system! The reason for the crash is that the code does not assign to **p** the address that **malloc( )** returns, but rather assigns the address to the memory location that **p** points to, which is 0. This is most certainly not what is wanted. To correct this program, you must substitute

```
p = malloc(100); /* this is correct */
```

for the wrong line.

The program also has a second, more insidious, error. There is no run-time check on the address that **malloc( )** returns. Remember, if memory is exhausted, then **malloc( )** will return NULL, which is never a valid pointer in C. The malfunction that this type of bug causes is difficult to find because it occurs rarely, when an allocation request fails. The best way to handle this error is to prevent it. Here is a corrected version of the program, which includes a check for pointer validity:

```
#include "stdlib.h"

main()  /* this program is now correct */
{
  char *p;

  p = malloc(100); /* this is correct */

  if(p==NULL) {
    printf("out of memory\n");
    exit(1);
  }

  gets(p);
  printf(p);
}
```

The terrible problem with "wild" pointers is that they are so hard to track down. If you are making assignments to a pointer variable that does not contain a valid pointer address, then your program may appear to function correctly some of the time and crash at other times. The smaller your program is, the more likely it will run correctly, even with a stray pointer, because very little memory is in use and the odds of that memory being used by something else are statistically small. As your program grows, failures will become more common—but you will be thinking about current additions or changes to your program, and not about pointer errors. Hence, you will tend to look in the wrong spot for the bug.

The sign of a pointer problem is that errors tend to be erratic. Your program will work correctly one time, and incorrectly another. Sometimes other variables will contain garbage for no explainable reason. If these problems occur, check your pointers. As a matter of procedure, you should always check all pointers when bugs begin to occur.

As consolation, remember that, while pointers can be troublesome, they are also one of the most powerful and useful aspects of the C language and are worth whatever trouble they may occasionally cause you. Make the effort early on to learn to use them correctly.

One final point to remember about pointers is that you must initialize them before you use them. Consider the following code fragment:

```
int *x;

*x = 100;
```

Using this code will be a disaster because you do not know where **x** is pointing and, if you assign a value to that unknown location, you are probably destroying something of value —such as other code or data for your program.

Redefining Functions

You can, but you should not, call your functions by the same names as those used in the C standard library. Turbo C will use your function over the one in the library. One of the worst occurrences of the redefinition problem happens when you redefine a standard library function but do *not* use the standard function directly in your program. Instead, another standard function uses it indirectly.

The only way to avoid redefinition problems is never to give a function that you write the same name as one in the standard library. If you are unsure, append your initials to the beginning of the name, such as **hs_getc( )** instead of **getc( )**.

One-Off Errors

As you should know, all array indexes in C start at 0. A common error involves the use of a **for** loop to access the elements of an array. Consider the following program that is supposed to initialize an array of 100 integers:

```
main()  /* this program will not work */
{
   int x, num[100];

   for(x=1; x<=100; ++x) num[x]=x;
}
```

The **for** loop in this program is wrng for two reasons. First, the loop will not initialize **num[0]**, the first element of array **num**. Second, the loop goes one past the end of the array: **num[99]** is the last element in the array and the loop runs to 100. The correct way to write this program is

```
main()  /* this is right */
{
   int x, num[100];

   for(x=0; x<100; ++x) num[x]=x;
}
```

Remember that an array of 100 has elements 0 through 99.

Boundary Errors

The Turbo C run-time environment and many standard library functions have little or no run-time bounds checking. For this reason, you can overwrite arrays. For example, consider the following program that is supposed to read a string from the keyboard and display it on the screen:

```
main()
{
  int var1;
  char s[10];
  int var2;

  var1 = 10;  var2 = 10;
  get_string(s);
  printf("%s %d %d", s, var1, var2);
}

get_string(string)
char *string;
{
  register int t;

  printf("enter twenty characters\n");
  for(t=0; t<20; ++t) {
    *s++ = getchar();
  }
}
```

Here, there are no direct coding errors. However, there is an indirect error: calling **get—string()** with s will cause a bug. Although the code declares s to be 10 characters long, **get—string()** will read 20 characters, which will cause s to be overwritten. The problem is that s may display all 20 characters correctly, but **var2** will not contain the correct value. Here is the reason: all C compilers, including Turbo C, must allocate a region of memory for local variables. This region is usually the stack region. The variables **var1**, **var2**, and s will be located in memory as shown in Figure 16-2.

Turbo C compilers on non-8086-based computers may exchange the order of **var1** and **var2**, but they will still bracket s. When overwriting s, the code places the additional information into the area that is supposed to be **var2**, a process that destroys any previous contents. Therefore, instead of printing the number 10 for both integer variables, Turbo C will display something else for the one destroyed by the overrun of s. This will cause you to look for

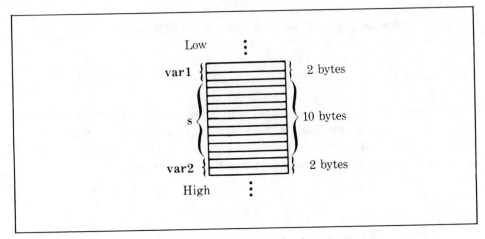

Figure 16-2. The variables **var1**, **var2**, and s in memory

the problem in the wrong place. Also, in this specific instance, the code may overwrite the return address of the function call, which will cause a crash.

Function-Declaration Omissions

Any time that a function returns a value type other than **int**, you must declare the function as such inside each function that uses it. Consider the following program that multiplies two floating-point numbers together:

```
main() /* this is wrong */
{
   float x, y;

   scanf("%f%f", &x, &y);
   printf("%f", mul(x, y));

}

float mul(a, b)
float a, b;
{
   return a*b;
}
```

Here, **main()** expects an integer value back from **mul()**, but **mul()** will return a floating-point number. You will get meaningless answers because **main()** will only copy two bytes out of the four needed for a **float**. Although Turbo C will catch this error if these functions are in the same file, it cannot if they are in separately compiled modules.

The way to correct this program is to declare **mul()** in **main()**, as shown in this corrected version:

```
main() /* this is correct */
{
  float x, y, mul();

  scanf("%f%f", &x, &y);
  printf("%f", mul(x, y));
}

float mul(a, b)
float a, b;
{
  return a*b;
}
```

This version adds **mul()** to the **float** declaration list, which tells **main()** to expect a floating-point value to be returned from **mul()**.

Calling-Argument Errors

Be sure to match whatever type of argument a function expects with the type that you give it. An important example is **scanf()**. Remember that **scanf()** expects to receive the *addresses* of its arguments, and not their values. For example,

```
int x;
char string[10];

scanf("%d%s", x, string);
```

is wrong, while

```
scanf("%d%s", &x, string);
```

is correct. Remember that strings already pass their addresses to functions, so you should not use the & operator on them.

If a function's formal parameters are of type **float,** then you must pass floating-point variables to the function. For example, the following program will not function correctly:

```
main() /* this program is wrong */
{
   int x,y;

   scanf("%d%d", x, y);
   printf("%d",div_it(x, y));

}

float div_it(a, b)
float a, b;
{
   return a/b;
}
```

You cannot use a floating-point function, such as **div__it( ),** to return an integer value. Furthermore, you cannot expect **div__it( )** to operate correctly when you pass integers to it because it is expecting floating-point numbers. (Remember, however, that you can always use a cast to coerce one type to another if necessary.)

Stack-Heap Collisions

When the stack overruns the heap, the process is called a *stack-heap collision.* Turbo C gives you the option of checking for stack overflow, which happens when the stack overruns the heap. However, this check does slow down program execution. Generally, you use this option only when you have strong reason to suspect that a stack overflow is occurring. Diagnosing a stack overflow takes a little intuition. Usually, the program either completely dies or continues executing at a bizarre point. This second symptom is due to the program using data accidentally as a return address. The worst thing about stack-heap collisions is that they generally occur without any warning and kill the program so completely that debugging code cannot execute.

Another problem is that a stack-heap collision often seems to be a wild pointer and, thus, misleads you. The only advice that can be offered is that runaway recursive functions cause most stack-heap collisions. If your program uses recursion and you experience unexplainable failures, check the terminating conditions in your recursive functions.

Parting Words

If you have read and worked through the examples in this book, you now have a good understanding of Turbo C. However, as much as you know about Turbo C—and C in general—there is still much to learn. The best way to become an expert C programmer is, first, to study the way that other expert C programmers write code. There are many excellent C programmers with over a decade of experience from whom you can learn a lot by reading their code. Second, write several programs in C. Each new programming task will challenge both your imagination and your programming skills.

Good luck, and may your programs be free of bugs!

Installing Turbo C

A P P E N D I X

Turbo C is supplied on four diskettes. The first diskette contains the integrated environment version of Turbo C. The second diskette has the command-line version. The third diskette holds the header files and part of the library files. The fourth diskette contains the rest of the library files.

Like many other programs, installing Turbo C is easier if your system has a hard disk. For this reason, let's first see how you can install Turbo C on a hard disk and then how floppy-based systems can use Turbo C.

Turbo C Hard-Disk Installation: Quick and Dirty

As the name of the section implies, the easiest way to get Turbo C to run on your hard disk is not the best in the long run. However, if you are the impatient type, or if you just need to bring Turbo C up on a system for a short period of time—perhaps to fix a bug in a program at a customer's site—this is the way to do it.

The first step is to create a Turbo C directory. The Turbo C user's guide recommends that you call this directory TURBOC, but the name TC will work just as well and is shorter. The second step is to copy the contents of all four diskettes into this directory if you want both the integrated-environment version and the command-line version of Turbo C. Copy the first, third, and fourth diskettes if you want only the integrated-environment version. Copy the second, third, and fourth if you need only the command-line version.

The major drawback to this installation method is that you have a large number of files in the directory. These files can make it cumbersome to work with Turbo C.

Hard-Disk Installation: Squeaky Clean

If you are installing Turbo C on your system and plan to leave it there, then you owe it to yourself to install Turbo C correctly.

First, create a special directory for Turbo C. For now, assume that this directory is called TURBOC, but you can give the directory any name that you want. Next, create two subdirectories called LIB and INCLUDE. Into the INCLUDE directory, copy all of the .H files from the third diskette. Into the LIB directory, place all of the files on the fourth diskette and all of those files on the third diskette that are not .H files. Into the TURBOC directory, put all files found on the first and second diskettes.

If you set up Turbo C in this way, you must specify where the include files and the library files are by using either the **Options/Environment** integrated-environment command or the −**I** command-line option.

Installing Turbo C
on a One-Floppy-Drive System

Running Turbo C on a system with a single floppy drive is not recommended and will not be much fun! However, it can be done and sometimes, in a pinch, it is better to have one floppy drive that works than a hard disk that doesn't.

You will need at least two diskettes. On the first diskette, place a copy of the first Turbo C diskette. With only one floppy drive, you must use the integrated-environment version.

The second diskette will hold the include files from the third Turbo C diskette plus these library and .OBJ files:

> C0*model*.OBJ
> C*model*.LIB
> EMU.LIB
> FP87.LIB
> MATH*model*.LIB

Here, *model* is the letter that specifies the memory model that you want to work with. For the beginning, the small model is best, so substitute s for *model*.

To run the Turbo C integrated environment, insert your first diskette in the drive and execute Turbo C. Next, put your second diskette in the drive and develop your programs. If you need Turbo C's help, you must put your first diskette back in the drive.

Using Turbo C with
Two Floppy Drives

If you wish to use the integrated environment, then follow the steps just given for the single-floppy-drive system, but place your first diskette in drive A and your second diskette in drive B.

To run the command-line version of Turbo C on two floppy drives, copy the contents of TCC.EXE and TLINK.EXE from the second Turbo C disk. If you like, create two directories, called LIB and INCLUDE. Put these files into LIB:

C0*model*.OBJ
C*model*.LIB
EMU.LIB
FP87.LIB
MATH*model*.LIB

Here, *model* is the letter that specifies the memory model that you want to work with. For the beginning, the small model is best, so substitute s for *model*.

Into the INCLUDE directory, put all of the header files (.H extensions) found on the third Turbo C diskette.

You can use drive B for the work disk.

T R A D E M A R K S

DEC™	Digital Equipment Corporation
Forth®	FORTH, Inc.
IBM®	International Business Machines Corporation
MicroPro®	MicroPro International Corporation
SideKick®	Borland International, Inc.
Turbo C®	Borland International, Inc.
Turbo Pascal®	Borland International, Inc.
Turbo Prolog®	Borland International, Inc.
UNIX®	AT&T
WordStar®	Micropro International Corporation

END FILE TM.1
gz
Machine A

INDEX

The manuscript for this book was prepared and submitted to Osborne/McGraw-Hill in electronic form. The acquisitions editor for this project was Jeffrey Pepper, the technical editor was Paul Chui, the copy editor was Lorraine Aochi, and the project editor was Fran Haselsteiner.

Text design uses Century Expanded for text body and Univers Bold for display.

Cover art by Bay Graphics Design Associates. Color separation by colour image. Cover supplier, Phoenix Color Corp. Book printed and bound by R.R. Donnelley & Sons Company, Crawfordsville, Indiana.